EXAM CRAM™

MCSE
SMS 2

Ian Turek

CORIOLIS

MCSE SMS 2 Exam Cram

Limits Of Liability And Disclaimer Of Warranty

The author and publisher of this book have used their best efforts in preparing the book and the programs contained in it. These efforts include the development, research, and testing of the theories and programs to determine their effectiveness. The author and publisher make no warranty of any kind, expressed or implied, with regard to these programs or the documentation contained in this book.

The author and publisher shall not be liable in the event of incidental or consequential damages in connection with, or arising out of, the furnishing, performance, or use of the programs, associated instructions, and/or claims of productivity gains.

Trademarks

Trademarked names appear throughout this book. Rather than list the names and entities that own the trademarks or insert a trademark symbol with each mention of the trademarked name, the publisher states that it is using the names for editorial purposes only and to the benefit of the trademark owner, with no intention of infringing upon that trademark.

The Coriolis Group, LLC
14455 N. Hayden Road, Suite 220
Scottsdale, Arizona 85260

480/483-0192
FAX 480/483-0193
http://www.coriolis.com

Library of Congress Cataloging-in-Publication Data
Turek, Ian
    MCSE SMS 2 exam cram / by Ian Turek.
        p. cm.
    ISBN 1-57610-424-9
    1. Electronic data processing personnel—Certification.
2. Microsoft software—Examinations Study guides.   3. SMS (Computer
file) I. Title.
QA76.3.T87   1999
005.7'1—dc21   99-32816
                                                    CIP

Printed in the United States of America
10 9 8 7 6 5 4 3

President, CEO
Keith Weiskamp

Publisher
Steve Sayre

Acquisitions Editor
Jeff Kellum

Marketing Specialist
Cynthia Caldwell

Project Editor
Ann Waggoner Aken

Technical Reviewer
Roland Perreaux

Production Coordinator
Wendy Littley

Cover Design
Jesse Dunn

Layout Design
April Nielsen

 CORIOLIS

14455 North Hayden Road, Suite 220 • Scottsdale, Arizona 85260

Coriolis: The Training And Certification Destination™

Thank you for purchasing one of our innovative certification study guides, just one of the many members of the Coriolis family of certification products.

Certification Insider Press™ has long believed that achieving your IT certification is more of a road trip than anything else. This is why most of our readers consider us their *Training And Certification Destination*. By providing a one-stop shop for the most innovative and unique training materials, our readers know we are the first place to look when it comes to achieving their certification. As one reader put it, "I plan on using your books for all of the exams I take."

To help you reach your goals, we've listened to others like you, and we've designed our entire product line around you and the way you like to study, learn, and master challenging subjects. Our approach is *The Smartest Way To Get Certified™*.

In addition to our highly popular *Exam Cram* and *Exam Prep* guides, we have a number of new products. We recently launched Exam Cram Live!, two-day seminars based on *Exam Cram* material. We've also developed a new series of books and study aides—*Practice Tests Exam Crams* and *Exam Cram Flash Cards*—designed to make your studying fun as well as productive.

Our commitment to being the *Training And Certification Destination* does not stop there. We just introduced *Exam Cram Insider*, a biweekly newsletter containing the latest in certification news, study tips, and announcements from Certification Insider Press. (To subscribe, send an email to **eci@coriolis.com** and type "subscribe insider" in the body of the email.) We also recently announced the launch of the Certified Crammer Society and the Coriolis Help Center—two new additions to the Certification Insider Press family.

We'd like to hear from you. Help us continue to provide the very best certification study materials possible. Write us or email us at **cipq@coriolis.com** and let us know how our books have helped you study, or tell us about new features that you'd like us to add. If you send us a story about how we've helped you, and we use it in one of our books, we'll send you an official Coriolis shirt for your efforts.

Good luck with your certification exam and your career. Thank you for allowing us to help you achieve your goals.

Keith Weiskamp
President, CEO, The Coriolis Group

To my family and friends, for always believing in me.
To the memory of my father.

಄

About The Author

Ian Turek has been involved in the computer industry since 1994. After migrating from Poland and graduating with an MS degree in Aeronautics and Astronautics from the University of Washington, Ian began a career as a computer systems engineer, consultant, and trainer. He has worked for a wide variety of companies including health care facilities, medical centers, banks, and government agencies. In 1998, Ian established Gravity Square Inc., a Microsoft Certified Solution Provider firm specializing in infrastructure design, systems integration, and training. Recently, he has worked as part of the Microsoft SMS team on the scalability and performance of Systems Management Server 2. Ian specializes in large-scale SMS deployments and systems performance analysis as well as implementations and migrations to Microsoft technologies in medium and large environments. He has also been a technical consultant for several MS Press publications. Ian can be found at several snowboarding and windsurfing spots and on the Internet at **iant@gravitysquare.com**.

Acknowledgments

Everyone I have run into during my life should receive a part of the credit for putting this book together.

First of all, I would like to thank the staff of the Coriolis Group. Many thanks to Jeff Kellum, acquisition editor, for initiating the project and helping me gain the momentum. Words of appreciation to Ann Waggoner Aken, project editor, for her patience and lots of help with writing, editing, deadlines, and project management. Rolly Pereaux did a great job of finding technical bugs in my writing. Thanks a lot Rolly. Copyeditor, Bonnie Trenga, must have had a fun time with a text written by a Pole—just ask me and I will send you the name of my English language teacher. Many thanks Bonnie. Wendy Littley, Cynthia Caldwell, and Jesse Dunn did a great production, marketing, and design job. Thanks.

I also would like to thank the Microsoft System Management Server team for their assistance with finding answers to many questions, keeping me around for a while, and lots of free sodas. Special thanks to Roger, Ken, Christine, Renee, Brett, Linda, Wally, Luke, and many other software engineers, test engineers, and technical writers. Glen, you helped me a lot as well—thanks.

Finally, I want to thank my family and friends for guiding me through life and giving me the best they could have: my wife Margaret, my mom and dad, sister and nephew, Spagnoli family (grazie tante!), and friends from Seattle and all over the world.

One way or the other, each of you helped me write a part of this book.

Ian Turek
July 1999

Contents At A Glance

Table Of Contents

Introduction

Welcome to *Systems Management Server 2 Exam Cram*! This book aims to help you get ready to take—and pass—the Microsoft certification Exam 70-086, titled "Implementing and Supporting Microsoft Systems Management Server 2.0." This Introduction explains Microsoft's certification programs in general and talks about how the *Exam Cram* series can help you prepare for Microsoft's certification exams.

Exam Cram books help you understand and appreciate the subjects and materials you need to pass Microsoft certification exams. *Exam Cram* books are aimed strictly at test preparation and review. They do not teach you everything you need to know about a topic (such as the ins and outs of tuning SQL Server for SMS, or all the nitty-gritty details involved in creating a software distribution package). Instead, I (the author) present and dissect the questions and problems I've found that you're likely to encounter on a test. I've worked from Microsoft's own training materials, preparation guides, and tests, and from a battery of third-party test preparation tools. My aim is to bring together as much information as possible about Microsoft certification exams.

Nevertheless, to completely prepare yourself for any Microsoft test, I recommend that you begin by taking the Self-Assessment included in this book immediately following this Introduction. This tool will help you evaluate your knowledge base against the requirements for an MCSE under both ideal and real circumstances.

Based on what you learn from that exercise, you might decide to begin your studies with some classroom training or some background reading. On the other hand, you might decide to pick up and read one of the many study guides available from Microsoft or third-party vendors on certain topics, including The Coriolis Group's *Exam Prep* series.

I also strongly recommend that you install, configure, and fool around with the software that you'll be tested on, because nothing beats hands-on experience and familiarity when it comes to understanding the questions you're likely to encounter on a certification test. Book learning is essential, but hands-on experience is the best teacher of all!

The Microsoft Certified Professional (MCP) Program

The MCP Program currently includes seven separate tracks, each of which boasts its own special acronym (as a would-be certificant, you need to have a high tolerance for alphabet soup of all kinds):

➤ **MCP (Microsoft Certified Professional)** This is the least prestigious of all the certification tracks from Microsoft. Passing any of the major Microsoft exams (except the Networking Essentials exam) qualifies an individual for MCP credentials. Individuals can demonstrate proficiency with additional Microsoft products by passing additional certification exams.

➤ **MCP+I (Microsoft Certified Professional + Internet)** This midlevel certification is attained by completing three core exams: "Implementing and Supporting Microsoft Windows NT Server 4.0," "Internetworking Microsoft TCP/IP on Microsoft Windows NT 4.0," and "Implementing and Supporting Internet Information Server 3.0 and Microsoft Index Server 1.1" or "Implementing and Supporting Microsoft Internet Information Server 4.0."

➤ **MCP+SB (Microsoft Certified Professional + Site Building)** This certification program is designed for individuals who are planning, building, managing, and maintaining Web sites. Individuals with the MCP+SB credential will have demonstrated the ability to develop Web sites that include multimedia and searchable content and Web sites that connect to and communicate with a back-end database. It requires one MCP exam, plus two of these three exams: "Designing and Implementing Commerce Solutions with Microsoft Site Server, 3.0, Commerce Edition," "Designing and Implementing Web Sites with Microsoft FrontPage 98," and "Designing and Implementing Web Solutions with Microsoft Visual InterDev 6.0."

➤ **MCSE (Microsoft Certified Systems Engineer)** Anyone who has a current MCSE is warranted to possess a high level of expertise with Windows NT (version 3.51 or 4.0) and other Microsoft operating systems and products. This credential is designed to prepare individuals to plan, implement, maintain, and support information systems and networks built around Microsoft Windows NT and its BackOffice family of products.

To obtain an MCSE, an individual must pass four core operating system exams, plus two elective exams. The operating system exams require individuals to demonstrate competence with desktop and server operating systems and with networking components.

You must pass at least two Windows NT-related exams to obtain an MCSE: "Implementing and Supporting Microsoft Windows NT Server" (version 3.51 or 4.0) and "Implementing and Supporting Microsoft Windows NT Server in the Enterprise" (version 3.51 or 4.0). These tests are intended to indicate an individual's knowledge of Windows NT in smaller, simpler networks and in larger, more complex, and heterogeneous networks, respectively.

Note: The NT 3.51 version is scheduled to be retired by Microsoft sometime in 1999.

You must pass two additional tests as well. These tests are related to networking and desktop operating systems. At present, the networking requirement can be satisfied only by passing the Networking Essentials test. The desktop operating system test can be satisfied by passing a Windows 95, Windows NT Workstation (the version must match the NT version for the core tests), or Windows 98 test.

The two remaining exams are elective exams. An elective exam may fall in any number of subject or product areas, primarily BackOffice components. These include tests on Internet Explorer 4, SQL Server, IIS, Proxy Server, SNA Server, Exchange Server, Systems Management Server, and the like. However, it is also possible to test out on electives by taking advanced networking topics like "Internetworking with Microsoft TCP/IP on Microsoft Windows NT 4.0" (but here again, the version of Windows NT involved must match the version for the core requirements taken). If you are on your way to becoming an MCSE and have already taken some exams, visit **www.microsoft.com/mcp/certstep/ mcse.htm** for information about how to proceed with your MCSE certification.

Note that the exam covered by this book can be used as the elective for the MCSE certification.

Whatever mix of tests is completed toward MCSE certification, individuals must pass six tests to meet the MCSE requirements. It's not uncommon for the entire process to take a year or so, and many individuals find that they must take a test more than once to pass. The primary goal of the *Exam Cram* series is to make it possible, given proper study and preparation, to pass all Microsoft certification tests on the first try. Table 1 shows the required and elective exams for the MCSE certification.

Table 1 MCSE Requirements*

Core

All 3 of these are required	
Exam 70-067	Implementing and Supporting Microsoft Windows NT Server 4.0
Exam 70-068	Implementing and Supporting Microsoft Windows NT Server 4.0 in the Enterprise
Exam 70-058	Networking Essentials
Choose 1 from this group	
Exam 70-064	Implementing and Supporting Microsoft Windows 95
Exam 70-073	Implementing and Supporting Microsoft Windows NT Workstation 4.0
Exam 70-098	Implementing and Supporting Microsoft Windows 98

Elective

Choose 2 from this group	
Exam 70-088	Implementing and Supporting Microsoft Proxy Server 2.0
Exam 70-079	Implementing and Supporting Microsoft Internet Explorer 4.0 by Using the Internet Explorer Administration Kit
Exam 70-087	Implementing and Supporting Microsoft Internet Information Server 4.0
Exam 70-081	Implementing and Supporting Microsoft Exchange Server 5.5
Exam 70-059	Internetworking with Microsoft TCP/IP on Microsoft Windows NT 4.0
Exam 70-028	Administering Microsoft SQL Server 7.0
Exam 70-029	Designing and Implementing Databases on Microsoft SQL Server 7.0
Exam 70-056	Implementing and Supporting Web Sites Using Microsoft Site Server 3.0
Exam 70-086	Implementing and Supporting Microsoft Systems Management Server 2.0
Exam 70-085	Implementing and Supporting Microsoft SNA Server 4.0

* This is not a complete listing—you can still be tested on some earlier versions of these products. However, we have included mainly the most recent versions so that you may test on these versions and thus be certified longer. We have not included any tests that are scheduled to be retired.

➤ **MCSE+I (Microsoft Certified Systems Engineer + Internet)** This is a newer Microsoft certification and focuses not just on Microsoft operating systems, but also on Microsoft's Internet servers and TCP/IP.

To obtain this certification, an individual must pass seven core exams plus two elective exams. The core exams include not only the server operating systems (Windows NT Server and Server in the Enterprise) and a desktop OS (Windows 95, Windows 98, or Windows NT Workstation), but also include Networking Essentials, TCP/IP, Internet Information Server (IIS), and the Internet Explorer Administration Kit (IEAK).

The two remaining exams are elective exams. These elective exams can be in any of four product areas: SQL Server, SNA Server, Exchange Server, or Proxy Server.

➤ **MCSD (Microsoft Certified Solution Developer)** The MCSD credential reflects the skills required to create multitier, distributed, and COM-based solutions, in addition to desktop and Internet applications, using new technologies. To obtain an MCSD, an individual must demonstrate the ability to analyze and interpret user requirements; select and integrate products, platforms, tools, and technologies; design and implement code and customize applications; and perform necessary software tests and quality assurance operations.

To become an MCSD, you must pass a total of four exams: three core exams and one elective exam. Each candidate must also choose one of these two desktop application exams—"Designing and Implementing Desktop Applications with Microsoft Visual C++ 6.0" or "Designing and Implementing Desktop Applications with Microsoft Visual Basic 6.0"—*plus* one of these two distributed application exams—"Designing and Implementing Distributed Applications with Microsoft Visual C++ 6.0" or "Designing and Implementing Distributed Applications with Microsoft Visual Basic 6.0."

Note: Microsoft is planning to release desktop application and distributed application exams on Visual J++ and Visual FoxPro in the spring of 1999.

Elective exams cover specific Microsoft applications and languages, including Visual Basic, C++, the Microsoft Foundation Classes, Access, SQL Server, Excel, and more.

➤ **MCDBA (Microsoft Certified Database Administrator)** The MCDBA credential reflects the skills required to implement and administer Microsoft SQL Server databases. To obtain an MCDBA, an individual must demonstrate the ability to derive physical database designs, develop logical data models, create physical databases, create data services by using Transact-SQL, manage and maintain databases, configure and manage security, monitor and optimize databases, and install and configure Microsoft SQL Server.

To become an MCDBA, you must pass a total of five exams: four core exams and one elective exam. The required core exams are "Administering Microsoft SQL Server 7.0," "Designing and Implementing Databases with Microsoft SQL Server 7.0," "Implementing and Supporting Microsoft Windows NT Server 4.0," and "Implementing and Supporting Microsoft Windows NT Server 4.0 in the Enterprise."

The elective exams that you can choose from cover specific uses of SQL Server and include "Designing and Implementing Distributed Applications with Visual Basic 6.0," "Designing and Implementing Distributed Applications with Visual C++ 6.0," "Designing and Implementing Data Warehouses with Microsoft SQL Server 7.0 and Microsoft Decision Support Services 1.0," and two exams that relate to NT: "Internetworking with Microsoft TCP/IP on Microsoft Windows NT 4.0" and "Implementing and Supporting Microsoft Internet Information Server 4.0".

➤ **MCT (Microsoft Certified Trainer)** Microsoft Certified Trainers are individuals who are deemed able to deliver elements of the official Microsoft curriculum, based on technical knowledge and instructional ability. Thus, it is necessary for an individual seeking MCT credentials (which are granted on a course-by-course basis) to pass the related certification exam for a course and complete the official Microsoft training in the subject area, and to demonstrate an ability to teach.

This latter criterion may be satisfied by proving that one has already attained training certification from Novell, Banyan, Lotus, the Santa Cruz Operation, or Cisco, or by taking a Microsoft-sanctioned workshop on instruction. Microsoft makes it clear that MCTs are important cogs in the Microsoft training channels. Instructors must be MCTs before Microsoft will allow them to teach in any of its official training channels, including Microsoft's affiliated Certified Technical Education Centers (CTECs) and the Microsoft Online Institute (MOLI).

Certification is an ongoing activity. Once a Microsoft product becomes obsolete, MCPs typically have 12 to 18 months in which they may recertify on current product versions. (If individuals do not recertify within the specified time period, their certifications become invalid.) Because technology keeps changing and new products continually supplant old ones, this should come as no surprise.

The best place to keep tabs on the MCP Program and its various certifications is on the Microsoft Web site. The current root URL for the MCP program is **www.microsoft.com/mcp/**. But Microsoft's Web site changes often, so if this URL doesn't work, try using the Search tool on Microsoft's site with either "MCP" or the quoted phrase "Microsoft Certified Professional Program" as a search string. This will help you find the latest and most accurate information about Microsoft's certification programs.

Taking A Certification Exam

Alas, testing is not free. Each computer-based MCP exam costs $100, and if you don't pass, you may retest for an additional $100 for each additional try. In the United States and Canada, tests are administered by Sylvan Prometric and by Virtual University Enterprises (VUE). Here's how you can contact them:

➤ **Sylvan Prometric** You can sign up for a test through the company's Web site at **www.slspro.com**. Or, you can register by phone at 800-755-3926 (within the United States or Canada) or at 410-843-8000 (outside the United States and Canada).

➤ **Virtual University Enterprises** You can sign up for a test or get the phone numbers for local testing centers through the Web page at **www.microsoft.com/train_cert/mcp/vue_info.htm**.

To sign up for a test, you must possess a valid credit card, or contact either company for mailing instructions to send them a check (in the U.S.). Only when payment is verified, or a check has cleared, can you actually register for a test.

To schedule an exam, call the number or visit either of the Web pages at least one day in advance. To cancel or reschedule an exam, you must call before 7 P.M. pacific standard time the day before the scheduled test time (or you may be charged, even if you don't appear to take the test). When you want to schedule a test, have the following information ready:

➤ Your name, organization, and mailing address.

➤ Your Microsoft Test ID. (Inside the United States, this means your Social Security number; citizens of other nations should call ahead to find out what type of identification number is required to register for a test.)

➤ The name and number of the exam you wish to take.

➤ A method of payment. (As I've already mentioned, a credit card is the most convenient method, but alternate means can be arranged in advance, if necessary.)

Once you sign up for a test, you'll be informed as to when and where the test is scheduled. Try to arrive at least 15 minutes early. You must supply two forms of identification—one of which must be a photo ID—to be admitted into the testing room.

All exams are completely closed-book. In fact, you will not be permitted to take anything with you into the testing area, but you will be furnished with a blank sheet of paper and a pen or, in some cases, an erasable plastic sheet and an erasable pen. I suggest that you immediately write down on that sheet of paper all the information you've memorized for the test. In *Exam Cram* books, this information appears on a tear-out sheet inside the front cover of each book. You will have some time to compose yourself, to record this information, and even to take a sample orientation exam before you begin the real thing. I suggest you take the orientation test before taking your first exam, but because they're all more or less identical in layout, behavior, and controls, you probably won't need to do this more than once.

When you complete a Microsoft certification exam, the software will tell you whether you've passed or failed. Results are broken into several topic areas. Even if you fail, I suggest you ask for—and keep—the detailed report that the test administrator should print for you. You can use this report to help you prepare for another go-round, if needed.

If you need to retake an exam, you'll have to schedule a new test with Sylvan Prometric or VUE and pay another $100.

The first time you fail a test, you can retake the test the next day. However, if you fail a second time, you must wait 14 days before retaking that test. The 14-day waiting period remains in effect for all retakes after the first failure.

Tracking MCP Status

As soon as you pass any Microsoft exam other than Networking Essentials, you'll attain Microsoft Certified Professional (MCP) status. Microsoft also generates transcripts that indicate which exams you have passed and your corresponding test scores. You can order a transcript by email at any time by sending an email to **mcp@msprograms.com**. You can also obtain a copy of your transcript by downloading the latest version of the MCT Guide from the Web site and consulting the section titled "Key Contacts" for a list of telephone numbers and related contacts.

Once you pass the necessary set of exams (one for MCP, six for MCSE, or nine for MCSE+I), you'll be certified. Official certification normally takes anywhere from four to six weeks, so don't expect to get your credentials overnight. When the package for a qualified certification arrives, it includes a Welcome Kit that contains a number of elements:

➤ An MCP, MCSE, or MCSE+I certificate, suitable for framing, along with a Professional Program Membership card and lapel pin.

➤ A license to use the MCP logo, thereby allowing you to use the logo in advertisements, promotions, and documents, and on letterhead, business cards, and so on. Along with the license comes an MCP logo sheet, which includes camera-ready artwork. (Note: Before using any of the artwork, individuals must sign and return a licensing agreement that indicates they'll abide by its terms and conditions.)

➤ A subscription to *Microsoft Certified Professional Magazine*, which provides ongoing data about testing and certification activities, requirements, and changes to the program.

➤ A one-year subscription to the Microsoft Beta Evaluation program. This subscription will get you all beta products from Microsoft for the next year. (This does not include developer products. You must join the MSDN program or become an MCSD to qualify for developer beta products.)

Many people believe that the benefits of MCP certification go well beyond the perks that Microsoft provides to newly anointed members of this elite group. More and more job listings are requesting or requiring applicants to have an MCP, MCSE, MCSE+I, and so on, and many individuals who complete the program can qualify for increases in pay and/or responsibility. As an official recognition of hard work and broad knowledge, one of the MCP credentials is a badge of honor in many IT organizations.

How To Prepare For An Exam

Preparing for any Windows NT Server-related test (including TCP/IP) requires that you obtain and study materials designed to provide comprehensive information about the product and its capabilities that will appear on the specific exam for which you are preparing. The following list of materials will help you study and prepare:

➤ The Windows NT Server product CD includes comprehensive online documentation and related materials; it should be a primary resource when you are preparing for the test.

➤ The exam prep materials, practice tests, and self-assessment exams on the Microsoft Training And Certification Download page (**www.microsoft.com/train_cert/download/downld.htm**). Find the materials, download them, and use them!

In addition, you'll probably find any or all of the following materials useful in your quest for SMS expertise:

➤ **Microsoft Training Kits** Microsoft Press offers a training kit that specifically targets Exam 70-086. For more information, visit: **http://mspress.microsoft.com/prod/books/1360.htm**. This training kit contains information that you will find useful in preparing for the test.

➤ **Microsoft TechNet CD** This monthly CD-based publication delivers numerous electronic titles that include coverage of SMS and related topics on the Technical Information (TechNet) CD. Its offerings include product facts, technical notes, tools and utilities, and information on how to access the Seminars Online training materials for SMS. A subscription to TechNet costs $299 per year, but it is well worth the price. Visit **www.microsoft.com/technet/** and check out the information under the "TechNet Subscription" menu entry for more details.

➤ **The *Exam Cram* series** These books give you information about the material you need to know to pass the tests.

➤ **Classroom Training** CTECs, MOLI, and unlicensed third-party training companies (like Wave Technologies, American Research Group, Learning Tree, Data-Tech, and others) all offer classroom training on SMS. These companies aim to help you prepare to pass the SMS test. Although such training runs upwards of $350 per day in class, most of the individuals lucky enough to attend find them to be quite worthwhile.

➤ **Other Publications** You'll find direct references to other publications and resources in this book. To help you sift through some of the publications out there, I end each chapter with a "Need To Know More?" section that provides pointers to more complete and exhaustive resources covering the chapter's information. This should give you an idea of where I think you should look for further discussion.

By far, this set of required and recommended materials represents a nonpareil collection of sources and resources for SMS and related topics. I anticipate that you'll find that this book belongs in this company. In the next section, I explain how this book works and give you some good reasons why this book counts as a member of the required and recommended materials list.

About This Book

Each topical *Exam Cram* chapter follows a regular structure, along with graphical cues about important or useful information. Here's the structure of a typical chapter:

➤ **Opening Hotlists** Each chapter begins with a list of the terms, tools, and techniques that you must learn and understand before you can be fully conversant with that chapter's subject matter. I follow the hotlists with one or two introductory paragraphs to set the stage for the rest of the chapter.

➤ **Topical Coverage** After the opening hotlists, each chapter covers a series of topics related to the chapter's subject title. Throughout this section, I highlight topics or concepts likely to appear on a test using a special Exam Alert layout, like this:

> This is what an Exam Alert looks like. Normally, an Exam Alert stresses concepts, terms, software, or activities that are likely to relate to one or more certification test questions. For that reason, I think any information found offset in Exam Alert format is worthy of unusual attentiveness on your part. Indeed, most of the information that appears on The Cram Sheet appears as Exam Alerts within the text.

Pay close attention to material flagged as an Exam Alert; although all the information in this book pertains to what you need to know to pass the exam, I flag certain items that are really important. You'll find what appears in the meat of each chapter to be worth knowing, too, when preparing for the test. Because this book's material is very condensed, I recommend that you use this book along with other resources to achieve the maximum benefit.

In addition to the Exam Alerts, I have provided tips that will help you build a better foundation for SMS knowledge. Although the information may not be on the exam, it is certainly related and will help you become a better test-taker.

> This is how tips are formatted. Keep your eyes open for these, and you'll become an SMS guru in no time!

➤ **Practice Questions** Although I talk about test questions and topics throughout each chapter, this section presents a series of mock test questions and explanations of both correct and incorrect answers. I also try to point out especially tricky questions by using a special icon, like this:

Ordinarily, this icon flags the presence of a particularly devious inquiry, if not an outright trick question. Trick questions are calculated to be answered incorrectly if not read more than once, and carefully, at that.

Although they're not ubiquitous, such questions make regular appearances on the Microsoft exams. That's why exam questions are as much about reading comprehension as they are about knowing your material inside out and backwards.

➤ **Details And Resources** Every chapter ends with a section titled "Need To Know More?". This section provides direct pointers to Microsoft and third-party resources offering more details on the chapter's subject. In addition, this section tries to rank or at least rate the quality and thoroughness of the topic's coverage by each resource. If you find a resource you like in this collection, use it, but don't feel compelled to use all the resources. On the other hand, I recommend only resources that I use on a regular basis, so none of my recommendations will be a waste of your time or money (but purchasing them all at once probably represents an expense that many network administrators and would-be MCPs, MCSEs, and MCSE+Is might find hard to justify).

The bulk of the book follows this chapter structure slavishly, but there are a few other elements that I'd like to point out. Chapter 12 includes a sample test that provides a good review of the material presented throughout the book to ensure you're ready for the exam. Chapter 13 provides an answer key to the sample test that appears in Chapters 12. Additionally, you'll find the Glossary, which explains terms, and an index that you can use to track down terms as they appear in the text.

Finally, the tear-out Cram Sheet attached next to the inside front cover of this *Exam Cram* book represents a condensed and compiled collection of facts and tips that I think you should memorize before taking the test. Because you can dump this information out of your head onto a piece of paper before taking the exam, you can master this information by brute force—you need to remember it only long enough to write it down when you walk into the test room. You might even want to look at it in the car or in the lobby of the testing center just before you walk in to take the test.

How To Use This Book

If you're prepping for a first-time test, I've structured the topics in this book to build on one another. Therefore, some topics in later chapters make more sense after you've read earlier chapters. That's why I suggest you read this book from front to back for your initial test preparation. If you need to brush up on a topic or you have to bone up for a second try, use the index or table of contents to go straight to the topics and questions that you need to study. Beyond helping you prepare for the test, I think you'll find this book useful as a tightly focused reference that will assist you in becoming a first-rate SMS Administrator.

Given all the book's elements and its specialized focus, I've tried to create a tool that will help you prepare for—and pass—Microsoft Exam 70-086, "Implementing and Supporting Systems Management Server 2.0." Please share your feedback on the book with me, especially if you have ideas about how I can improve it for future test-takers. I'll consider everything you say carefully and will respond to all suggestions.

Send your questions or comments to me at **cipq@coriolis.com**. Please remember to include the title of the book in your message; otherwise, we'll be forced to guess which book you're writing about. And we don't like to guess—we want to *know*! Also, be sure to check out the Web page at **www.certificationinsider.com**, where you'll find information updates, commentary, and certification information.

Thanks, and enjoy the book!

Self-Assessment

Based on recent statistics from Microsoft, as many as 250,000 individuals are at some stage of the certification process but haven't yet received an MCP or other Microsoft certification. We also know that three or four times that number may be considering whether or not to obtain a Microsoft certification of some kind. That's a huge audience!

The reason we included a Self-Assessment in this *Exam Cram* book is to help you evaluate your readiness to tackle MCSE (and MCSE+I) certification. It should also help you understand what you need to master the topic of this book—namely, Exam 70-086, "Implementing and Supporting Microsoft Systems Management Server 2.0." But before you tackle this Self-Assessment, let's talk about concerns you may face when pursuing an MCSE, and what an ideal MCSE candidate might look like.

MCSEs In The Real World

In the next section, we describe an ideal MCSE candidate, knowing full well that only a few real candidates will meet this ideal. In fact, our description of that ideal candidate might seem downright scary. But take heart: Although the requirements to obtain an MCSE may seem pretty formidable, they are by no means impossible to meet. However, you should be keenly aware that it does take time, requires some expense, and consumes substantial effort to get through the process.

More than 90,000 MCSEs are already certified, so it's obviously an attainable goal. You can get all the real-world motivation you need from knowing that many others have gone before, so you will be able to follow in their footsteps. If you're willing to tackle the process seriously and do what it takes to obtain the necessary experience and knowledge, you can take—and pass—all the certification tests involved in obtaining an MCSE. In fact, we've designed these *Exam Crams*, and the companion *Exam Preps*, to make it as easy on you as possible to prepare for these exams. But prepare you must!

The same, of course, is true for other Microsoft certifications, including:

➤ MCSE+I, which is like the MCSE certification but requires seven core exams, and two electives drawn from a specific pool of Internet-related topics, for a total of nine exams.

➤ MCSD, which is aimed at software developers and requires one specific exam, two more exams on client and distributed topics, plus a fourth elective exam drawn from a different, but limited, pool of options.

➤ Other Microsoft certifications, whose requirements range from one test (MCP or MCT) to many tests (MCP+I, MCP+SB, MCDBA).

The Ideal MCSE Candidate

Just to give you some idea of what an ideal MCSE candidate is like, here are some relevant statistics about the background and experience such an individual might have. Don't worry if you don't meet these qualifications, or don't come that close—this is a far from ideal world, and where you fall short is simply where you'll have more work to do.

➤ Academic or professional training in network theory, concepts, and operations. This includes everything from networking media and transmission techniques through network operating systems, services, and applications.

➤ Three-plus years of professional networking experience, including experience with Ethernet, token ring, modems, and other networking media. This must include installation, configuration, upgrade, and troubleshooting experience.

➤ Two-plus years in a networked environment that includes hands-on experience with Windows NT Server, Windows NT Workstation, and Windows 95 or Windows 98. A solid understanding of each system's architecture, installation, configuration, maintenance, and troubleshooting is also essential.

➤ A thorough understanding of key networking protocols, addressing, and name resolution, including TCP/IP and IPX/SPX.

➤ A thorough understanding of NetBIOS naming, browsing services, and file and print services.

➤ Familiarity with key Windows NT-based TCP/IP-based services, including DHCP and WINS.

➤ Working knowledge of NetWare 3.*x* and 4.*x*, including IPX/SPX frame formats, NetWare file, print, and directory services, and both Novell and Microsoft client software. Working knowledge of Microsoft's Client Service for NetWare (CSNW), Gateway Service for NetWare (GSNW), and the NetWare Client for Windows (NT, 95, and 98) is very helpful.

➤ Working knowledge of batch files, logon script processing, and application installation on Windows machines including secured Windows NT Workstations and Servers. An intermediate knowledge of Registry editing, the system directory and file structure of Windows operating systems, and user-specific settings and profiles is essential.

Fundamentally, this boils down to a bachelor's degree in information technology, plus three years of work experience in a technical position involving network design, installation, configuration, and maintenance. We believe that well under half of all certification candidates meet these requirements, and that, in fact, most meet less than half of these requirements—at least, when they begin the certification process. But because all 90,000 people who already have been certified have survived this ordeal, you can survive it too—especially if you heed what our Self-Assessment can tell you about what you already know and what you need to learn.

Put Yourself To The Test

The following series of questions and observations is designed to help you figure out how much work you must do to pursue Microsoft certification and what kinds of resources you may consult on your quest. Be absolutely honest in your answers, or you'll end up wasting money on exams you're not yet ready to take. There are no right or wrong answers, only steps along the path to certification. Only you can decide where you really belong in the broad spectrum of aspiring candidates.

Two things should be clear from the outset, however:

➤ Even a modest background in information technology will be helpful.

➤ Hands-on experience with Microsoft products and technologies is an essential ingredient to certification success.

Educational Background

1. Have you ever taken any computer-related classes? [Yes or No]

   If Yes, proceed to question 2; if No, proceed to question 4.

2. Have you taken any classes on computer operating systems? [Yes or No]

   If Yes, you will probably be able to handle Microsoft's architecture and system component discussions. If you're rusty, brush up on basic operating system concepts, especially processes and threads, virtual memory, multitasking regimes, and general computer security topics.

   If No, consider some basic reading in this area. We strongly recommend a good general operating systems book, such as *Operating System Concepts*, by Abraham Silberschatz and Peter Baer Galvin (Addison-Wesley, 1997, ISBN 0-201-59113-8). If this title doesn't appeal to you, check out reviews for other, similar titles at your favorite online bookstore.

3. Have you taken any networking concepts or technologies classes? [Yes or No]

   If Yes, you will probably be able to handle Microsoft's networking terminology, concepts, and technologies (brace yourself for frequent departures from normal usage). If you're rusty, brush up on basic networking concepts and terminology, especially networking media, transmission types, the OSI Reference Model, and networking technologies such as Ethernet, token ring, FDDI, and WAN links.

   If No, you might want to read one or two books in this topic area. The two best books that we know of are *Computer Networks*, *3rd Edition*, by Andrew S. Tanenbaum (Prentice-Hall, 1996, ISBN 0-13-349945-6) and *Computer Networks and Internets*, by Douglas E. Comer (Prentice-Hall, 1997, ISBN 0-13-239070-1).

   Skip to the next section, "Hands-On Experience."

4. Have you done any reading on operating systems or networks? [Yes or No]

   If Yes, review the requirements stated in the first paragraphs after questions 2 and 3. If you meet those requirements, move on to the next section, "Hands-On Experience." If No, consult the recommended reading for both topics. A strong background will help you prepare for the Microsoft exams better than just about anything else.

Hands-On Experience

The most important key to success on all of the Microsoft tests is hands-on experience, especially with Windows NT Server and Workstation, plus the many add-on services and BackOffice components around which so many of the Microsoft certification exams revolve. If we leave you with only one realization after taking this Self-Assessment, it should be that there's no substitute for time spent installing, configuring, and using the various Microsoft products upon which you'll be tested repeatedly and in depth.

5. Have you installed, configured, and worked with:

➤ Windows NT Server? [Yes or No]

If Yes, make sure you understand basic concepts as covered in Exam 70-067 and advanced concepts as covered in Exam 70-068. You should also study the TCP/IP interfaces, utilities, and services covered in Exam 70-059.

 You can download objectives, practice exams, and other information about Microsoft exams from the company's Training and Certification page on the Web at **www.microsoft.com/train_cert/**. Use the "Find an Exam" link to get specific exam info.

If you haven't worked with Windows NT Server, TCP/IP, and IIS (or whatever product you choose for your final elective), you must obtain one or two machines and a copy of Windows NT Server. Then, learn the operating system, and do the same for TCP/IP and whatever other software components on which you'll also be tested.

In fact, we recommend that you obtain two computers, each with a network interface, and set up a two-node network on which to practice. With decent Windows NT-capable computers selling for about $500 to $600 apiece these days, this shouldn't be too much of a financial hardship. You can order a BackOffice Trial Kit from Microsoft, which includes evaluation copies of both Workstation and Server, for under $50 from **www.backoffice.microsoft.com/downtrial/**.

➤ Windows NT Workstation? [Yes or No]

If Yes, make sure you understand the concepts covered in Exam 70-073.

If No, you will want to obtain a copy of Windows NT Workstation and learn how to install, configure, and maintain it. You can use *MCSE NT Workstation 4 Exam Cram* to guide your activities and studies, or work straight from Microsoft's test objectives if you prefer.

For any and all of these Microsoft exams, the Resource Kits for the topics involved are a good study resource. You can purchase softcover Resource Kits from Microsoft Press (search for them at **http://mspress.microsoft.com/**), but they're also included on the TechNet CD subscription (**www.microsoft.com/technet**). We believe that Resource Kits are among the best preparation tools available, along with the *Exam Crams* and *Exam Preps*, that you can use to get ready for Microsoft exams.

You have the option of taking the Window 95 (70-064) exam or the Windows 98 (70-098) exam, instead of Exam 70-073, to fulfill your desktop operating system requirement for the MCSE. Although we don't recommend these others (because studying for Workstation helps you prepare for the Server exams), we do recommend that you obtain Resource Kits and other tools to help you prepare for those exams if you decide to take one or both of them for your own reasons.

6. For any specific Microsoft product that is not itself an operating system (for example, FrontPage 98, SQL Server, SMS, and so on), have you installed, configured, used, and upgraded this software? [Yes or No]

If the answer is Yes, skip to the next section, "Testing Your Exam-Readiness." If it's No, you must get some experience. Read on for suggestions on how to do this.

Experience is a must with any Microsoft product exam, be it something as simple as FrontPage 98 or as challenging as SMS 2 or SQL Server 7. You can grab a download of BackOffice at **www.backoffice.microsoft.com/downtrial/**; for trial copies of other software, search Microsoft's Web site using the name of the product as your search term.

If you have the funds, or your employer will pay your way, consider taking a class at a Certified Training and Education Center (CTEC) or at an Authorized Academic Training Partner (AATP). In addition to classroom exposure to the topic of your choice, you get a copy of the software that is the focus of your course, along with a trial version of whatever operating system it needs (usually, NT Server), with the training materials for that class.

Before you even think about taking any Microsoft exam, make sure you've spent enough time with the related software to understand how it may be installed and configured, how to maintain such an installation, and how to troubleshoot that software when things go wrong. This will help you in the exam, and in real life!

Testing Your Exam-Readiness

Whether you attend a formal class on a specific topic to get ready for an exam or use written materials to study on your own, some preparation for the Microsoft certification exams is essential. At $100 a try, pass or fail, you want to do everything you can to pass on your first try. That's where studying comes in.

We have included one practice exam in this book. If you don't hit a score of at least 80 percent after the practice exam, you'll want to investigate the other practice test resources we mention in this section.

For any given subject, consider taking a class if you've tackled self-study materials, taken the test, and failed anyway. The opportunity to interact with an instructor and fellow students can make all the difference in the world, if you can afford that privilege. For information about Microsoft classes, visit the Training and Certification page at **www.microsoft.com/train_cert/** (use the "Find a Course" link).

If you can't afford to take a class, visit the Training and Certification page anyway, because it also includes pointers to free practice exams and to Microsoft Certified Professional Approved Study Guides and other self-study tools. And even if you can't afford to spend much at all, you should still invest in some low-cost practice exams from commercial vendors, because they can help you assess your readiness to pass a test better than any other tool. All of the following Web sites offer practice exams online for less than $100 apiece (some for significantly less than that):

➤ Beachfront Quizzer at **www.bfq.com/**

➤ CramSession at **www.cramsession.com/**

➤ Hardcore MCSE at **www.hardcoremcse.com/**

➤ LANWrights at **www.lanw.com/books/examcram/order.htm**

➤ MeasureUp at **www.measureup.com/**

7. Have you taken a practice exam on your chosen test subject? [Yes or No]

If Yes, and you scored 70 percent or better, you're probably ready to tackle the real thing. If your score isn't above that crucial threshold, keep at it until you break that barrier.

If No, obtain all the free and low-budget practice tests you can find (see the list above) and get to work. Keep at it until you can break the passing threshold comfortably.

 When it comes to assessing your test readiness, there is no better way than to take a good-quality practice exam and pass with a score of 70 percent or better. When we're preparing ourselves, we shoot for 80-plus percent, just to leave room for the "weirdness factor" that sometimes shows up on Microsoft exams.

Assessing Readiness For Exam 70-086

In addition to the general exam-readiness information in the previous section, there are several things you can do to prepare for the SMS 2 exam. As you're getting ready for Exam 70-086, visit the MCSE mailing list. Sign up at **www.sunbelt-software.com** (look for the "Subscribe to..." button). You will also find a great source of questions and related information at the CramSession site at **www.cramsession.com.** These are great places to ask questions and get good answers, or simply to watch the questions that others ask (along with the answers, of course).

You should also cruise the Web looking for "braindumps" (recollections of test topics and experiences recorded by others) to help you anticipate topics you're likely to encounter on the test. The MCSE mailing list is a good place to ask where the useful braindumps are, or you can check Shawn Gamble's list at **www.commandcentral.com** (he's also got some peachy—and free—practice tests on this subject) or Herb Martin's Braindump Heaven at **http://209. 207.167.177/.**

 When using any braindump, it's OK to pay attention to information about questions. But you can't always be sure that a braindump's author will also be able to provide correct answers. Thus, use the questions to guide your studies, but don't rely on the answers in a braindump to lead you to the truth. Double-check everything you find in any braindump.

Microsoft exam mavens also recommend checking the Microsoft Knowledge Base (available on its own CD as part of the TechNet collection, or on the Microsoft Web site at **http://support.microsoft.com/support/**) for "meaningful technical support issues" that relate to your exam's topics. Although we're not sure exactly what the quoted phrase means, we have also noticed some overlap between technical support questions on particular products and troubleshooting questions on the exams for those products.

For SMS 2 preparation in particular, we'd also like to recommend that you check out one or more of these resources as you prepare to take Exam 70-086:

➤ Microsoft Corporation. *Microsoft Systems Management Server Administrator's Guide, version 2.0.* Microsoft Corporation, Redmond, WA, 1999.

➤ Microsoft Press. *Microsoft Systems Management Server Resource Guide.* Microsoft Press, Redmond, WA, 1999. ISBN 0-7356-0583-1. This is one volume of the *Microsoft BackOffice 4.5 Resource Kit.*

Stop by your favorite bookstore or online bookseller to check out one or more of these resources.

One last note: Hopefully, it makes sense to stress the importance of hands-on experience in the context of the SMS 2 exam. As you review the material for that exam, you'll realize that hands-on experience with SMS 2 services, features, and operations is invaluable.

Onward, Through The Fog!

Once you've assessed your readiness, undertaken the right background studies, obtained the hands-on experience that will help you understand the products and technologies at work, and reviewed the many sources of information to help you prepare for a test, you'll be ready to take a round of practice tests. When your scores come back positive enough to get you through the exam, you're ready to go after the real thing. If you follow our assessment regime, you'll not only know what you need to study, but when you're ready to make a test date at Sylvan or VUE. Good luck!

Microsoft
Certification Exams

. . . .

Terms you'll need to understand:

✓ Radio button

✓ Checkbox

✓ Exhibit

✓ Multiple-choice question formats

✓ Careful reading

✓ Process of elimination

✓ Fixed-length tests

✓ Adaptive tests

✓ Short-form tests

✓ Combination tests

✓ Simulations

Techniques you'll need to master:

✓ Assessing your exam-readiness

✓ Preparing to take a certification exam

✓ Practicing (to make perfect)

✓ Making the best use of the testing software

✓ Budgeting your time

✓ Guessing (as a last resort)

Exam taking is not something that most people anticipate eagerly, no matter how well prepared they may be. In most cases, familiarity helps offset test anxiety. In plain English, this means you probably won't be as nervous when you take your fourth or fifth Microsoft certification exam as you'll be when you take your first one.

Whether it's your first exam or your tenth, understanding the details of exam taking (how much time to spend on questions, the environment you'll be in, and so on) and the exam software will help you concentrate on the material rather than on the setting. Likewise, mastering a few basic exam-taking skills should help you recognize—and perhaps even outfox—some of the tricks and snares you're bound to find in some of the exam questions.

This chapter, besides explaining the exam environment and software, describes some proven exam-taking strategies that you should be able to use to your advantage.

Assessing Exam Readiness

We strongly recommend that before you take any Microsoft exam, you read through and take the Self-Assessment included with this book (it appears just before this chapter, in fact). Doing so will allow you to pinpoint areas that you need to study more to obtain an Microsoft Certified Systems Engineer (MCSE). If you get the right set of basics under your belt, obtaining Microsoft certification will be that much easier.

Once you've worked through an *Exam Cram*, read the supplementary materials, and taken the practice test, you'll have a pretty clear idea of whether you are ready to take the real exam. Although we strongly recommend that you keep practicing until your scores top the 80 percent mark, 85 percent would be a good goal, to give yourself some margin for error in a real exam situation (where stress will play more of a role than when you practice). Once you hit that point, you should be ready to go. However, if you get through the practice exam in this book without attaining that score, you should keep taking practice tests and studying the materials until you get there. In the Self-Assessment, you'll find more information about other practice test vendors, along with even more pointers on how to study and prepare. But now, on to the exam itself!

The Exam Situation

When you arrive at the testing center where you scheduled your exam, you'll need to sign in with an exam coordinator. He or she will ask you to show two forms of identification, one of which must be a photo ID. After you've signed in and your time slot arrives, you'll be asked to deposit any books, bags, or other items you brought with you. Then, you'll be escorted into a closed room. Typically, the room will be furnished with anywhere from one to half a dozen computers, and each workstation will be separated from the others by dividers designed to keep you from seeing what's happening on someone else's computer.

You'll be furnished with a pen or pencil and a blank sheet of paper, or, in some cases, an erasable plastic sheet and an erasable pen. You're allowed to write down anything you want on both sides of this sheet. Before the exam, you should memorize as much of the material that appears on The Cram Sheet (in the front of this book) as you can, so you can write that information on the blank sheet as soon as you are seated in front of the computer. You can refer to your rendition of The Cram Sheet anytime you like during the test, but you'll have to surrender the sheet when you leave the room.

Most test rooms feature a wall with a large picture window or video camera. This permits the exam coordinator to monitor the room, to prevent exam-takers from talking to one another, and to observe anything out of the ordinary that might go on. The exam coordinator will have preloaded the appropriate Microsoft certification exam—for this book, that's Exam 70-086, "Implementing and Supporting Microsoft Systems Management Server 2.0"—and you'll be permitted to start as soon as you're seated in front of the computer.

All Microsoft certification exams allow a certain maximum amount of time in which to complete your work (this time is indicated on the exam by an on-screen counter/clock, so you can check the time remaining whenever you like). All Microsoft certification exams are computer generated, and most use a multiple-choice format. Although this may sound quite simple, the questions are constructed not only to check your mastery of basic facts about SMS, but they also require you to evaluate one or more sets of circumstances or requirements. Often, you'll be asked to give more than one answer to a question. Likewise, you might be asked to select the best or most effective solution to a problem from a range of choices, all of which are technically correct. Taking the exam is quite an adventure, and it involves real thinking. This book shows you what to expect and how to deal with the potential problems, puzzles, and predicaments.

In the next section, you'll learn more about how Microsoft test questions look and how they must be answered.

Exam Layout And Design

Some exam questions require you to select a single answer; others ask you to select one or more correct answers. The following multiple-choice question requires you to select a single correct answer. Following the question is a brief summary of each potential answer and why it is either right or wrong.

Question 1

> You want to find out which client agents have been enabled for SMS clients in your site. Which SMS Administrator console node will provide you with this information?
>
> ○ a. Client Agents node (under Site Systems)
>
> ○ b. Windows NT Logon Client Installation node
>
> ○ c. Advertisement Status to see which clients have received client agent software
>
> ○ d. Express setup

Answer a is correct. To view which client agents are enabled, you use the Client Agents node under Site Settings in the SMS Administrator console. Answer b is incorrect because Windows NT Logon Client Installation allows you to enable a method of installing SMS client software; it does not control client agent installation. Answer c is incorrect because you do not use advertisements to install client agents. Answer d is incorrect because Express setup is not a node in the SMS Administrator console.

This sample question format corresponds closely to the Microsoft certification exam format—the only difference on the exam is that answer keys do not follow the questions. To select an answer, position the cursor over the radio button next to the answer. Then, click the mouse button to select the answer.

Let's examine a question where you must select more than one answer. This type of question provides checkboxes rather than radio buttons for marking all appropriate selections.

Question 2

> After using Custom setup, which of the following must you do before Windows Networking Logon Client Installation will successfully install SMS client software on clients in your site? [Choose all correct answers]
>
> ❑ a. Enable Windows Networking Logon Discovery.
>
> ❑ b. Enable Windows Networking Logon Client Installation.
>
> ❑ c. Modify logon scripts.
>
> ❑ d. Configure client status message reporting.

Answers b and c are correct. Enabling Windows Networking Logon Client Installation causes SMS to install logon points. Then, you must modify the user logon scripts to allow SMS to be installed when users logon to the network. Answer a is incorrect because you do not need to enable logon discovery for logon installation to work. Answer d is incorrect because configuring client status message reporting is totally irrelevant to the installation process.

For this particular question, two answers are required. Such questions are scored as wrong unless all the required selections are chosen. In other words, a partially correct answer does not result in partial credit when the test is scored. For Question 2, you have to check the boxes next to answers b and c to obtain credit for a correct answer. Notice that picking the right answers also means knowing why the other answers are wrong! Although these two basic types of questions can appear in many forms, they constitute the foundation on which all the Microsoft certification exam questions rest.

Other questions involve exhibits and use charts or network diagrams to help document a workplace scenario that you'll be asked to troubleshoot or configure. Careful attention to such exhibits is the key to success. Be prepared to toggle frequently between the exhibit and the question as you work.

Microsoft's Testing Formats

Currently, Microsoft uses four testing formats:

➤ Fixed-length

➤ Adaptive

➤ Short-form

➤ Combination

Microsoft tests can come in any one of these forms. You must take the test in whichever form it appears; you can't choose one form over another.

Some Microsoft exams employ more advanced testing capabilities than might immediately meet the eye. Although the questions that appear are still multiple choice, the logic that drives them is more complex than that of older Microsoft tests (which use a fixed sequence of questions) called *fixed-length tests*. Other exams employ a sophisticated user interface, which Microsoft calls a *simulation*, to test your knowledge of the software and systems under consideration in a more or less "live" environment that behaves just like the original. At the time of this writing, the SMS exam was fixed-length.

Adaptive Tests

For many upcoming exams, Microsoft is turning to a well-known technique, called *adaptive testing*, to establish a test-taker's level of knowledge and product competence. Adaptive exams look the same as fixed-length exams, but they discover the level of difficulty at which an individual test-taker can correctly answer questions. Microsoft is also in the process of converting some of its older fixed-length exams into adaptive exams.

In adaptive tests, test-takers with differing levels of knowledge or ability see different sets of questions. Individuals with high levels of knowledge or ability are presented with a smaller set of more difficult questions; individuals with lower levels of knowledge are presented with a larger set of easier questions. Two individuals may answer the same percentage of questions correctly, but the test-taker with a higher knowledge or ability level will score higher because his or her questions are worth more. Also, the lower-level test-taker will probably answer more questions than his or her more-knowledgeable colleague. This explains why adaptive tests use ranges of values to define the number of questions and the amount of time it takes to complete the test.

Adaptive tests work by evaluating the test-taker's most recent answer. A correct answer leads to a more difficult question (and the test software's estimate of the test-taker's knowledge and ability level is raised). An incorrect answer leads to a less difficult question (and the test software's estimate of the test-taker's knowledge and ability level is lowered). This process continues until the test targets the test-taker's true ability level. The exam ends when the test-taker's level of accuracy meets a statistically acceptable value (in other words, when his or her performance demonstrates an acceptable level of knowledge and ability) or when the maximum number of items has been presented (in which case, the test-taker is almost certain to fail). Currently, the SMS exam is not adaptive.

Short-Form Tests

Microsoft has recently introduced the short-form test for its most popular tests. As of this writing, only Networking Essentials (Exam 70-058) and TCP/IP (Exam 70-059) have appeared in this format. A short-form test delivers approximately 30 questions to its takers, giving them exactly 60 minutes to complete the exam. This type of exam is similar to a fixed-length test in that it allows readers to jump ahead or return to earlier questions, and to cycle through the questions until the test is done. Microsoft does not use adaptive logic in this test, but claims that statistical analysis of the question pool is such that the 30 questions delivered during a short-form exam will conclusively measure a test-taker's knowledge of the subject matter in much the same way as an adaptive test will. You can think of the short-form test as a kind of "greatest hits" version of the adaptive exam on the same topic (that is, the most important questions).

Combination Tests

A fourth kind of test you could encounter is what we've dubbed the combination exam. Several test-takers have reported that some of the Microsoft exams—including Windows NT Server (Exam 70-067), Windows NT Server in the Enterprise (Exam 70-068), and Windows NT Workstation (Exam 70-073)—can appear as combination exams. Such exams begin with a set of 15 through 25 adaptive questions, followed by 10 fixed-length questions. In fact, many test-takers have reported that although some combination tests claim that they will present both adaptive and fixed-length portions, when the test-taker has finished the adaptive portion (usually in exactly 15 questions), the test ends there. Because such users have all attained passing scores, it may be that a high enough passing score on the adaptive portion of a combination test obviates the fixed-length portion. However, we're not completely sure about this, and Microsoft won't comment. Most combination exams allow a maximum of 60 minutes for the testing period.

The biggest difference between an adaptive test and a fixed-length or short-form test is that on a fixed-length or short-form test, you can revisit questions after you've read them over one or more times. On an adaptive test, you must answer the question when it's presented and will have no opportunities to revisit that question thereafter.

Strategies For Different Testing Formats

Before you can choose a test-taking strategy, you need to know if your test is fixed-length, adaptive, short-form, or combination. When you begin your exam, the software will tell you the test is adaptive, if in fact the version you're taking is presented as an adaptive test. If your introductory materials fail to mention this, you're probably taking a fixed-length test. If the total number of questions involved is exactly 30, then you're taking a short-form test. Combination tests announce themselves by indicating that they will start with a set of adaptive questions, followed by fixed-length questions. However, they don't actually call themselves "combination tests" or "combination exams"—we've adopted this nomenclature for descriptive reasons.

You'll be able to tell for sure if you are taking a fixed-length, adaptive, short-form, or combination test by the first question. If it includes a checkbox that lets you mark the question for later review, you're taking a fixed-length or short-form test. If the total number of questions is 30, it's a short-form test; if there are more than 30, it's a fixed-length test. Adaptive test questions (and the first set of questions on a combination test) can be visited (and answered) only once, and they include no such checkbox.

The Fixed-Length And Short-Form Exam Strategy

A well-known strategy when taking fixed-length or short-form exams is to first read over the entire exam from start to finish while answering only those questions you feel absolutely sure of. On subsequent passes, you can dive into more complex questions more deeply, knowing how many such questions you have left.

Fortunately, the Microsoft exam software for fixed-length and short-form tests makes the multiple-visit approach easy to implement. At the top-left corner of each question is a checkbox that permits you to mark that question for a later visit.

> *Note: Marking questions makes review easier, but you can return to any question by clicking on the Forward or Back button repeatedly.*

As you read each question, if you answer only those you're sure of and mark for review those that you're not sure of, you can keep working through a decreasing list of questions as you answer the trickier ones in order.

 There's at least one potential benefit to reading the exam over completely before answering the trickier questions: Sometimes, information supplied in later questions will shed more light on earlier questions. Other times, information you read in later questions might jog your memory about SMS facts or behavior that also will help with earlier questions. Either way, you'll come out ahead if you defer answering those questions about which you're not absolutely sure.

Here are some question-handling strategies that apply to fixed-length and short-form tests. Use them if you have the chance:

➤ When returning to a question after your initial read-through, read every word again—otherwise, your mind can fall quickly into a rut. Sometimes, revisiting a question after turning your attention elsewhere lets you see something you missed, but the strong tendency is to see what you've seen before. Try to avoid that tendency at all costs.

➤ If you return to a question more than twice, try to articulate to yourself what you don't understand about the question, why the answers don't appear to make sense, or what appears to be missing. If you chew on the subject for a while, your subconscious might provide the details that are lacking or you might notice a "trick" that will point to the right answer.

As you work your way through the exam, another counter that Microsoft provides will come in handy—the number of questions completed and questions outstanding. For fixed-length and short-form tests, it's wise to budget your time by making sure that you've completed one-quarter of the questions one-quarter of the way through the exam period. For a short-form test, this means you must complete one-quarter of the questions one-quarter of the way through (the first 8 questions in the first 15 minutes) and three-quarters of the questions three-quarters of the way through (24 questions in 45 minutes).

If you're not finished when only five minutes remain, use that time to guess your way through any remaining questions. Remember: Guessing is potentially more valuable than not answering, because blank answers are always wrong, but a guess may turn out to be right. If you don't have a clue about any of the remaining questions, pick answers at random, or choose all a's, b's, and so on. The important thing is to submit an exam for scoring that has an answer for every question.

 At the very end of your exam period, you're better off guessing than leaving questions unanswered.

The Adaptive Exam Strategy

If there's one strategy that applies to taking an adaptive test, it could be summed up as "Get it right the first time." You cannot elect to skip a question and move on to the next one when taking an adaptive test, because the testing software uses your answer to the current question to select whatever question it plans to present next. Nor can you return to a question once you've moved on, as the software gives you only one chance to answer the question. You can, however, take notes, because sometimes information supplied in earlier questions will shed more light on later questions.

Also, when you answer a question correctly, you are presented with a more difficult question next, to help the software gauge your level of skill and ability. When you answer a question incorrectly, you are presented with a less difficult question, and the software lowers its current estimate of your skill and ability. This continues until the program settles into a reasonably accurate estimate of what you know and can do, and takes you on average through somewhere between 15 and 30 questions as you complete the test.

The good news is that if you know your stuff, you'll probably finish most adaptive tests in 30 minutes or so. The bad news is that you must really, really know your stuff to do your best on an adaptive test. That's because some questions are so convoluted, complex, or hard to follow that you're bound to miss one or two, at a minimum, even if you do know your stuff. So the more you know, the better you'll do on an adaptive test, even accounting for the occasionally weird or unfathomable questions that appear on these exams.

Because you can't tell in advance if a test is fixed-length, short-form, adaptive, or combination, you will be best served by preparing for the exam as if it were adaptive. That way, you should be prepared to pass no matter what kind of test you take. But if you do take a fixed-length or short-form test, remember our tips from the preceding section. They should help you improve on what you could do on an adaptive test.

If you encounter a question on an adaptive test that you can't answer, you must guess an answer immediately. Because of the way the software works, you may have to suffer for your guess on the next question if you guess right, because you'll get a more difficult question next!

The Combination Exam Strategy

When it comes to studying for a combination test, your best bet is to approach it as a slightly longer adaptive exam, and to study as if the exam were adaptive only. Because the adaptive approach doesn't rely on rereading questions, and suggests that you take notes while reading useful information on test questions, it's hard to go wrong with this strategy when taking any kind of Microsoft certification test.

Exam-Taking Basics

The most important advice about taking any exam is this: Read each question carefully. Some questions use terminology in incredibly precise ways. We have taken numerous exams—both practice and live—and in nearly every one, have missed at least one question because we didn't read it closely or carefully enough.

Here are some suggestions on how to deal with the tendency to jump to an answer too quickly:

➤ Make sure you read every word in the question. If you find yourself jumping ahead impatiently, go back and start over.

➤ As you read, try to restate the question in your own terms. If you can do this, you should be able to pick the correct answer(s) much more easily.

Above all, try to deal with each question by thinking through what you know about SMS—the characteristics, behaviors, and facts involved. By reviewing what you know (and what you've written down on your information sheet), you'll often recall or understand things sufficiently to determine the answer to the question.

Question-Handling Strategies

Based on exams we've taken, some interesting trends have become apparent. For those questions that take only a single answer, usually two or three of the answers will be obviously incorrect, and two of the answers will be plausible—of course, only one can be correct. Unless the answer leaps out at you (if it does, reread the question to look for a trick; sometimes those are the ones you're most likely to get wrong), begin the process of answering by eliminating those answers that are most obviously wrong.

Things to look for in obviously wrong answers include spurious menu choices or utility names, irrelevant software options, and terminology you've never seen. If you've done your homework for an exam, no valid information should be completely new to you. In that case, unfamiliar or bizarre terminology probably indicates a totally bogus answer.

Numerous questions assume that the default behavior of a particular utility is in effect. Knowing the defaults and understanding what they mean will help you cut through many Gordian knots.

Mastering The Inner Game

In the final analysis, knowledge breeds confidence, and confidence breeds success. If you study the materials in this book carefully and review all the practice questions at the end of each chapter, you should become aware of those areas where additional learning and study are required.

Next, follow up by reading some or all of the materials recommended in the "Need To Know More?" section at the end of each chapter. The idea is to become familiar enough with the concepts and situations you find in the sample questions that you can reason your way through similar situations on a real exam. If you know the material, you have every right to be confident that you can pass the exam.

After you've worked your way through the book, take the practice exam in Chapter 12. This will provide a reality check and help you identify areas to study further. Make sure you follow up and review materials related to the questions you miss on the practice exam before scheduling a real exam. Only when you've covered all the ground and feel comfortable with the whole scope of the practice exam should you take the online exam. Only if you score 85 percent or better should you proceed to the real thing (otherwise, obtain some additional practice tests so you can keep trying until you hit this magic number).

Armed with the information in this book and with the determination to augment your knowledge, you should be able to pass the certification exam. However, you need to work at it, or you'll spend the exam fee more than once before you finally pass. If you prepare seriously, you should do well. Good luck!

Additional Resources

A good source of information about Microsoft certification exams comes from Microsoft itself. Because its products and technologies—and the exams that go with them—change frequently, the best place to go for exam-related information is online.

If you haven't already visited the MCP site, do so right now. The MCP home page resides at **www.microsoft.com/mcp/** (see Figure 1.1).

> *Note: This page might not be there by the time you read this, or it may be replaced by something new and different, because things change regularly on the Microsoft site. Should this happen, please read the sidebar titled "Coping With Change On The Web."*

The menu options in the left column of the home page point to the most important sources of information in the MCP pages. Here's what to check out:

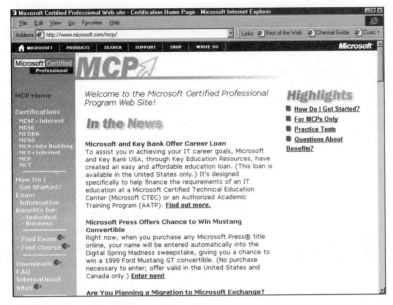

Figure 1.1   The MCP home page.

➤ **Certifications** Use this menu entry to read about the various certification programs that Microsoft offers.

➤ **Find Exam** Use this menu entry to pull up a search tool that lets you list all Microsoft exams and locate all exams relevant to any Microsoft certification (MCP, MCSE, MCSD, and so on) or those exams that cover a particular product. This tool is quite useful not only to examine the options but also to obtain specific exam preparation information, because each exam has its own associated preparation guide. This is Exam 70-086.

➤ **Downloads** Use this menu entry to find a list of the files and practice exams that Microsoft makes available to the public. These include several items worth downloading, especially the Certification Update, the PEP exams, various assessment exams, and a general exam study guide. Try to make time to peruse these materials before taking your first exam.

These are just the high points of what's available in the MCP pages. As you browse through them—and we strongly recommend that you do—you'll probably find other informational tidbits that are every bit as interesting and compelling.

Coping With Change On The Web

Sooner or later, all the information we've shared with you about the MCP pages and the other Web-based resources mentioned throughout the rest of this book will go stale or be replaced by newer information. In some cases, the URLs you find here might lead you to their replacements; in other cases, the URLs will go nowhere, leaving you with the dreaded "404 File Not Found" error message. When that happens, don't give up. If you can't find something where the book says it lives, intensify your search.

There's always a way to find what you want on the Web if you're willing to invest some time and energy. Most large or complex Web sites—and Microsoft's qualifies on both counts—offer a search engine. On all of Microsoft's Web pages, a Search button appears along the top edge of the page. As long as you can get to Microsoft's site (it should stay at **www.microsoft.com** for a long time), use this tool to help you find what you need.

The more focused you can make a search request, the more likely the results will include information you can use. For example, you can search for the string

```
"training and certification"
```

to produce a lot of data about the subject in general. However, if you're looking for the preparation guide for Exam 70-086, "Implementing and Supporting Microsoft Systems Management Server 2.0," you'll be more likely to get there quickly if you use a search string similar to the following:

```
"Exam 70-086" AND "preparation guide"
```

Likewise, if you want to find the Training and Certification downloads, try a search string such as this:

```
"training and certification" AND "download page"
```

Finally, feel free to use general search tools—such as **www.search.com**, **www.altavista.com**, and **www.excite.com**—to look for related information. Although Microsoft offers great information about its certification exams online, there are plenty of third-party sources of information and assistance that need not follow Microsoft's party line.

Introduction To SMS 2

Terms you'll need to understand:

- √ Client
- √ Resource discovery
- √ Site server
- √ Site hierarchy
- √ Site boundaries
- √ SMS site database
- √ SQL Server database
- √ Primary site
- √ Secondary site

- √ Child site
- √ Parent site
- √ Site system
- √ Site system role
- √ SMS Administrator console
- √ Windows Management Instrumentation (WMI)
- √ Central site

Techniques you'll need to master:

- √ Understanding how to construct site hierarchies
- √ Choosing where in your company you should install primary and secondary sites

- √ Understanding the functions of site systems
- √ Understanding the relationship between the SMS Administrator console, the SMS Provider, WMI, and the SMS site database

Before you can successfully learn the principles you need to succeed on the SMS 2 exam, you must firmly understand the terminology and the various SMS features you can install and configure. This chapter introduces SMS terminology and important concepts, as well as the basic change and configuration management features SMS provides for IT departments. In addition, we will highlight some important concepts that you'll need to know when you take the SMS certification exam.

Overview Of SMS Features

SMS is a client-server application that runs on the Microsoft Windows NT operating system and utilizes a Microsoft SQL Server database. To be fully functional, SMS is installed on both servers and clients on your network. After you have installed and configured your SMS server or servers, you install SMS client software on client computers. Then, SMS becomes a feedback system, with the clients responding to instructions from the SMS servers. You can configure SMS to perform many management tasks. In the following sections, we explain the main ones.

Resource Discovery And Client Installation

Before SMS can assist you in electronically managing the computers in your company, SMS needs to collect information about the various computers and network devices in use on your network. SMS determines to which sites clients and/or resources belong and then installs SMS client software on client computers. SMS accomplishes these goals using the processes of discovering resources and installing clients.

> *Note:*   *See Chapter 3 for information on the client operating systems that SMS supports for resource discovery and client installation.*

Resource Discovery

Resource discovery is the process of discovering any device on your network that has an Internet Protocol (IP) or Internetwork Packet Exchange (IPX) address. In addition, SMS can discover the supported operating systems that are running on discovered client computers as well Windows NT user accounts and user groups. There are three major types of resource discovery:

➤ Network Discovery

➤ Logon client discovery

➤ User Account and User Group Discovery

Network Discovery uses Simple Network Management Protocol (SNMP), Microsoft DHCP servers, and LAN Manager calls to detect devices such as routers, hubs, bridges, and printers, as well as computers. When you use Network Discovery, SMS does not install any software on the computers that are discovered. Network Discovery is simply a mechanism for gathering data about devices on your network.

Logon client discovery provides methods for discovering client computers on your network. During logon discovery, SMS finds computers and installs the SMS client discovery software (including the Systems Management Control Panel applet) on client computers. Several types of discovery methods are available to accommodate the differences in network operating systems and resources in use in various organizations.

User Account and User Group Discovery methods allow you to distribute software to Windows NT domain users and user groups as well as to target software installation or to check on the need for a hardware upgrade based on employee job function. These methods collect discovery data from the Windows NT Primary Domain Controller (PDC).

All discovery methods create Discovery Data Records (DDRs), which contain several fields of information about discovered resources. During the discovery process, DDRs are passed to the primary site server, where they are processed and stored in the SQL Server database.

> *Note:*   *The specific discovery types and the Systems Management Control Panel applet are discussed in more detail in Chapter 5.*

Client Installation

As with resource discovery, there are different methods for installing clients to accommodate differing networks and operating systems. A computer is considered an SMS client when core SMS client software has been installed on it. This software allows SMS clients to do the following:

➤ Communicate with SMS site systems

➤ Learn of client configuration and site server changes

➤ Send status messages to the site server

➤ Perform SMS client functions

SMS supports all 32-bit Windows operating systems for SMS client software. Windows 2000 was in beta testing phase at the time SMS was released, so SMS does support Windows 2000 beta 2 clients that participate in a Windows

NT 4 domain. SMS also supports Windows 3.1 and Windows for Workgroups 3.1x. Macintosh, OS/2, and DOS clients are not supported.

SMS can install many client components. Those that are selectively installed and provide various management features are called *client agents*; they are visible in the Systems Management Control Panel applet.

> *Note:*   *Client installation and configuration are discussed in more detail in Chapters 5 and 6.*

Site Boundaries

SMS sites are defined by site boundaries. All computers discovered within the site boundaries are assigned to the site and can then be installed as clients for the site. The site boundaries of two or more separate SMS sites can overlap. In such cases, client computers located in the shared boundary region are assigned to all of the sites, therefore becoming SMS clients of multiple sites. You can then manage them from any of these SMS sites.

You define site boundaries based on IP network IDs and/or Internetwork Packet Exchange (IPX) network numbers. SMS does not support sites that span slow wide area network (WAN) links. This site boundary requirement is imposed because you need fast and reliable network links between all SMS site systems and SMS site clients within a site.

When a computer system DDR is produced, SMS compares the computer's location on the network to the defined SMS site boundaries and either assigns the computer to its appropriate site (or sites) or leaves it unassigned. The same holds true for the DDRs stored in the SMS site database for all discovered resources. If the IP network ID of a discovered resource is not within the specified site boundaries, a resource is not assigned to the SMS site. Whenever the SMS administrator changes the SMS site boundaries, the DDRs are reevaluated and corresponding resources are appropriately assigned.

 Network Discovery is not limited to searching for resources within the SMS site boundaries. Network Discovery scans the network regions defined in the Network Discovery Properties dialog box and produces DDRs based on discovered IP devices. DDRs are stored in the SMS site database and the devices from within the site boundaries are then assigned to the site, whereas others are marked as unassigned. Note that the SMS site database of the site initiating the discovery is the one that will have the stored DDRs. If Network Discovery is initiated from a secondary site, the DDRs will be stored at its parent site.

Note: See Chapter 4 for more detailed information about creating and using site boundaries.

Inventory

You can configure SMS 2 to collect both hardware and software inventory information from SMS client computers. The inventory information is then processed on the site server and stored in the SMS site database. You can use the inventory information you gather to determine which computers are running specific types of software and software versions. You can use hardware inventory information to determine which client computers are physically capable of installing and running newer software versions. You can also create administrative reports with inventory data and use these reports to help audit your computer systems.

Hardware Inventory

Hardware inventory is enabled (or disabled) for all clients in an entire SMS site. The 32-bit hardware inventory agent is based on WMI (covered in detail later in this chapter). The Hardware Inventory Client Agent collects the data and stores it on both the client computer and the site server (in the SMS site database). During the next inventory cycle, the Hardware Inventory Client Agent collects new hardware data, compares it to the previously stored inventory data, and writes the new inventory data to a local repository. If a client is connected to the network, the client sends only the incremental update to the appropriate SMS site system. The site system then forwards the update to the site server, where it gets processed and stored in the SMS site database.

For 16-bit inventory, the Hardware Inventory Client Agent always collects inventory directly by scanning the hardware and the operating system of the client and always uploads the entire file to the site server. Both types of inventory, 16- and 32-bit, collect data based on a predefined template—the SMS_DEF.MOF file. You can modify this file to allow filtering options to collect either more or less inventory data.

Hardware inventory on computers that run 32-bit operating systems is processed through the Win32 Provider. When hardware inventory is enabled and installed on SMS clients, the Hardware Inventory Client Agent on each client reads the SMS_DEF.MOF file to obtain the hardware inventory classes it should inventory. It then queries the Common Information Model (CIM) Object Manager, which collects the data through the Win32 Provider. The hardware inventory information for each client is stored on the client in the CIM repository.

> For 16-bit clients, the same SMS_DEF.MOF file is used;
> however, the collected inventory information is not as
> extensive.

Software Inventory

Software inventory is enabled (or disabled) for all clients in an entire SMS site. SMS collects software inventory information from the headers of the program files installed on computers in your site. You can configure the Software Inventory Client Agent to inventory files by file extension (.EXE, .DLL, .DOC, and so on). You can also collect files from SMS client computers based on their file names (wildcard characters are allowed).

The hardware inventory and software inventory processes are similar. The Software Inventory Client Agent collects software inventory data at each client. This data is then stored in a software inventory complete file (which uses the .SIC file extension) and in a software inventory delta file (which uses the .SID file extension). The first collected data file (with the .SIC extension) is passed to the client access point (CAP), forwarded to the site server, and stored in the SMS site database. Each consecutive time software inventory is run, only the incremental update file (with the .SID extension) is uploaded to the CAP and forwarded to the SMS site server for processing.

Note: *For more detailed information on hardware and software inventory, see Chapters 6 and 7.*

Software Distribution

The software distribution feature allows you to automate software distribution and installation at client computers based on collected discovery and/or inventory data. In other words, you can target software to specific client computers, users, and user groups. You can use this feature to perform the following tasks:

➤ Install service packs

➤ Run customized batch files

➤ Install complete software packages, such as operating systems or word processing packages

➤ Distribute software to clients running both 16- and 32-bit operating systems

When a new machine gets installed with SMS client software, if the new user fits predefined software distribution rules, the user automatically receives advertised software. You can make the software available to run on only specific client machines, to be assigned to clients to run at a specified time, or to run on a schedule repetitively. Additionally, using SMS Installer scripting capabilities, you can silently install software that isn't compatible with unattended installation. Uninstall functionality is also supported.

> *Note:*   *For more detailed information on the software distribution process, see Chapter 8.*

Software Metering

Software metering allows you to monitor and manage software license usage in your company. You can use software metering to monitor software use on Windows NT, 95, and 98 clients in your SMS site. You can configure software metering to keep track of which software applications are used, as well as which computers and users are using them. This information can help you verify that you are within the software licensing agreement limits for concurrent use of applications your company has purchased.

You can also configure software metering to actually grant or deny access to specific applications. This feature allows you to restrict particular software use to only the number allowed in your licensing agreements. Additionally, you can restrict application use by user, user group, workstation, and time.

> *Note:*   *For more detailed information on software metering, see Chapter 7.*

Product Compliance

You can use the Product Compliance feature and its accompanying Product Compliance database to verify your company's software into Year 2000 (Y2K) and Euro compliance. Microsoft has a Web site (**www.microsoft.com/technet/ year2k/product/prodcomp.txt**) where it maintains the most recent compliance database for Microsoft products. The downloadable compliance database is stored in a text file and can be easily imported into the SMS Product Compliance database.

Each Microsoft product is assigned a compliance value in the Product Compliance database. To determine Y2K/Euro software compliance in your company, follow these steps:

1. First, run software inventory to find which software is currently installed on your company's computers.

2. Next, use predefined queries that first compare software inventory data with the compliance data and then report all machines with non-compliant software.

3. After you verify the compliance status of the software in your organization, you might want to use the software distribution feature to send Y2K- and Euro-compliant software upgrades to SMS clients.

Note: For more detailed information on Product Compliance, see Chapter 8.

Remote Tools

SMS provides several tools for help desk personnel to use from a central management location. You configure remote tools settings for an entire site, and all client computers in your site use the same configuration. If you want specific clients to have a different client configuration, you need to create a separate SMS site to assign them to. The remote tools feature includes remote control, remote reboot, remote chat, remote file transfer, and remote execute. You can dramatically enhance remote control of Windows NT clients by using screen compression and accelerated video drivers.

Note: For more detailed information on remote tools, see Chapter 6.

Crystal Reports

You can create reports based on data stored in the SMS site database, the software metering database, and the Product Compliance database using the Crystal Info snap-in utility. SMS ships with several predefined reports, or you can create your own. You can run Crystal Reports on a schedule, print them, or save them as templates for use at other SMS sites. Microsoft recommends installing the Crystal Info snap-in only on a single site server with fewer than 500 clients. If you want to use Crystal Info for reporting at a large site or as part of a site hierarchy, you should consider using different SMS data access methods.

Note: For more information on SMS reporting, see the Microsoft Systems Management Server Resource Guide, version 2 in the Microsoft BackOffice 4.5 Resource Kit.

Network Diagnostic Tools

SMS provides several network tools that can assist you in monitoring your network. These tools are:

➤ Network Monitor (NetMon)

➤ Health Monitor (HealthMon)

➤ Network Trace

NetMon

NetMon is a tool you can use to monitor network traffic patterns and to find network-related problems. It can help you detect and troubleshoot problems on local area networks (LANs), WANs, or serial links that run Microsoft Remote Access Server (RAS). Monitors and Experts, new features of NetMon, make network troubleshooting even easier than using the previous versions of NetMon included in SMS 1.2. Monitors looks for particular patterns in network traffic that may be problematic and then reports them in real time. You can also use NetMon to capture data packets directly from the network on a local segment or on remote segments. Once you capture data packets, you can edit, display, and filter them. Experts analyzes captured data and gives you expert information to help solve network problems.

HealthMon

HealthMon is another SMS utility that uses WMI and data provided by the CIM Object Manager. It is a client-server application where the server runs the HealthMon management console (a Microsoft Management Console—MMC—snap-in) and the clients run HealthMon Agent software. HealthMon Agents query their local CIM repositories for Windows NT and BackOffice critical status information. The agent then uploads this information to the HealthMon console on the HealthMon server. The console is configured with critical and warning threshold settings that visually inform SMS administrators about the condition of their systems.

Network Trace

Network Trace uses data obtained from Network Discovery to create connectivity diagrams between an SMS site server and either a selected SMS site system or all of the site systems in your SMS site (depending on whether you select Site view or Trace view). In Site view, Network Trace diagrams also display the SMS site system roles assigned to each server, IP network IDs and addresses, and network devices such as routers and switches. If one of the SMS site systems is not currently responding, you can use Network Trace to verify whether the current network connection is functioning.

Note: For more detailed information on network diagnostic tools, see Chapter 9.

SMS Toolkit

The SMS Toolkit provides the information you need to create custom applications that integrate with SMS and operate on data made available through WMI. The toolkit contains SMS Provider and CIM schema information, including definitions and the relationship between SMS objects (their classes and attributes). The toolkit allows you to write applications that utilize any of the three WMI access methods:

➤ WMI open database connectivity (ODBC) adapter

➤ WMI application programming interfaces (APIs)

➤ WMI component object model (COM) APIs

With this information, you can create custom applications as MMC snap-ins and attach them to the SMS Administrator console, write scripts to automate SMS administrative tasks, and create other simple or complex applications utilizing WMI and the SMS Provider.

> *Note:*   *You can download the SMS Toolkit from the Microsoft*
> *Developer's Network (MSDN) Web site (**http://msdn.microsoft.com/**
> **developer/sdk/platform.htm**). It is also available as part of the*
> *BackOffice 4.5 Resource Kit.*

Elements Of An SMS Site

An SMS site contains three main elements: site systems, the SMS Administrator console, and data stores. Each of these elements works in concert with the others to provide SMS functionality. The following sections provide more detail about each of the three elements.

SMS Site Systems And Site System Roles

An SMS site is composed of one or more servers that act on behalf of SMS. The servers, which host any of the SMS components or provide SMS functions, are called *site systems*. These servers perform functions for SMS that are called *site system roles*. You can install various SMS components on multiple servers by assigning the following site system roles:

➤ SMS site servers

➤ Site database servers

➤ Logon points

➤ CAPs

➤ Distribution points

➤ Software metering servers

➤ Software metering database servers

➤ Senders

SMS Site Servers

SMS is designed to automate systems management tasks in your organization. In order to accomplish this goal, you must install at least one SMS site server to manage all SMS functions. There are two types of SMS site servers: primary and secondary. *Primary site servers* use Microsoft SQL Server to store data. They have an SMS Administrator console installed that allows administrators to perform management tasks.

The SMS Administrator console is an MMC snap-in with many extensions. Because the extensions are optional, you can create SMS Administrator consoles with the selected extensions to perform only specific management tasks, such as software distribution or remote control. You should remember, though, that these consoles do not provide adequate security for your SMS data. Any user can install additional extensions and gain access to the initially hidden SMS functionality. You need to configure SMS security as described in Chapter 3 to fully protect your network when using MMC snap-ins.

Secondary site servers do not have SQL Server installed and, therefore, do not have their own SMS site database for data storage. Secondary site servers store their data in the site database of their parent sites, which must be primary site servers. Secondary sites do not have an SMS Administrator console either; thus, administrators manage secondary sites from their parent sites.

Secondary sites are often used in locations that do not require a local administrator. This type of site server uses fewer system resources than a primary site server and does not require Microsoft SQL Server. They are therefore less expensive to install and maintain than primary site servers; yet they still perform all of the automated SMS management functions.

A secondary site must be attached to a primary site, where all administrative tasks for that secondary site are performed and all data for the site is stored. A secondary site does not have an SMS Administrator console or a SQL Server database (SMS site database); be careful of tricks on the exam.

Both primary and secondary sites have SMS clients in their site boundaries. The data from primary site clients is stored in the primary site's SMS site database. The data from secondary site clients is stored in the SMS site database of the parent primary site attached to the secondary site.

Site Database Servers

Every primary site requires a site database server to store SMS data. You must install either Microsoft SQL Server 6.5 or 7 before or during the installation of a primary site server. You must configure SQL Server to communicate using either named pipes or multiprotocol network library. Although both versions of SQL Server work very well with SMS, SQL 7 is the preferred choice for SMS because of its advanced management features as well as improved performance and scalability.

The different types of data stored in the SMS site database include:

➤ DDRs

➤ Hardware inventory

➤ Software inventory

➤ Site configuration settings

➤ Status messages

➤ Data from all SMS subsites

 "SMS site database" and "SQL Server database" are interchangeable terms used to refer to the database where SMS data is stored. SMS requires that SQL Server be present with an SMS primary site, either on the same computer or on another computer on the network. The data is stored in a SQL Server database, so "SQL Server database" is frequently used to refer to the SMS site database. Likewise, the term "SQL Server" is interchangeable with the term "site database server" when you are referring to the computer on which SQL Server is installed and that maintains the SMS site database.

Logon Points

If you want to use your existing Windows NT domain structure to discover and/or install SMS clients, you can configure SMS to modify domain controllers and optionally modify user logon scripts so that SMS client software is installed on computers when users log on to the network. SMS provides three logon discovery and installation methods (one for Windows and two for NetWare: Bindery and Novell Directory Services [NDS]).

If you decide to use either networking logon method for client discovery and/ or installation, you need to configure SMS to create and configure SMS logon points. Because logon discovery and logon installation methods are domain-wide, SMS configures all domain controllers (the Primary Domain Controllers [PDCs] and all Backup Domain Controllers [BDCs]) of each enumerated NT domain as logon points. In NetWare environments, you can configure NDS volumes and Bindery servers as logon points.

SMS creates logon points when you enable a logon discovery or logon client installation method. When SMS creates logon points on Windows NT domain controllers, it creates the SMSLOGON share and then copies all necessary files, including the relevant site configuration information and client core installation files.

When you enable logon discovery, a logon discovery agent is created and started as an NT service on each domain controller. You can also configure SMS to modify logon scripts for you, or you can modify them yourself. Alternately, you can discover and/or install clients without having to modify logon scripts. To do so, execute the manual installation process using SMSMAN.EXE. If logon scripts are modified and processed by the network client or SMSMAN.EXE is executed, discovery files are copied to the client computer, a DDR is created, and site membership is evaluated. If the client is assigned to the site (or sites), the SMS client software is installed as well as all of the enabled client agents.

Enabling logon discovery or logon client installation does not actually affect your clients; doing so only configures the SMS logon points. To discover and/or install clients, you must configure SMS to modify logon scripts, or you must do so manually. Another option is to distribute the manual installation process file to your clients and have them execute it.

SMS logon points are managed entirely by SMS. Although the name of the domain configured with either a logon discovery or logon installation method does not change, all domain controllers in that domain are continuously updated and synchronized. These updates are independent of the number and names of the domain controllers. If the name of a NetWare Bindery server changes, you must reflect this change in the MMC; the same applies to the NDS tree, container, and volume names.

Client Access Points (CAPs)

CAPs, as the name implies, are the points of contact between a client and a site server. A CAP (installed under the CAP_*sitecode* share) is automatically created on the site server when you install SMS. You can have multiple CAPs in one site by assigning their roles to other Windows NT or NetWare servers. You can also remove the CAP role from the site server once you have installed another CAP in the site.

Clients access CAPs for a number of reasons:

➤ To finish the SMS client installation process.

➤ To report their discovery records.

➤ To report their inventory and status information files. An SMS component that runs on the CAP (Windows NT site systems only) then forwards these data files to the site server.

➤ To determine whether any advertised programs are available.

You may want to assign the CAP role to additional servers in your site depending on these factors:

➤ The number of clients you have assigned to each site server

➤ The volume of client activities

➤ The resulting stress applied to the CAP

➤ The amount of network traffic

Each client in your site should be able to access at least one CAP using a fast and stable network connection.

 The contents of the CAP_*sitecode* share are maintained entirely by SMS. If a CAP site systems fails and its contents get damaged, you only need to restore the server. You do not need to restore the CAP share content. If you change the name of an NT Server or NDS or Bindery volume configured as a CAP, you should complete this change by deleting the old CAP and creating a new CAP server site system in the SMS Administrator console.

Distribution Points

Distribution points are used to store software packages that might also be advertised. You can distribute packages to Windows NT Servers and shares, NetWare Bindery volumes, and NetWare NDS volumes. Depending on the size of the distributed packages and the number of simultaneous client downloads, you might want to create multiple distribution points in your site to balance the load. Each client in your site should be able to access at least one distribution point through a fast and reliable network connection.

> *Note: If a distribution point site system fails and packages get damaged, you need to restore the distribution point server and then update all defined packages by using the SMS Administrator console. (See Chapter 8 for details about updating or refreshing distribution points.)*

Software Metering Servers

Software metering is an optional SMS feature that allows you to meter software application use on your SMS client computers. You also use it to enforce the number of applications being used at one time, allowing you to make sure you use them according to your licensing agreements. The metering functionality is built into SMS through a number of metering components: the software metering site server, the software metering database server, and the SMS site server itself.

 The SMS administrator must always configure the software metering server through the SMS Administrator console. It is the only site system role that is not configured by default when you use SMS Express setup. See Chapter 4 for more information on SMS setup methods and how to configure software metering site systems.

Software metering servers perform the following functions:

➤ Listen for client requests to run applications

➤ Record those requests in a local data cache storage

➤ Check for available licenses (if licensing is enabled)

➤ Reply back to the client with a grant or deny response

If the client has been denied the runtime of an application, it might request a callback to receive a license when one becomes available. You can use multiple software metering servers to accommodate a larger number of application runtime requests. The data stored in the software metering data cache is periodically moved to the software metering database server (SQL Server) for summarization and replication with other SMS sites.

The software metering role is not supported on Alpha servers. Also, SMS site servers running on Alpha servers cannot participate in license balancing between multiple sites.

Software metering uses two databases: the SMS site database and the software metering database. The SMS site database is used to store license-balancing data among SMS sites; the software metering database is used to store all other software metering data.

Software Metering Database Servers

The computer that performs this role must have Microsoft SQL Server 6.5 or 7 installed to host the software metering database server. You determine the location of this server while you are installing the software metering optional component, and you can change it by running setup again. Depending on the intensity with which you plan to use the software metering feature, you should create the metering database on either the SMS site server, the site database server, or a separate remote computer with SQL Server installed. If you plan to use the software metering feature to monitor many different software titles used on your network and to frequently generate metering reports, you may want to consider installing it on a separate computer.

Senders

SMS uses senders for site-to-site communication. By default, each site is configured with a standard sender. This sender is used to communicate over established LAN or WAN connections. SMS sites can also communicate over RAS connections: Asynchronous, Systems Network Architecture (SNA), X.25, and ISDN. Additionally, large software distribution packages can be transmitted between sites using Courier Sender and removable media. An SMS site system can have only one sender of a single kind. If your site requires multiple senders of the same type, you must install them on separate site systems.

There is no SMS sender site system role; a computer configured with a sender and no other SMS roles appears in the SMS Administrator console as a component server site system.

The SMS Administrator Console

The SMS Administrator console, shown in Figure 2.1, is an MMC snap-in that you use to configure and maintain your site and subsites. It also allows you

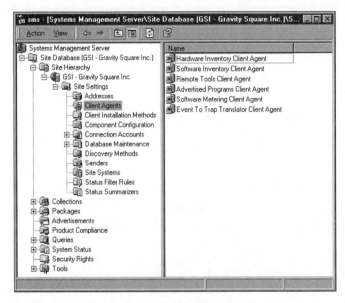

Figure 2.1   The SMS Administrator console.

to manage your SMS clients. The SMS Administrator console has two panes: The left one contains the SMS console tree, and the right one contains details. When you select an item on the console tree, the details for that item appear in the details pane.

The SMS Administrator console is not designed to be feature based. In other words, you do not select a feature, such as software distribution, and from there access everything related to software distribution. In fact, you will notice that most of the items listed in the console tree are not the same as the features described earlier in this chapter.

With the console, you select a task you want to accomplish (such as client installation) and then access various console functions to configure various client installation methods. Due to this design, the server and client configuration tasks are all under one function (Site Hierarchy), all security-related tasks are available under another function (Security Rights), all status messages can be viewed in one place (System Status), and so on.

You can install SMS Administrator consoles on computers other than the site server for convenient administration. The SMS Administrator console requires both MMC and WMI to operate. A computer must be running a 32-bit Windows operating systems to have WMI successfully installed. However, only computers running Windows NT 4 or above can run the SMS version of the MMC.

Data Stores

A data store is a program or object that stores data in some form. A data store can be part of the program or an outside program (such as SQL Server) that works in concert with a program. SMS uses two basic types of data stores in its day-to-day function:

➤ Configuration data stores

➤ Object data stores

For configuration data, SMS uses a file called the *site control file*, which contains all of the site configuration data SMS uses for daily function. SMS also uses the Windows NT Registry to store configuration data. Finally, a mirror copy of the site control file is stored in the SMS site database.

 Direct modifications to the site control file are not supported. You make changes to it when you make configuration changes through the SMS Administrator console or WMI applications.

Object data stores that SMS uses include:

➤ **SMS site database** Used by SMS for configuration and data storage. Software metering only uses the site database for storing license-balancing information.

➤ **Software metering database** Used by the software metering feature. Mirror data is not stored in the SMS site database.

➤ **Product Compliance database** Used by the Product Compliance feature to determine the compliance level of software in use in your site.

➤ **CIM Object Manager** Used by the SMS Administrator console, NetMon and HealthMon monitors, the 32-bit Hardware Inventory Agent, and Network Discovery. It acts as a pass-through between SMS components or utilities and the data stored in the SMS site database or made available through providers. It is the data store part of WMI.

SMS Site Hierarchy

An SMS *site hierarchy* is a collection of one or more SMS sites related to each other by parent-child relationships. It includes one or more SMS site servers (both primary and secondary) and all SMS clients installed within the site boundaries of their sites. An SMS hierarchy is made up of at least one central site. In addition, a hierarchy might have one or more child sites, and one or more parent sites. The following definitions will help you better understand each of these terms:

➤ **Central site** The primary site at the top of an SMS hierarchy to which all other SMS sites report. Thus, the central site's database stores information from site systems and clients in all sites in the hierarchy. A central site is a parent site but cannot be a child site.

➤ **Child site** A primary or a secondary site that reports to another SMS site in the hierarchy.

➤ **Parent site** A primary SMS site that has at least one attached child site. A primary site can be a parent site, but a secondary site cannot because it doesn't have an SMS site database.

An SMS hierarchy allows you to distribute SMS sites to accommodate various networking conditions, international settings, and client agent configurations, and then to have them cooperate in one continuous structure. Figure 2.2 illustrates an SMS site hierarchy.

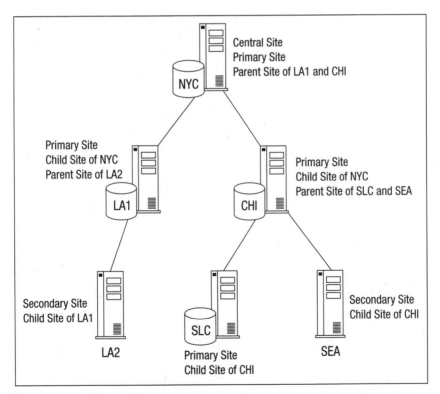

Figure 2.2 An SMS site hierarchy.

WMI

WMI provides an interface through which you can access various management data using a common access method. The data available through WMI can be both read and written and is consolidated in the CIM Object Manager data store. The store uses the Desktop Management Task Force (DMTF) CIM format and complies with the Web Based Enterprise Management (WBEM) initiative. WBEM supports many standard and proprietary management protocols, such as DMI and SNMP, as well as the Windows Registry and performance counters. You can store all of this data in the CIM Object Manager and access it using WMI.

 The Hardware Inventory Client Agent uses WMI and CIM to collect hardware information. The HealthMon Agent also uses them to pull system status, and the SMS Administrator console uses them to access data stored in the SMS site database, as shown in Figure 2.3.

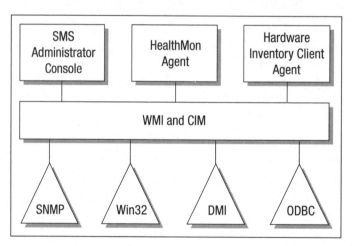

Figure 2.3 SMS and WMI.

Practice Questions

Question 1

> Which of the following resources can become SMS clients?
>
> O a. A Windows NT User Account
>
> O b. A computer running Windows NT 4 Workstation configured with the NetBEUI protocol
>
> O c. A network switch with an IP address
>
> O d. A Power Macintosh computer configured with the TCP/IP protocol
>
> O e. A computer running Windows 95 configured with the IPX/SPX protocol

Answer e is correct. SMS supports Windows 95 and 98, Windows NT 3.51 and 4, Windows 3.1, and Windows for Workgroups 3.11 or later. Only Windows computers can be installed as SMS clients, which makes answers a, c, and d incorrect. SMS clients must be configured with either the TCP/IP or the IPX/SPX protocol, so answer b is incorrect.

Question 2

> Which SMS clients can store hardware and software inventory history locally?
>
> O a. All Windows clients
>
> O b. All Windows NT clients
>
> O c. Only Windows 98 and NT clients
>
> O d. All 32-bit Windows SMS clients
>
> O e. All SMS clients

Answer d is correct. SMS stores hardware and software inventory history locally only on computers running 32-bit Windows operating systems (including Windows 95, 98, and NT). Therefore, at first glance, answers b and c both seem correct. However, answers b and c are both subsets of answer d and Windows NT clients are not the only clients running 32-bit operating systems. Therefore, answer d is the most accurate. Answers a and e are incorrect because they include 16-bit operating system clients that don't store inventory history locally.

Question 3

Which SMS features does Product Compliance (Y2K) use to determine software compliance? [Choose all correct answers]

❏ a. Hardware inventory

❏ b. Software inventory

❏ c. Metered software

❏ d. Y2K compliance database

❏ e. Registry of an SMS client computer

Answers b and d are correct. Y2K software verification compares collected client software inventory with the data stored in the Product Compliance database. You can then use pre-configured queries and the Crystal Reports feature to view the compliance status of software in use in your company. Product Compliance does not use hardware inventory data, metered software data, or client Registries to analyze software compliance. Therefore, answers a, c, and e are incorrect.

Question 4

Which role do distribution points provide?

○ a. Receive inventory files from clients and forward them to the SMS site server

○ b. Collect discovery data records from clients and forward them to SMS logon points

○ c. Store distributed packages and make them available to clients for installation

○ d. Participate in the inter-site communication process

Answer c is correct. Distributed software packages are placed on distribution points. SMS client components then access distribution points to access advertised program files for installation. Answer a is incorrect because CAPs—not distribution points—receive inventory files as well as discovery data records from clients and forward them to the site server. Answer b is incorrect because discovery data is sent to SMS logon points directly from client computers (using the logon discovery method). Distribution points do not participate in the inter-site communication process; therefore, answer d is incorrect.

Question 5

What framework is the SMS Administrator console based on?

O a. WBEM

O b. WMI

O c. MMC

O d. CIM

Answer c is correct. The SMS Administrator console is an MMC snap-in. SMS MMC snap-ins use WMI to access data available in CIM (an implementation of WBEM) and pulled from the SMS site database. The subject of the question is the console's framework, not the connectivity between the console and SMS data stores. Therefore, answers a, b, and d are incorrect.

Question 6

Which operating system can successfully run an installed SMS Administrator console?

O a. Any Windows computer

O b. Any 32-bit Windows computer

O c. Any Windows NT 4 Server computer

O d. Any Windows NT 4 computer

O e. Any computer configured with WMI

Answer d is correct. The SMS Administrator console requires both MMC and WMI to operate. Every computer running a 32-bit Windows operating system can have WMI successfully installed, but only computers running Windows NT 4 or above can run the MMC. Therefore, answers a, b, and e are incorrect. Both answers c and d appear to be correct, but the SMS Administrator console can run on any NT 4 computer, not just servers. So, answer c is a subset of answer d, making d the most correct answer

Question 7

Two SMS secondary site servers with site codes SA1 and SA2 report their data directly to an SMS site server with site code SA0. An SMS site server with site code NY1 has its own SMS site database and reports directly to SA0. An SMS site server with site code PH2 has only one directly reporting site— SA0. Which of the following statements are true? [Choose all correct answers]

- ❑ a. SA0, SA1, SA2, and NY1 are child sites.
- ❑ b. NY1 and PH2 are both primary sites.
- ❑ c. SA0, SA1, and SA2 are secondary site servers.
- ❑ d. PH2 and NY1 are the parent sites.

Answers a and b are correct. The best way to answer this question is to draw a site hierarchy diagram (like the one in Figure 2.4) and label all primary sites, secondary sites, child sites, parent sites, and the central site. Then, read the question again to verify the accuracy of your drawing and search for the correct answers.

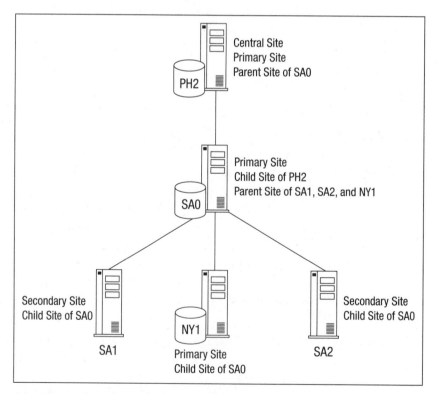

Figure 2.4 Sample site hierarchy drawing.

Answer a is correct because site SA0 is a child site of PH2, and sites SA1, SA2, and NY1 are all child sites of SA0. Answer b is also correct because both the NY1 and PH2 sites have site databases. The question states that NY1, SA1, and SA2 report to site SA0, so SA0 must be a parent of these sites, and therefore it cannot be a secondary site. Remember that only primary sites can have child sites. Therefore, answer c is incorrect. Answer d is incorrect because the question does not list any child sites for NY1.

Question 8

Which of the following are valid reasons for creating multiple sites? [Choose all correct answers]

- ❏ a. Several company offices are separated by slow WAN links.
- ❏ b. Computers in each department need to be configured with different desktop settings.
- ❏ c. Computers in each department are managed by different help desk operators. Company policy does not allow operators to access computers in any department except the ones they belong to.
- ❏ d. Several locations require different SMS client configurations.

Answers a and d are correct. Slow WAN links (answer a) are the main requirement for separating management zones into multiple SMS sites. In addition, SMS client agent configuration (answer d) is site-wide. You can configure different desktop settings and different security privileges within a single site; therefore, answers b and c are incorrect.

Question 9

Which SMS components use WMI? [Choose all correct answers]

- ❏ a. The 32-bit hardware inventory agent
- ❏ b. The 32-bit software inventory agent
- ❏ c. The SMS Administrator console
- ❏ d. Product Compliance (Y2K software verification)

Answers a and c are correct. Thirty-two-bit hardware inventory (answer a) uses WMI to collect hardware information using the Win32 Provider. An SMS Administrator console (answer c) communicates with the SMS site database

(SQL database) via WMI and the SMS Provider. Answer b is incorrect because the Software Inventory Agent does not use WMI to collect inventory data. Answer d is incorrect because Product Compliance uses the Product Compliance database and software inventory data, neither of which use WMI.

Need To Know More?

 Microsoft Corporation. *Microsoft Systems Management Server 2.0 Administrator's Guide.* Microsoft Corporation, Redmond, WA, 1998. This book ships with SMS and provides more detailed information on each of the topics discussed in this chapter.

 Microsoft Corporation. *Microsoft Systems Management Server Resource Guide*, one volume of the *Microsoft BackOffice 4.5 Resource Kit.* Microsoft Press, Redmond, WA, 1999. ISBN 0-7356-0583-1. The chapters in this volume contain advanced information on the concepts discussed in this chapter.

 www.microsoft.com/smsmgmt/ is a good place to start to get general information on SMS.

 www.microsoft.com/ntserver/management/ will give you background on WMI and CIM.

 www.dmtf.org is a good place to go for DMTF and WBEM standards.

 www.microsoft.com/msdn/ contains WMI API documentation.

Planning And Design

Terms you'll need to understand:

√ Sender
√ Address
√ Client connection account
√ Site system connection account
√ WBEMPERM
√ Class
√ Instance

Techniques you'll need to master:

√ Establishing site boundaries
√ Deciding which type of SMS site to install under different circumstances
√ Understanding how sites communicate
√ Calculating the number of licenses required for an SMS site and hierarchy
√ Securing your SMS environment using both SMS and Windows NT security
√ Understanding interoperability between SMS 1.2 and SMS 2 sites
√ Planning an upgrade from SMS 1.2 to SMS 2
√ Understanding interoperability with NetWare systems

Before you install your first SMS site server, you need to select the appropriate SMS infrastructure for your environment. Your SMS hierarchy might be composed of a single site that manages thousands of users or several smaller sites connected in a hierarchical structure. Several factors dictate the appropriate design. This chapter explains how SMS manages large distributed environments, enumerates the computer platforms and operating systems that SMS 2 supports, and explains SMS licensing guidelines.

Site Boundaries

SMS uses site boundaries to determine which resources belong to each site. *Site boundaries* are the lists of IP subnets and IPX network numbers that define the boundaries of the site. In SMS 2, managed resources are assigned to SMS sites based on their IP network IDs and/or IPX network numbers. You can configure each SMS site to manage resources located on multiple IP segments and IPX networks. The set of IP network IDs and IPX network numbers defined at the SMS site level creates a site's boundaries. Different SMS sites usually have unique site boundaries; however, you can create sites whose boundaries overlap. When this occurs, more than one SMS site can manage the same resources.

Although it is easier to manage resources in one site, you often must install multiple SMS sites in one organization. When a company requires more than one site, you create a site hierarchy where sites communicate with each other through a reporting structure that leads up to one central site. Each primary SMS site stores its data as well as the data stored at its subsites. The central site stores data for the entire hierarchy. The most common reasons for installing multiple sites are:

➤ **Network performance** When the links that connect different physical locations within your company are slow, you need to consider establishing different SMS sites on each side of the slow links.

➤ **International settings** When SMS client computers and/or SMS administrators are using different international configurations and settings, you might want to install multiple SMS sites to accommodate language preferences.

➤ **Features required by users** If multiple groups of clients require conflicting SMS feature configurations, you'll need to separate them into different SMS sites because you can configure client settings on a site-wide basis only.

➤ **IS administrative structure** When multiple IS administrator groups require restricted access to resources, each group might need its own SMS site.

➤ **Number of resources** Although SMS 2 is very scalable and can manage hundreds of thousands of users, you may want to divide the number of managed resources and assign them to different SMS sites.

Although you could use a company's IS administrative structure to create multiple sites, SMS provides granular security settings that allow you to strictly structure security privileges within one site. Therefore, you do not need to create multiple sites to accommodate different IS administrative structures.

You must specify the SMS site boundaries explicitly in the Boundaries tab of the Site Properties dialog box. You can open this dialog box from the SMS site server node in the SMS Administrator console as shown in Figure 3.1.

IP network IDs entered as site boundaries can be of the full class A, B, or C IP networks as well as any valid subnetted and supernetted IP networks. Figure 3.2 illustrates site boundaries composed of subnetted class A IP networks.

When establishing SMS site boundaries, you need to be familiar with the concepts of IP addresses, IP subnet masks, and IP network IDs. Incorrectly configured site boundaries might cause an unwanted client to become a member of your SMS site.

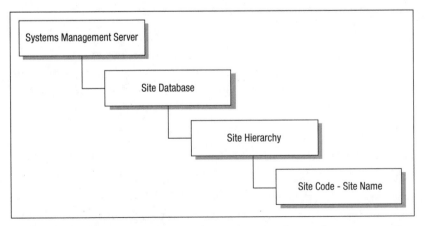

Figure 3.1   SMS Administrator console location for configuring site boundaries.

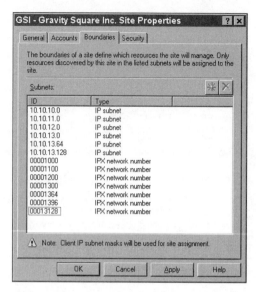

Figure 3.2 The Site Boundaries dialog box.

Hierarchy Layout

After your computing environment is appropriately divided into SMS sites, you need to decide how to connect them to form a single SMS hierarchy. Before you can fully understand the benefits, requirements, and limitations of an SMS hierarchy, it is important that you learn about the different types of SMS sites.

Types Of SMS Sites

There are two classifications of SMS sites: One is based on the location of the site's main data store, and the other is based on the site's location in an SMS hierarchy. Primary sites and secondary sites are the two site types based on location of the database. Parent site, child site, and central site designations are determined by a site's location in the hierarchy. Each of these site types is described below.

Primary Sites

An SMS *primary site* has its own Microsoft SQL Server 6.5 or 7 database to store its own data and data for all of its subsites. A primary site also has at least one SMS Administrator console, which contains the administrative tools. Local SMS administrators use the console to manage the site, its subsites, and the information stored in the site database. You can install an SMS primary site and the corresponding SQL Server on the same server or on separate servers.

Secondary Sites

An SMS *secondary site* does not have a local site database. A secondary site stores its data in the SMS site database of the site it reports to—its parent primary site. A secondary site does not have administrative tools either; an administrator must manage it from any primary site above it in the hierarchy. A secondary site is particularly useful for locations that do not require local administration.

Parent Sites

Any SMS site that has at least one SMS site directly attached beneath it is called a *parent site*. Only a primary site can be a parent site because a parent site must have a site database. SMS data flows up the hierarchy, so the administrator at a parent site can view all of the parent site's resource data as well as those of each of its subsites.

Child Sites

A *child site* is any SMS site with a parent. A secondary site requires a parent site, so a secondary site is always a child site. Primary sites can be child sites as well. In fact, a primary site can be both a child site and a parent site. It is important to remember that a child site can have only one parent, although a parent site can have multiple child sites in an SMS hierarchy.

Central Sites

The topmost site in the hierarchy is called the *central site*. The central site must be a primary site; therefore, it stores its own site data as well as the site data from all of its subsites. An administrator at the central site can view and manage all of the resources in the hierarchy, including the resources its subsites manage. Within the site hierarchy, management instructions and software distribution packages flow from the top down the hierarchy structure; whereas SMS site database data (site configuration, inventory data, status messages, discovery data records [DDRs], and so on) flows up the hierarchy—from SMS site servers up to the central site.

Constructing A Site Hierarchy

Figure 3.3 shows an SMS hierarchy with five sites. The London site is a central site. Its two child sites, New York and Paris, are both primary sites. The Paris site has two child sites: Florence (a primary site) and Berlin (a secondary site). Although the SMS administrators at the London central site can manage all of the computers in the hierarchy, the administrators at the New York and Florence sites can manage only their own clients and resources. Administrators at

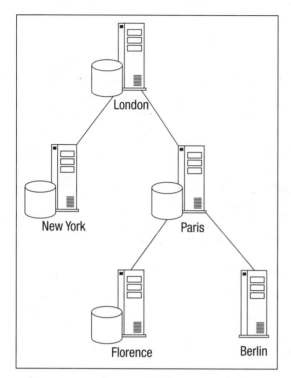

Figure 3.3 Sample SMS site hierarchy.

the Paris site can manage their own resources as well as the resources belonging to both the Florence and Berlin sites. The Berlin site does not require a local administrator because it is a secondary site.

When designing a site hierarchy, you should consider the administrative needs of your company and your network. For example, in Figure 3.3, if the administrators at the New York site had to manage the London site, they would need to restructure the hierarchy so that the New York site became the central site.

Inter-Site Communication

In addition to your network's administrative needs, you need to consider inter-site communication when designing an SMS hierarchy. For an SMS hierarchy to function correctly, parent sites must be directly connected to their child sites and vice versa. No other site-to-site communication links are required. For example, the central site needs to communicate with its child sites, but it does not need to directly contact child sites that belong to its child sites (grandchild sites). SMS has routing functionality that allows a hierarchy to operate with connections between parent and child sites only (rather than from all sites to all sites).

SMS sites communicate with each other using functioning physical connectivity, senders, and addresses. A *sender* is an SMS component that uses an existing physical link to manage site-to-site communication. An *address* consists of the site code of the site to contact and the name of the server to connect to. A set of two addresses allows two sites to accurately connect to each other. SMS provides three different types of senders:

➤ **Standard Sender** Used to communicate over local area network (LAN) or wide area network (WAN) links. Standard Sender is installed and configured by default on every SMS site. If two sites that need to communicate with each other are configured with a common networking protocol (TCP/IP or IPX/SPX) and are on the same LAN or WAN, you can use Standard Sender for inter-site communication. You do not need to install an additional sender.

➤ **RAS Sender (Asynchronous, ISDN, X.25, and SNA)** Used for dial-up RAS communication. You must install Windows NT RAS to use a RAS Sender. If you use SNA RAS sender, be aware that it requires additional configuration to accommodate connectivity over an SNA link. When installing secondary sites, you can select any RAS Sender or the Standard Sender as your default sender.

➤ **Courier Sender** Used only to distribute software packages on removable media to subsites. Courier Sender is installed by default on every SMS site. You cannot configure Courier Sender through the SMS Administrator console. To configure and transfer packages to removable media to be sent to other SMS sites, use SMS Courier Sender Manager, a utility accessible from the Systems Management Server program group on the Start menu.

You configure addresses to use specific senders for site-to-site communication.

There can be only one instance of a specific sender on each site system as well as only one address to a single site using a specific sender type. For example, an SMS site server can only have one Standard Sender with only one Standard Sender Address that connects a primary site to a child site. However, there can also be a RAS Sender configured with one address from the primary site to the same child site or another Standard Sender address configured to communicate with a different child site.

You can have multiple addresses to a site, but each one has to use a different type of sender. For example, you might want to use the Standard Sender or an ISDN RAS Sender for connectivity between two SMS sites. You may also want to use the Courier Sender to send large packages to child sites connected by slow or unreliable links.

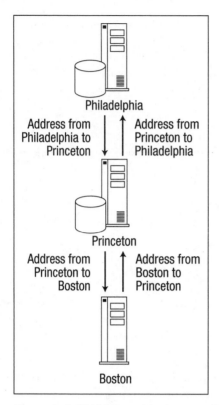

Figure 3.4 SMS hierarchical connectivity.

Figure 3.4 shows site-to-site communication. All sites are connected over a frame relay network and are configured only with the Standard Sender. Philadelphia, the central site, has an address to the Princeton site only. Princeton, a child site of Philadelphia and a parent site to Boston, has two addresses: one to Philadelphia and one to Boston. Boston, a secondary site, has an address to the Princeton site only. Management data that the Philadelphia site sends to Boston is routed through the Princeton site.

You may sometimes want to establish a direct communication channel between two sites that are not directly configured into a parent-child relationship. If the Philadelphia-Princeton-Boston hierarchy layout shown in Figure 3.4 were created based on a company's organizational structure rather than its network connectivity, you might need to create an address from the Philadelphia site to the Boston site. Then, the management data would not have to be routed via the Princeton site.

Hardware And Software Requirements

Before you install SMS 2, you need to prepare your hardware by first making sure you have equipment that meets the minimum requirements for SMS. Then, you need to confirm that you have the required supporting software for SMS servers (Windows NT 4, Internet Explorer 4.01, and SQL Server 6.5 or 7). Finally, you need to verify that SMS 2 supports your client operating systems.

 During the SMS installation process (described in detail in Chapter 4), SMS installs its components on one or more servers, based on the selections you make during setup. After the installation process, you might want to configure additional servers with the SMS roles or move some roles created during the installation process. Make sure that all servers configured as SMS site systems meet the minimum software recommendations.

SMS 2 Server Requirements

The following hardware is required to install SMS 2 (only the processor platform and the disk space requirements are required to initiate the installation process):

➤ An x86 or Alpha system that is included in the Microsoft Windows NT 4 hardware compatibility list

➤ A Pentium 133MHz or faster processor (within the Intel platform family)

➤ 96MB of physical memory (64MB for a secondary site server)

➤ 500MB of available hard disk space on an NTFS-formatted drive (additional space is required to store software distribution packages)

➤ 100MB of available hard disk space on any formatted system partition (FAT or NTFS)

 Due to the differences in disk requirements when you install SMS with a remote SQL Server, Microsoft recommends a minimum of 1GB of available disk space on an NTFS-formatted drive.

The following supporting software must be installed on the SMS site server and/or the SQL Server before you can install SMS 2:

➤ Microsoft Windows NT Server 4 (Service Pack 4—SP4 including the Microsoft Data Access Components—MDAC and Y2K upgrade) or later configured as a domain controller or a member server participating in an NT domain.

➤ Microsoft Internet Explorer 4.01 (Service Pack 1—SP1) or later

➤ Microsoft SQL Server 6.5 (SP4) or later (for remote SQL Server installations only)

Supported-Site System Platforms

SMS site systems have unique hardware and software requirements depending on the role they are configured to serve. As a result, you can assign some site system roles to computers that run operating systems other than Windows NT Server 4. Table 3.1 lists the operating systems supported for specific site systems.

 Software metering, a feature that allows you to meter software use in your site, is not supported on Alpha servers. It is also not supported for a full integration with NetWare. SMS clients must be able to connect to Windows NT Servers in order to have their software usage metered.

Table 3.1   Supported operating systems for SMS site systems.

Server Operating System	Site System(s)
Windows NT 3.51 (x86 only)	Distribution point
Windows NT 4	Distribution point
Windows NT 4, Terminal Server Edition	Distribution point
Windows NT 4, SP3 (x86 only)	Distribution point, logon point, and client access point (CAP)
Windows NT 4, SP4	All
Windows NT 4, Enterprise Edition	All
NetWare 3.12 and 3.2	Distribution point, logon point, and CAP
NetWare 4.1x (Bindery or NDS)	Distribution point, logon point, and CAP

Supported Client Platforms

The following operating systems are supported for SMS client software:

➤ Windows NT 4 (Workstation, Server, and Server Enterprise Edition)

➤ Windows NT 3.51 (Workstation and Server, SP5a or later)

➤ Windows 98

➤ Windows 95

➤ Windows for Workgroups 3.11 (using MS Windows Network Client for MS-DOS)

➤ Windows 3.1 (using MS Windows Network Client for MS-DOS or LAN Manager Enhanced version 2.2c)

Additionally, only the following client functions are supported on the Windows NT 4 Server, Terminal Server Edition:

➤ Remote Windows NT client installation

➤ Manual installation (requires you to change **user /install** command execution prior to executing SMSMAN.EXE)

➤ Hardware inventory

➤ Software inventory

SMS Server And Client Licensing

SMS 2 is a client-server application, so it requires licenses for both servers and clients. Table 3.2 lists the different SMS licenses available and explains where you are required to use each license.

Table 3.2 SMS license requirements.	
License	**Requirements**
SMS Server	Each SMS site server (includes both primary and secondary site servers)
SQL Server	Each SMS SQL Server (site database server)
SMS Client Access	Each computer with SMS 2 client software installed (including all SMS site servers and site systems with SMS client software installed)

SMS licensing is not concurrent. You must have as many client licenses as there are machines with client software installed. So even though you have purchased a server license for a site server, you still need to purchase a client license for the same computer. This rule applies to all site systems except NetWare servers because SMS client software is not installed on them. You do not need a separate SMS Server license for each site system you install. When you install site systems on different computers in your site, the SMS Server license covers their use as site systems.

Security

Security is an important issue for networks. Since SMS is installed on both servers and clients throughout your network, it is important for you to understand how security can be configured to offer the protection you desire. SMS provides several layers of security that allow you to configure the security level in your SMS environment. The three security layers offered by SMS are listed below:

➤ SMS files and directories are protected with the standard Windows NT Share and NTFS Access permissions.

➤ Data stored in the SQL database is secured by either a SQL account or an integrated Windows NT account, depending on the configuration you choose when installing SMS.

➤ Access to the SMS data from the SMS Administrator console is protected with the permissions stored in Windows Management Instrumentation (WMI) and controlled via the SMS Provider. The SMS Provider provides the interface between SMS and WMI.

Additionally, SMS 2 uses multiple accounts for different site and client functions. Finally, you can configure security on SMS Administrator console objects that allows you to determine which SMS administrators in your company can access different SMS features and resources.

SMS security is automatically created by the installation process and by the SMS components creating and/or modifying site systems. This security system maintains itself; only experienced Windows NT administrators should alter it. Most of the SMS security features are associated with specific tasks: SMS setup, site configuration, software distribution, and so on. Table 3.3 lists and briefly describes the configurable accounts that SMS uses. More information about these accounts and specifically how you use them will be detailed in subsequent chapters.

Table 3.3   Configurable accounts that SMS uses.

Account	Description
SMS Service	Used to run the main SMS services on the site server and on some site systems. This account requires access rights to all SMS site systems unless a Site Systems Connection account is used. When you use the Site Systems Connection account, the SMS Service account requires administrator privileges to only the SMS site server and the SQL server (if present).
SMS Site Address	Used by senders to connect to another SMS site (or sites). Each address has to be configured with the SMS Site Address account. This account requires Write permissions to the SMS_SITE share on the SMS site server for which the address is configured.
Software Metering	Used to run the software metering service. This account is automatically created and configured during the software metering server configuration as long as the SMS Service can connect to the metering server using administrative rights.
Site Systems Connection	Optional account(s) SMS uses to connect to SMS site systems. This account(s) requires administrative rights to distribution points, CAPs, domain controllers, and NetWare servers. It does not have to be a Domain Admin account. If this account is not configured, SMS uses the SMS Service account to connect to site systems.
NT Client Software Installation	An account necessary for software distribution to logged off NT machines. This account is not used to run the advertised software; it is used to access network resources used during the runtime of distributed software, and it should have access rights to them.
Client Connection	An account used by SMS client components to access CAP(s) and distribution points. You can have multiple Client Connection accounts to accommodate CAPs and distribution points located in different NT domains and on NetWare servers.

(continued)

Table 3.3 Configurable accounts that SMS uses (continued).	
Account	**Description**
SMS Client Remote Installation	An optional account used to install SMS client software on Windows NT account machines. This account requires administrative privileges to Windows NT machines. If this account is not configured, SMS uses the SMS Service account.

Understanding SMS Administrator Console Security

SMS administrators can access objects and data available through the SMS Administrator console only if the administrators have the following security rights:

➤ A Windows NT user account that has access to the computer configured with the SMS Provider (for more information on the location of the SMS Provider, see Chapter 4)

➤ Access to the SMS Administrator console files

➤ WMI Permissions

➤ Permissions to the appropriate SMS Administrator console objects

Although almost every domain user can install an SMS Administrator console and point it to the computer configured with the SMS Provider, not everyone has WMI permissions that allow them to access SMS Administrator console objects. Only the domain user who installed the site server has, by default, full access to all SMS secured objects. This user has the responsibility of granting appropriate SMS security rights to other SMS administrators or help desk operators.

Web-Based Enterprise Management (WBEM)/WMI Access Permissions

You need to have WBEM/WMI pass-through permissions to access data in the SMS site database when you are using the SMS Administrator console. By default, only the SMS Admins local group has appropriate access to WMI. These rights include:

➤ Attributes enabled

➤ Execute Methods with the Write Instance Schema Access Level

After the SMS site server installation process is complete, only one user account is a member of the SMS Admins local group—the account of the administrator who installed the SMS site server. This user must add additional user accounts or global Windows NT groups to the SMS Admins local group in order for them to gain access to WMI. Alternately, by using the Web Based Enterprise Management Permission Tool—WBEMPERM (WBEMPERM.EXE)—an administrator can give specific user accounts or user groups direct access rights to WMI. Figure 3.5 shows a screenshot of WBEMPERM and the required SMS WMI access rights.

 If you installed your SMS site server with the SMS Provider on a remote SQL Server, the SMS Admin group is created in the local security databases of both computers. The SMS Admin group on the SQL server guards access to WMI.

Class- And Instance-Level Security Permissions

The user who installed the site server is also the only one with access rights to all security objects in the SMS Administrator console. Again, this user has the responsibility of granting console objects access rights to other NT users or user groups. The SMS Administrator console security rights can be granted at two levels:

➤ **Class** Grants security rights to all objects that are members of a specific class

➤ **Instance** Grants security rights to a single instance of an object

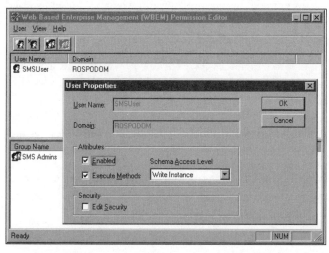

Figure 3.5 Web Based Enterprise Management Permission Editor.

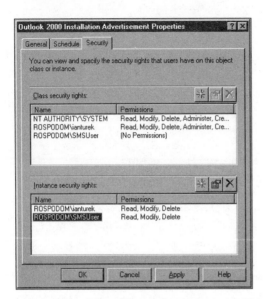

Figure 3.6 SMS Class and Instance security access rights.

Figure 3.6 shows an example of the Class and Instance security rights. One user, ROSPODOM\ianturek, has both Class and Instance rights to the Outlook 2000 Installation advertisement. The other user, ROSPODOM\SMSUser, has been granted only Instance rights to the Outlook 2000 Installation advertisement. He might be given security rights to other advertisements, but he cannot manage them all. You can see in Figure 3.6 that SMSUser has the No Permissions right to the Advertisements Class security object. The SMS security system automatically entered this permission right when SMSUser received Instance-level rights without having Class-level rights. Class-level permission rights do not have to be entered implicitly.

Users can see only objects to which they have Instance-level rights. Each Class and Instance permission has additional access rights such as Read, Modify, and Administer. Many permissions are specific to an object. For instance, a Collection object has a Use Remote Tools permission right and a Package object has a Distribute permission right. Table 3.4 lists all of the object permissions and the security object to which they apply.

Note that each object must have at least one user with the Administer permission. The SMS security system prevents you from deleting the last user with Administer permissions to an object.

Table 3.4   Permissions by security object type.

Permission	Security Object	Purpose
Administer	All object types	Manage objects
Advertise	Collection class and instances	Advertise to resources (requires Read Resource permission)
Create	All object types	Create an instance
Delete	All object types except status message instances	Delete an instance
Delete Resource	Collection class and instances	Delete resources from a collection
Distribute	Package class and instances	Send a package to distribution points
Modify	All object types except status	Modify an instance of an object type
Modify Resource	Collection class and instances	Modify a resource in a collection
Read	All object types except status message instances	View an instance and its properties
Read Resource	Collection class and instances	View resources in a collection
Use Remote Tools	Collection class and instances	Start a remote session with a resource (requires the Read Resource permission)
View Collected Files	Collection class and instances	View files collected for a resources (requires the Read Resource permission)

Interoperability

SMS 2 includes built-in features that allow for limited interoperability with SMS 1.2. SMS administrators gradually upgrading their SMS 1.2 environment can still manage their systems centrally and provide support to clients that SMS 2 does not directly support: DOS, IBM OS/2, and Macintosh clients. Additionally, SMS 2 includes optional NetWare integration modules that allow you to manage supported clients in a NetWare environment.

Upgrading SMS 1.2 To SMS 2

SMS 2 supports upgrades from the last version of SMS—SMS 1.2. Because the two versions of SMS have different database schemas and forward data differently to the parent site, Microsoft built a data forwarding conversion algorithm and included it in Service Pack 4 (SP4) for SMS 1.2. This algorithm allows SMS 1.2 sites to be attached to SMS 2 sites and still function properly. Because of this change, you must apply SP4 to an SMS 1.2 site server before you upgrade the SMS 1.2 site server to SMS 2.

 Only SMS 1.2 SP4 can be upgraded to SMS 2. If you are upgrading SMS 1.2 sites to SMS 2, make sure that all child sites of the upgraded site have SP4 installed as well.

Due to the compatibility limitation, an SMS 2 site cannot be a child site of an SMS 1.2 or even an SMS 1.2 SP4 site; therefore, when you upgrade your hierarchy, you must upgrade from the top to the bottom.

The following data is converted when you upgrade SMS 1.2 SP4 to SMS 2:

➤ Hardware inventory data (except physical disk data)

➤ Machine groups

➤ Software packages

➤ Programs

➤ SQL Server views

 You should document all SMS 1.2 data that is not preserved because you may need this information after the upgrade.

The remaining data that is not converted includes:

➤ Available hard drive space on your SMS 1.2 client machines

➤ PDF files

➤ Software inventory and collected files

➤ Queries

➤ Jobs

➤ Most site settings, including client configuration

➤ Alerts

➤ Events

SMS 2 does not have an equivalent to the SMS 1.2 Share Package on Server job type and Program Group Control. You can use the advanced features of software distribution to supply similar functionality.

After you complete the upgrade process, an SMS 2 site's configuration is similar to that of a new custom installation with only the default options selected. All SMS 1.2 clients are temporarily orphaned until they go through the regular SMS 2 client discovery and/or installation process.

The SMS 2 client discovery and installation methods recognize the presence of SMS 1.2 SP4 client software and launch the client upgrade process. All components of SMS 1.2 client software are removed, and only the enabled components of SMS 2 sites are installed and started. The upgraded clients are not identified by the GUID (globally unique identifier of pure SMS 2 clients) but by the SMS 1.2 SMS Identifier (SMSID). The SMSID becomes the unique identifier for an upgraded client. SMS requires each client to have a unique ID. For proper SMS 2 client functionality, it doesn't matter whether the client uses the GUID or the SMSID.

Because SMS 2 does not support MS-DOS, IBM OS/2, or Macintosh system clients, the clients are not upgraded and are left orphaned. If you want to continue to manage these clients, you need to maintain one or more SMS 1.2 sites in your hierarchy. Alternatively, you might consider upgrading these computers to supported SMS 2 client operating systems.

Creating A Mixed SMS 1.2 And 2 Hierarchy

When a parent SMS 1.2 site is upgraded, its child site(s) is not automatically upgraded. You must manually upgrade each child site, whether primary or secondary. After a parent is upgraded, your hierarchy will be composed of mixed SMS versions. As explained previously, this interoperability is possible due to modifications included in SP4 for SMS 1.2; unfortunately, this interoperability is limited.

An SMS 2 site administrator can see all SMS 1.2 child sites down the hierarchy, but the administrator cannot configure them. Configuration for SMS 1.2 sites is available only from the SMS Administrator (SMS 1.2 Administrator console). This presents a particular problem when a child SMS 1.2 site is a secondary site; this site is unmanageable and can be upgraded only. You can upgrade secondary SMS 1.2 sites using the SMS 2 secondary site installation methods (see Chapter 4 for more information on secondary site installation).

The SMS 2 site administrator can still view the SMS 1.2 clients in any collections they belong to and can distribute software to them.

 SMS 1.2 sites don't use routing functionality for inter-site communication; therefore, they need to have an address to each site where software is being distributed. The same applies to an SMS 2 site with SMS 1.2 subsites. For instance, if in Figure 3.4, the Philadelphia site were upgraded from SMS 1.2 to SMS 2 and the remaining sites were still running SMS 1.2, Philadelphia would require an address to Boston in order to distribute software to Boston's clients.

Managing NetWare Clients

You can use SMS 2 to successfully manage Windows computers that are part of a NetWare networking environment. You still have to install SMS on a Windows NT Server and use SQL Server for its data storage; however, you can configure CAPs, logon points, and distribution points (which are the only SMS site systems with which clients have direct contact) on NetWare servers. This integration allows you to use SMS to manage clients that run only NetWare network redirectors. Table 3.5 lists supported clients and redirectors.

Table 3.5 Supported clients that connect to NetWare site systems.					
NetWare Client	NT 4 SP4	NT 3.51 SP5	Windows 95/98	Windows 3.1	Workgroups 3.11
Client Services for NetWare	x				
IntranetWare Client 2.5			x		
IntranetWare Client 4.11a		x			
IntranetWare Client 4.3	x^1				
IntranetWare Client 4.5	x				
VLM 1.21				x^2	x^2

[1] Not supported for bindery emulation site systems.

[2] Not supported for NDS site systems.

To communicate with NetWare systems, SMS must be installed on an appropriately configured Windows NT Server machine. SMS site systems that manage NetWare clients must be configured with an appropriate redirector and the IPX/SPX network protocol. Table 3.6 lists the supported redirectors you can use to connect to and configure NetWare servers.

 In order to manage NetWare clients, SMS must be configured with either the IPX/SPX or NWLink (Microsoft's implementation of IPX/SPX) network protocol to communicate with supported NetWare servers. Windows NT servers cannot communicate with NetWare servers over TCP/IP. If an SMS site server that is managing NetWare clients is part of a hierarchy operating with the TCP/IP protocol, it must be configured with both TCP/IP and IPX/SPX.

Once an SMS site server is installed with the optional NetWare components, the IPX/SPX protocol, and a supported redirector, you can configure the site server to modify NetWare servers to become SMS site systems. To do so, you need to create or configure the following items through the SMS Administrator console:

➤ NetWare NDS or Bindery Site Systems Connection accounts

➤ NetWare NDS or Bindery Client Connection accounts

➤ NetWare NDS or Bindery Logon Discovery (used to discover clients)

➤ NetWare NDS or Bindery Logon Client Installation (required to install SMS client software on NetWare client computers)

➤ A CAP on a NetWare NDS or bindery volume

➤ A distribution point on a NetWare NDS or bindery volume

Table 3.6 Supported redirectors for NetWare servers.			
	NDS	Bindery Emulation	Bindery
Gateway Services for NetWare		x	x
IntranetWare Client 4.3	x		x
IntranetWare Client 4.5	x	x	x

Practice Questions

Question 1

> You company is composed of three departments (Accounting, Sales, and Marketing) located on three fast IPX networks that are joined by a router. Company policy does not allow client machines that belong to the Accounting department to be remotely controlled. You want to use SMS to manage all client machines and to remotely control as many as possible. You also want to minimize the cost of implementing SMS. How many SMS sites should you install?
>
> ○ a. 1
>
> ○ b. 2
>
> ○ c. 3
>
> ○ d. You cannot manage this environment

Answer b is correct. Client agent configuration settings are site-wide, so you must separate users in the Accounting department from all other users. Therefore, you need at least two SMS sites. You could install more than two sites, but one of your requirements is to minimize the implementation costs. Answer a is one site, which would not allow you to have unique client settings for the accounting department. The fact that the IPX networks are divided by a router is not a reason to create a separate site, so answer c, which suggests three to match the number of IPX networks, is not correct. Finally, you can manage this environment, so answer d is incorrect.

Question 2

> Your company is located on seven floors of two buildings connected with a fast fiber-optic network that runs the TCP/IP protocol. You measured the network utilization on all segments and concluded that the available bandwidth supports the worst possible SMS traffic. Your budget is limited, but your first priority is to install and configure SMS according to the specifications. How many SMS sites should you install?
>
> ○ a. 1
>
> ○ b. 2
>
> ○ c. 7
>
> ○ d. SMS cannot operate on a fiber-optic network

Answer a is correct. You have tested your network and verified that it is very fast, so you need to install only one SMS site. Given your budget constraints, you should not consider installing additional sites that are not required. Therefore, answers b and c are incorrect. SMS can operate on a fiber-optic network, as long as it transmits TCP/IP or IPX/SPX protocol data. Therefore, answer d is incorrect.

Question 3

You plan to install SMS sites in three geographical locations connected by a frame relay network. One of the locations has no administrative staff. You need to decide whether to install a secondary site server or a primary site server at that location. Which of the following statements are true? [Choose all correct answers]

❑ a. A secondary site does not require an administrative staff.

❑ b. A primary child site requires an administrative staff.

❑ c. A secondary site can use its child site's database to store its configuration data.

❑ d. A primary site can administratively manage a secondary site and distribute software to a secondary site's clients.

Answers a and d are correct. Answer a is correct because a secondary site can be entirely managed from its parent site. Answer d is correct because any site and its clients can be managed from its parent site. (Note that a child site's clients can be remotely controlled from the parent site only if direct NT permissions are established.) Answer b is incorrect because any child site can be managed by any site located above it in the SMS hierarchy. Answer c is incorrect because a secondary site stores its configuration data in the SQL database of its parent site, not in the database of its child site.

Question 4

Your company has two locations: Seattle and Brisbane. Due to the time difference between the two locations, only 350 computers are operating on the company network at any give time. You plan to use SMS to distribute software to all computers during the local off-peak hours.

The Seattle site will have 200 client computers and will be managed by the SMS central site server. The central site server will use a remote SQL Server to store the hierarchy data. To improve performance, you also decided to install an additional primary site server (with a local database) in Brisbane. The Brisbane primary site will manage 30 secondary SMS site servers and their 350 SMS client workstations. SMS client software will be installed on all client machines and the site servers. How many SMS server, SQL Server, and SMS client licenses will you need to purchase without violating your licensing agreements?

- ○ a. 2 SMS server licenses, 2 SQL Server licenses, and 350 SMS client licenses

- ○ b. 32 SMS server licenses, 2 SQL Server licenses, and 600 SMS client licenses

- ○ c. 32 SMS server licenses, 1 SQL Server license, and 600 SMS client licenses

- ○ d. 32 SMS server licenses, no SQL Server licenses, and 600 SMS client licenses

- ○ e. 2 SMS server licenses, 2 SQL Server licenses, and 550 SMS client licenses

Answer b is correct. You will need to have SMS server licenses for all of your SMS servers, both primary and secondary. You will need to have SQL Server licenses for all of your SQL Servers, both local to the SMS site server and remote. You will need to have SMS client licenses for all computers configured with SMS client software. When you total it all up, you find that your company needs 32 SMS server licenses, 2 SQL Server licenses, and 583 SMS client access licenses (550 clients + 32 SMS servers + 1 remote SQL Server).

You can legally have more licenses than your company requires, but you cannot have fewer. None of the other answers provides the correct number of licenses.

Question 5

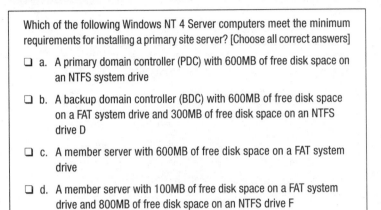

Which of the following Windows NT 4 Server computers meet the minimum requirements for installing a primary site server? [Choose all correct answers]

❑ a. A primary domain controller (PDC) with 600MB of free disk space on an NTFS system drive

❑ b. A backup domain controller (BDC) with 600MB of free disk space on a FAT system drive and 300MB of free disk space on an NTFS drive D

❑ c. A member server with 600MB of free disk space on a FAT system drive

❑ d. A member server with 100MB of free disk space on a FAT system drive and 800MB of free disk space on an NTFS drive F

Answers a and d are correct. An SMS primary site server requires 100MB of available disk space on any formatted system drive and 500MB of available disk space on an NTFS drive. Answer a suggests a PDC with 600MB of free disk space on an NTFS partition. Since you need to have at least 600MB of total free disk space to install SMS on one drive and that drive also needs to be formatted NTFS and be a system drive, answer a is correct. Answer d exceeds the minimum requirements with 100MB of free disk space on a FAT system drive and 800MB of free disk space on an NTFS drive. Answer b only provides for 300MB of free disk space on an NTFS drive. Since 500MB are required, it is incorrect. Answer c does not have an NTFS drive. You must have an NTFS drive to install SMS, so answer c is incorrect.

Question 6

Which of the following computers can be used as both a distribution point and a CAP?

○ a. An alpha server running Windows NT 3.51 Server (SP5a)

○ b. An x86 server running Windows NT 4 Server (SP2)

○ c. An x86 server running Windows NT 3.51 Server (SP5a)

○ d. An x86 server running Windows NT 4 Server (SP3)

Answer d is correct. An x86 server running Windows NT 4 Server SP3 supports both a distribution point and a CAP. Because x86 servers running Windows NT 3.51 are supported for distribution points only, answers a and c are both incorrect. Windows NT 4 Server SP2 is not supported for CAPs. Therefore, answer b is incorrect.

Question 7

> You have installed an SMS primary site server on a Windows NT Server con-
> figured as a PDC. Your assistant, Marian, has only Computer Operator rights
> on your Windows NT domain. You want Marian to manage all of the SMS
> clients using the SMS Administrator console. What should you do?
>
> ○ a. Add Marian to the Domain Admins global group.
>
> ○ b. Provide Marian with the SQL SA password.
>
> ○ c. Add Marian to the Administrators local group on the PDC.
>
> ○ d. Add Marian to the SMS Admins local group on the PDC.
>
> ○ e. Give Marian Change permissions to the SMS directories on the PDC.

Answer d is correct. By default, the SMS Admins local group is given access to
the WMI Administrator console, and you have to be a member of this group
to manage SMS resources. So, you need to add Marian to this local group. You
also will have to give Marian some Class and/or Instance access rights to the
SMS objects in the SMS Administrator console. Answers a and c are incorrect
because neither the Domain Admins global group nor the Administrators local group has rights to the SMS Administrator console by default. Answer b is
incorrect because providing Marian with rights to SQL Server may help her
access SQL, but it will not give her rights to the SMS Administrator console.
Answer e is incorrect because giving Marian permissions to SMS directories
does not give her any rights to the SMS Administrator console.

Question 8

> Your existing SMS 1.2 site hierarchy is composed of one central site and
> three secondary sites. There are 150 Windows 3 clients managed by one of
> the secondary sites and 700 Windows 95 clients managed by all of the other
> sites. You plan to upgrade the Windows 3 clients in six months, and you want
> to use SMS to manage them in the meantime. You want to install SMS 2 client
> software on all of the Windows 95 computers now. What should you do?
>
> ○ a. Upgrade the central site to SMS 2.
>
> ○ b   Upgrade all of the sites to SMS 2.
>
> ○ c. Upgrade all of the sites to SMS 2 except the secondary site that is
>   managing the Windows 3 clients.
>
> ○ d. Detach the secondary site that is managing the Windows 3 clients
>   from the hierarchy and upgrade all of the other sites to SMS 2.

Answer c is correct. Only an SMS 1.2 secondary site can manage Windows 3 clients because they are not supported by SMS 2. So, this site should not be upgraded to SMS 2. The SMS 1.2 site will not have any SMS 2 child sites because it's a secondary site.

Answer a is incorrect since it does not allow for installing SMS 2 client software on all of the Windows 95 machines. Answer b is incorrect. Since Windows 3 machines are not supported by SMS 2, you could not use SMS to manage them under these circumstances. Answer d is incorrect as well because a secondary site requires continuous access to its parent site. A secondary site cannot operate while it is detached.

Question 9

You have decided to use SMS 2 to manage your NetWare 3.12 Windows 98 clients. All NetWare 3.12 servers are configured with the IPX/SPX and TCP/IP protocols. What do you need to do to accomplish your task?

○ a. Install an SMS site server on an NT Server configured with the TCP/IP protocol.

○ b. Install an SMS site server on one of the NetWare 3.12 servers.

○ c. Install an SMS site server on all of the NetWare 3.12 servers.

○ d. Install an SMS site server on an NT Server configured with the IPX/SPX protocol.

○ e. Install an SMS site server on an NT Server configured with the IPX/SPX protocol and configure SQL Server to use NWLink IPX/SPX network library.

Answer d is correct. An SMS site server must be installed on an NT Server and must run the IPX/SPX protocol. Answer a is incorrect because any NT Server, including an SMS site server, can communicate with NetWare servers using the IPX/SPX protocol only. Answers b and c are incorrect because a SMS site server can be installed only on a Windows NT Server computer, not on a NetWare 3.12 server. Answer e is incorrect because an SMS site server can communicate with SQL Server using only the named pipes or multiprotocol network library.

Question 10

> Margaret is a member of the local SMS Admins group and has only the following Class and Instance permissions:
>
> - All rights to the Site Hierarchy class
> - Read and Read Resource rights to the Collections class
> - Advertise, Read, Read Resource to the All Users collection instance
>
> To which SMS resources can Margaret advertise programs?
>
> O a. All resources
>
> O b. Only resources listed in the All Users collection
>
> O c. Resources in the All Users collection and all SMS site systems
>
> O d. Margaret cannot advertise any programs

Answer d is correct. Margaret has no permissions to the Packages and Advertisements classes; therefore, she cannot advertise any programs. Answers a, b, and c list specific collections and resources to which Margaret could have access. Since she has no access rights to Packages and Advertisements, the collections and resources she has access to are irrelevant.

Need To Know More?

 Garms, Jason. *Windows NT Server 4 Unleashed*. Sams Publishing, Indianapolis, IN, 1996. ISBN 0-672-30933-5. Chapter 22 has some valuable information about connecting Windows NT to NetWare servers. Chapters 23 and 25 explain Windows NT security and give great examples of how to configure it properly.

 Tittel, Ed, Kurt Hudson, and J. Michael Stewart. *MCSE TCP/IP Exam Cram*. The Coriolis Group, Inc., Scottsdale, AZ, 1998. ISBN 1-57610-195-9. Chapters 4 and 5 explain IP addressing, subnetting, calculating network IDs, and the number of hosts per IP subnet.

 Microsoft Corporation. *Microsoft TCP/IP Training*. Microsoft Press, Redmond, WA, 1997. ISBN 1-57231-623-3. The entire book is a good source of information about internetworking using Windows NT and the TCP/IP protocol. Subnetting, supernetting, and NetBIOS name resolution are interesting topics that an SMS administrator planning an SMS deployment must understand.

 Microsoft Corporation. *Microsoft Systems Management Server Training*. Microsoft Press, Redmond, WA, 1997. ISBN 1-57231-614-4. This hands-on training manual is a great source of information about SMS 1.2. Anyone going through the upgrade process will find this publication handy during the site upgrade preparation phase.

 Microsoft Corporation. *Microsoft Systems Management Server Administrator's Guide, version 2.0*. Microsoft, Corporation, Redmond, WA, 1999. Chapter 4, "Creating Your SMS Security Strategy," contains more detail about the SMS security system. Chapter 5, "Upgrading from SMS 1.2 to SMS 2.0," contains more detailed information about interoperability between SMS 1.2 and SMS 2 sites.

 www.microsoft.com/smsmgmt/ is the Microsoft Systems Management Server Web page. This Web site contains the latest information about SMS 2, including supported operating systems, upgrade and interoperability information, white papers, and deployment case studies.

SMS Site Installation And Configuration

4

Terms you'll need to understand:

- √ SQL data device
- √ SQL transaction log device
- √ SQL tempdb database
- √ Systems Management Server Setup Wizard
- √ Express setup
- √ Custom setup
- √ SQL user connections
- √ Secondary Site Creation Wizard
- √ Windows NT Server site system
- √ Windows NT Share site system
- √ NetWare Bindery site system
- √ NetWare NDS (Novell Directory Services) site system
- √ NT Logon Discovery Agent
- √ Address priority
- √ Sender rate limit

Techniques you'll need to master:

- √ Configuring SQL Server for SMS integration
- √ Understanding the differences between the SMS setup options
- √ Selecting optional SMS features during both Custom and secondary site setup
- √ Choosing the appropriate secondary site setup method
- √ Installing an SMS Administrator console
- √ Configuring addresses to set up hierarchical relationships
- √ Configuring addresses to operate under different network conditions
- √ Creating and configuring various site system roles

When you install SMS, you need to make many decisions and choices that will determine how your site will be configured. SMS offers two primary site setup methods: Express and Custom. In this chapter, we will compare them as well as list the installed components and default configurations for each. Then, we will discuss the different secondary site installation methods and how to configure SMS site systems. Although this chapter doesn't include detailed installation steps or information about optimizing and maintaining an SMS site (discussed in Chapter 9), we will cover the main topics you should know for the test.

Getting Ready For Installation

Like many Microsoft BackOffice applications, SMS has two setup options: Express and Custom. Express setup installs and configures a select set of SMS features, whereas Custom setup installs the core SMS features, leaves configuration to the SMS administrator, and allows you to choose the optional SMS features you would like to install.

> *Note: For step-by-step SMS installation instructions, see the resources in the "Need To Know More?" section at the end of this chapter.*

Your SMS site will function based on which optional SMS components you install and how you configure your site. Therefore, before you begin installing SMS, you must fully understand the setup process as well as your choices and the configuration options. Some SMS features appear as if they provide you with a wealth of information about your managed systems. However, if you don't configure them properly, they might create unwanted loads on your existing systems and affect your network's stability.

Prior to installing an SMS 2 site server, you need to verify that your system meets the minimum hardware and software recommendations. These are listed in detail in Chapter 3 and are summarized below:

➤ A minimum of 100MB of free disk space on the system drive (formatted with either FAT (file allocation table) or NTFS (NT file system)

➤ A minimum of 500MB of free disk space on an NTFS partition

➤ Windows NT 4 Server Service Pack 4 (SP4) configured as a domain controller or a member server

➤ Internet Explorer 4.01 (SP1)

The SMS 2 CD-ROM includes SP4 for Windows NT 4 as well as Internet Explorer 4.01 (SP1). The installation files for SP4 are located in the \NTQFE\Nt4SP4A<l><platform> directory.

Installing SQL Server

A primary site server requires Microsoft SQL Server 6.5 (SP4) or 7 installed either locally or remotely. You need to either install a version of SQL Server before installing SMS or have access to the SQL Server installation source files. Both Express and Custom setup can install and configure SQL Server for you. If you install SQL Server prior to launching setup, you can preconfigure SQL Server for SMS. The following sections explain how to configure SQL Server before you install SMS.

 If you plan to use SQL Server on a separate computer from your site server (remote SQL), you must complete the steps listed in the following section before starting SMS setup.

 The Express setup option is available only on SMS server computers without SQL Server installed. Express setup installs SQL automatically, and therefore is not available if you have installed SQL Server on your site server prior to running setup.

Pre-Installing SQL Server

If you install SQL Server as part of your SMS installation, you cannot specify separate locations for SQL Server 6.5 devices or SQL Server 7 files. SMS administrators must create the database devices or files manually under either of the following conditions:

➤ SQL Server will be located on the same computer as the SMS site server, but the SMS administrator wants to create and store the data and transaction log devices/files on separate drives.

➤ SQL Server will be running on a remote computer.

Other reasons to install SQL Server manually are if:

➤ You want to use integrated Windows NT security.

➤ You want to control the location of the SQL master database.

➤ You want to specify a character set or sort order that SQL Server uses that is different from the SQL defaults.

The following sections—which assume that you have already used SQL setup to install SQL Server 6.5 or 7—describe the SQL Server configuration tasks you must accomplish after you install SQL Server and before you install SMS.

Creating Data And Transaction Log Devices

When you create the database and transaction logs devices manually, you might want to place them on separate drives for better SQL performance and fault-tolerance.

Both the SMS site database and the software-metering database require two separate devices. You cannot use one device to store both the data and the transaction logs.

The SMS installation procedure is preconfigured to point to the SQL 6.5 Server SMS site database and the software-metering devices with the following default names:

➤ **Database device** SMSData_<*sitecode*> is the default name of the SMS data device; Lic_Data_<*sitecode*> is the default name of the software-metering data device. (<*sitecode*> represents the actual three-letter site code of your site.)

➤ **Transaction log** SMSLog_<*sitecode*> is the default name of the SMS log device; Lic_Log_<*sitecode*> is the default name of the software-metering log device. (If you use SMS Express setup described later in the chapter, by default, the software-metering devices are called: LIC_DATA and LIC_LOG.)

A SQL Server 6.5 *data device* is a disk file used to store database objects and data. Similarly, the SQL Server 6.5 *transaction log device* is a disk file used to store the transaction log of a database. SQL Server 7 uses different terminology. Its operating system files (called *files*) are used for database objects, data storage, and the transaction log.

Although SQL Server 6.5 can use a data device to store both the database and its transaction log, SQL Server 7 requires a separate file for the transaction log. For simplicity, the term "device" is used to describe both a SQL 6.5 device and a SQL 7 file.

You may create the devices using these names, but feel free to use others. If you use other names, you must specify them during SMS setup.

If you are using SQL 7, the SMS installation procedure points to the SMS site database and software-metering database names instead of to their devices (or, rather, files).

 You cannot create SQL Server 7 files without creating the data-base. However, you can create SQL Server 6.5 devices with no database.

The default names for both SQL Server 6.5 and SQL Server 7 databases are:

➤ **SMS site database** Used to store inventory, discovery, client installation, configuration, and other types of data in your site. The default name is SMS_<*sitecode*>.

➤ **Software-metering database** Used to store software metering data in your site. The default name is Lic_DB_<*sitecode*>.

When creating SQL devices, use the following sizing guidelines:

➤ SMS database device should be at at least 50MB

➤ SMS database device should have at least 100K per each SMS client

➤ SMS transaction log device should contain at least 20 percent as much space as the corresponding data device

➤ Software-metering device should be at least 10MB

➤ Software-metering device should have at least 200K for each SMS client

➤ Software-metering transaction log device should contain at least 15 percent as much space as the corresponding data device

➤ Tempdb data device should contain at least 20 percent as much space as both the SMS and software-metering data devices

➤ Tempdb transaction log device should contain at least 20 percent as much space as the tempdb data device

By default, the SQL 6.5 tempdb data device, which is 2MB, is stored on the master device. Therefore, you might want to expand tempdb over the newly created separate data and transaction log devices. For better performance, you might also want to create these devices on different physical drives.

Figure 4.1 shows an example of both an SMS and a tempdb device for a 3,000-client site.

Creating The SQL Access Account

You can configure the account that SMS will use to access the SMS site database. SMS allows you to choose whether you want to use standard SQL Server security or integrated Windows NT security.

If you use standard SQL Server security, SMS can use the SA (SQL system administrator) account or any SQL account that has the following permissions:

➤ Create Database

➤ Dump Database

➤ Dump Transaction Log

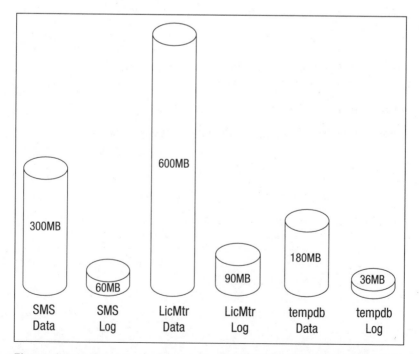

Figure 4.1 Minimum device size for an SMS installation with 3,000 clients.

If you use integrated Windows NT security, the Windows NT account that SMS uses to access SQL Server must have the appropriate rights as well. The account SMS uses to create, access, and manage the SMS site database requires the three permissions to the master database that we listed above.

Configuring SQL Server For SMS

You should configure SQL Server with the appropriate number of User Connections, Locks, and Open Objects. When you first install SMS, the following settings should be sufficient:

➤ Open Objects: 1,000

➤ Locks: 1,500

➤ User Connections: 75

You need to reconfigure the above settings—and possibly others—based on how intensely you use your database, what type of machine SQL runs on, and the version of SQL Server you use.

> *Note:* *Refer to Chapter 9 for more information on Open Objects, Locks, and User Connections.*

Installing Primary Sites

SMS provides an installation wizard that you will use for installing SMS sites. You can start the primary site installation process in three ways:

➤ Insert the SMS 2 CD-ROM into the CD-ROM drive and have it auto-start.

➤ Run AUTORUN.EXE from the root of the SMS 2 installation source directory.

➤ Run SETUP.EXE from the SMSSETUP\BIN*<platform>* directory.

The installation wizard will guide you through the installation process. You will be asked some questions, and depending on your answers, the installation routine will set up SMS differently. For example, if you're running setup on a computer without Microsoft SQL Server installed, you must select the installation method, as shown in Figure 4.2.

If your computer has Microsoft SQL Server installed, this screen does not appear; the Custom installation option is selected by default. Remember that Custom setup allows you to select whether or not to install the optional SMS features. Table 4.1 lists all of the default SMS components installed by the Express and Custom setup options.

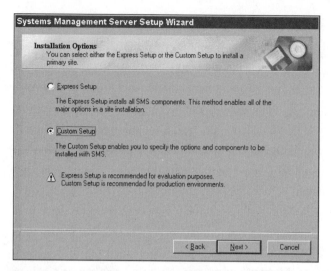

Figure 4.2 Installation options that appear when SQL Server is not previously installed.

Table 4.1 Default SMS components installed by each setup option.

SMS Component	Express Setup	Custom Setup
Alpha Site System Support	Installed	Optional
Crystal Reports	Installed	Optional
NetWare Bindery Support	Installed	Optional
NetWare NDS Support	Installed	Optional
Network Monitor	Installed	Optional
Package Automation Scripts	Installed	Optional
Product Compliance Database	Installed	Optional
Remote Tools	Installed	Optional
SMS Administrator console	Installed	Installed
SMS Installer	Installed	Optional
SMS Site Server	Installed	Installed
Software Metering Console	Installed	Optional
Software Metering	Installed[1]	Optional
SQL Server	Installed	Installed[2]

[1]The software-metering role is not assigned to any site system.

[2]The SQL Server role can be installed by either you or the setup.

Running Express Setup

You cannot remove or disable any of the optional SMS components, so the Express setup method is preferred primarily for installing a site simply to evaluate whether or not a company wants to install SMS. By default, Express setup does the following:

➤ Installs SQL Server and all optional SMS components

➤ Creates both the SMS site database and the software-metering database

➤ Enables most of the server features and client agents

 SMS setup will ask you to specify a three-character site code for your site. Make sure that the site code you choose is unique for each SMS site within your SMS hierarchy.

During setup, the wizard will ask for SMS Service account information. This account should be a member of the Domain Admins global group and the local Administrators group. The account also requires Logon as a service advanced user rights. You can create and configure this account prior to installation, or SMS can do it for you automatically.

You will need to specify the appropriate number of clients your site will manage. SMS uses this number to properly size the databases. If your databases run low on disk space after your site is operational, you can always expand the databases to accommodate more clients or more data being passed from each client.

Express setup will also ask you for the estimated number of SMS Administrator consoles that you will be using simultaneously. SMS uses this information to configure the number of SQL User Connections. SMS requires 50 SQL User Connections for the primary site server and 5 for each additional SMS Administrator console. The default number of User Connections is 75 (allowing for 5 SMS Administrator consoles). You can specify a larger number during the setup process. Or, after installation, you can increase the number by using SQL Enterprise Manager, ISQL, or any other utility that can run SQL commands.

When the Express Setup Installation Wizard is complete, SMS setup starts. Next, it asks you for the CD Key from your Microsoft SQL Server CD-ROM and the location of the SQL Server setup file. Once you have provided this information, SMS setup installs SQL Server and then SMS.

In addition to installing all of the optional components, Express setup enables many SMS features and configures them for operation. Table 4.2 lists the major configurable SMS features and their settings after Express setup successfully finishes installing SQL Server and SMS.

Table 4.2 Express setup configuration of SMS features.

SMS Feature	State	Notes
Hardware Inventory Client Agent	Enabled	Runs once a day
Software Inventory Client Agent	Enabled	Runs once a day
Remote Tools Client Agent	Enabled	
Advertised Programs Client Agent	Enabled	Runs once an hour
Software Metering Client Agent	Enabled	Starts with a 240-minute polling interval
Event To Trap Translator Client Agent	Enabled	
Windows Networking Logon Client Installation	Enabled	NT domain specified only if installed on a domain controller
Modify Windows NT Logon Scripts	Disabled	
NetWare NDS Logon Client Installation	Enabled	No logon points are specified
Modify NetWare NDS Logon Scripts	Disabled	
NetWare Bindery Logon Client Installation	Enabled	No logon points are specified
Modify NetWare Bindery Logon Scripts	Disabled	
Windows NT Remote Client Installation	Enabled	Enabled for all NT machines
Windows Networking Logon Discovery	Enabled	NT domain specified only if installed on a domain controller
Windows NT User Account Discovery	Enabled	NT domain specified if installed on a domain controller or a member server
Windows NT User Group Discovery	Enabled	NT domain specified if installed on a domain controller or a member server
NetWare NDS Logon Discovery	Enabled	No logon points are specified

(continued)

Table 4.2	Express setup configuration of SMS features (continued).	
SMS Feature	**State**	**Notes**
NetWare Bindery Logon Discovery	Enabled	No logon points are specified
Heartbeat Discovery	Enabled	Runs once a day
Network Discovery	Disabled	

Running Custom Setup

The Custom setup option allows you to install SMS components selectively (refer back to Table 4.1). Custom setup can install a local copy of SQL Server and it allows you to point to an existing local or remote SQL Server to work with SMS 2. As in Express setup, you must answer several questions. For example, you need to specify which account to use for the SMS Service account, how many SMS Administrator consoles will be used simultaneously, and where the SQL Server setup files will be located (if SMS is to install SQL Server for you).

You also have to specify whether SMS should install Alpha support files. You should select this option if some of your site systems will run on computers that use Alpha processors or if you are planning on remotely installing secondary sites that run on Alpha processor computers. In addition, Custom setup asks you which optional SMS features you wish to install. Use the guidelines presented in Table 4.3 to assist you in selecting optional SMS features.

Table 4.3	Optional SMS features.
SMS Feature	**Select If**
Software Metering	You are planning to meter software usage in your SMS site or secondary child site.
Software Metering Console	You are planning on managing the software licenses at your site and/or its subsites, or if you want to generate software-metering reports.
Remote Tools	You want to use remote control features in your site and/or its secondary child sites.
SMS Installer	You want to create simplified installation packages.

(continued)

Table 4.3 Optional SMS features (continued).	
SMS Feature	**Select If**
Network Monitor	You want to monitor and troubleshoot network-related problems.
Package Automation Scripts	You want to use predefined installation scripts for installing software.
Crystal Reports	You are planning on using the sample Crystal Reports Microsoft Management Console (MMC) snap-in to generate reports.
NetWare Bindery Support	Some or all of your clients connect only to supported NetWare bindery servers.
NetWare NDS Support	Some or all of your clients connect only to supported NetWare NDS servers.
Product Compliance Database	You want to verify Year 2000 (Y2K) software compliance for software installed on your client computers.

The last major set of questions the Systems Management Server Setup Wizard asks you is related to SQL Server and the database and log devices. You have to instruct the wizard to use either a pre-installed local or a remote SQL Server. Or, you can have Custom setup install a local copy of SQL Server automatically. If you are using a pre-installed version of SQL Server, you also need to specify the names of the SQL devices or instruct setup to create the devices.

 If you decide to use a remote SQL Server, you must specify the SMS Provider's location. You should place the SMS Provider on the server that will have the least stress (if only SMS will use your remote SQL Server, the SQL Server computer will qualify on this point). You cannot change the location of the SMS Provider without moving the SMS site database to a different SQL Server computer. Therefore, carefully consider any changes to applications that run on both servers as well as additional databases hosted on the SQL Server and databases that clients will actively access.

After you have filled in all of the data that setup requires, the installation wizard summarizes your selections. You should review and adjust any possible mistakes and then start the installation process.

As soon as the primary site is installed, the SMS client installation process begins on the site server, making the site server an SMS client.

Installing Secondary Sites

In Chapter 2, we delineated the differences between primary and secondary sites. We explained that secondary sites are frequently used in remote office locations that do not have a permanent IS staff. However, you can install secondary sites in other situations as well. SMS provides you with two convenient methods for installing secondary sites:

➤ From the SMS Administrator console at the parent primary site

➤ From the computer designated to be the secondary site server (direct installation)

Remember that a secondary site requires a connection to a primary parent site for data storage. The two sites must communicate with each other in order to function properly. The physical connection among the sites, SMS senders, and addresses provides this communication.

Before installing secondary sites, make sure that the target computer meets the minimum hardware and software requirements.

Local Secondary Site Setup

You can install a secondary site in the same way you installed your primary site (using Custom setup from the SMS 2 CD-ROM or any other SMS installation file source). The Systems Management Server Setup Wizard will guide you as well as ask you some questions.

Using the local secondary site setup option, you can install a secondary site without a physical link to the parent site. The Systems Management Server Setup Wizard will still create the sender and the address to the primary site, but the secondary site will not be operational until the physical link between the two sites is present.

After you select the option to install a secondary site, you must enter a site code for the secondary site; later, you will need to decide whether or not to install Alpha platform support. Next, you will be able to select the optional SMS features to install on the secondary site server.

A secondary site does not have its own site database, so only the following optional SMS features are available for installation at a secondary site:

➤ Software Metering

➤ Remote Tools

➤ NetWare Bindery Support

➤ NetWare NDS Support

The next SMS Setup Wizard screen (shown in Figure 4.3) will ask you to enter the site code and the NetBIOS name of the parent primary site. You will also be asked to select the type of SMS sender the secondary site will use to connect to its parent site. After specifying the sender and the Windows NT account that the secondary site will use to connect to the primary site, you will see a summary of your selections. After you review the selections and select Finish, the installation process will begin.

 After you install a secondary site using local installation, the parent site will be aware of its new child site (if the secondary site can physically connect to its parent). The parent site will still not be able to send configuration data to the secondary site until you configure the primary site with the sender and the address to the secondary site.

Figure 4.3 Secondary site Setup Wizard screen.

Setup From The SMS Administrator Console

Most secondary sites are in remote offices with no IS staff, so for convenience, you can install secondary sites remotely using the Secondary Site Creation Wizard at the parent site. This wizard is available in the SMS Administrator console, from the primary site's Action|New pull-down menu.

 You can initiate installation of a secondary site using the Secondary Site Creation Wizard only on a remote computer that is directly attached to a parent site. In order to install a secondary site as a grandchild site (or lower-level site), you need to attach the console directly to that site's parent (use the Connect To Site Database item).

Another way to start the Secondary Site Creation Wizard is by right-clicking on the *<site code>* - *<site name>* primary site object in the SMS Administrator console, shown in Figure 4.4.

After you start the wizard, it guides you through the process of creating an installation file that SMS will use to install the secondary site. The information you need to provide while running the wizard is similar to the answers you provide when running the Systems Management Server Setup Wizard to install a primary or a secondary site. In addition, you will need to indicate the processor platform of the secondary site (x86-compatible or Alpha) and create or specify an address from and to the secondary site. The primary site will use the later address to send installation instructions to the new secondary site.

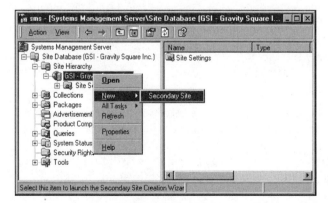

Figure 4.4 Launching the Secondary Site Creation Wizard from the SMS Administrator console at a parent site.

You must also specify an SMS Service account for the secondary site. This account needs to be a member of the Domain Admins global domain group and the Administrators local machine group. It also must have Logon as a service advanced user rights.

 During local secondary site installation, the setup wizard can create and grant appropriate permissions for the SMS Service account. When you install a secondary site remotely, you must create and configure the SMS Service account prior to installation.

The most important information you provide, from the point of network utilization (how much traffic will be on your network), is the answer about the installation source files. You can choose either to transfer all installation files from the parent site using the sender or to use the SMS 2 CD-ROM locally at the secondary site. The following guidelines will help you select the best option:

➤ Choose to install from the local CD-ROM if you have the means to create one, and if you have someone available to insert the CD-ROM into the CD-ROM drive at the secondary site.

➤ Choose to transfer installation files from the parent site if you have relatively fast connectivity between the primary site server and the secondary site server or if no one is available to load a CD-ROM into the secondary site server's CD-ROM drive.

 If you choose to transfer the files from the parent site, you should expect a minimum of 42MB of files to be transferred (after compression). The transferred package can be larger, depending on the platform support and the optional SMS features installed on the primary site server.

 You can install a secondary site server on an Alpha processor only if the parent site was installed with the Alpha support files. The same applies to the optional SMS features. For example, if you installed the primary site without the software-metering feature, you cannot install software metering at the secondary site.

Installing The SMS Administrator Console

The SMS Setup Wizard also allows you to install the SMS Administrator console and related tools. You can install the console on any computer that runs Windows NT 4 SP4 and Microsoft Internet Explorer 4.01. You need to have administrative privileges to the Windows NT 4 computer to install the console. Once you start the Setup Wizard and choose to install the SMS Administrator console, you will be asked to provide information about the SMS site server name, the directory you wish the supporting files to be copied to, and the optional console tools. You may choose from the following list of tools:

➤ Software Metering Console

➤ Network Monitor

➤ Crystal Reports Console

Once the console is installed, you can use it to connect to the primary site you specified or to any other primary site.

Modifying An SMS Installation

You can modify an SMS site server and an SMS Administrator console installation by re-running the SMS Setup Wizard. You can specify additional components to install; however, the Modify option of the SMS Setup Wizard does not allow you to remove any optional components.

In order to add additional components to your SMS site server, you should run SMS setup from the SMS CD-ROM or from any location that contains the full installation source files. You cannot add components if you run SMS setup from the Start menu because they are not located on your local disk drive.

Another way to remotely add components to the secondary site server is by first adding them to the primary site and then upgrading the secondary site installation from the Action|All Tasks menu (with the primary site server object highlighted). You can also upgrade a secondary site by right-clicking on the *<site code>* - *<site name>* primary site object in the SMS Administrator console.

Configuring Site System Roles

After installation, by default, every SMS site server is also configured as a client access point (CAP) and a distribution point. Other SMS roles are assigned depending on the type of setup you used, the role the SMS server plays as a Windows NT Server in the domain, and the location of the SQL Server. You can add or remove site system roles to or from your SMS site server and assign them to different Windows NT or NetWare servers to modify specific SMS functionality. You can also move site system roles for performance reasons. Only one server role cannot be moved from one site system to another—the SMS site server role.

The SMS Site Server Role

The SMS site server role (either primary or secondary) is permanently assigned to the computer on which you installed SMS. In order to move this role from one site system to another, you have to reinstall SMS. This role has a number of properties and is configurable under the Site Hierarchy node in the SMS Administrator console. The most important functions that the site server performs are:

➤ Maintaining site boundaries

➤ Processing objects that SMS clients produce

➤ Providing clients with distributed software

➤ Providing addresses to other sites in the SMS hierarchy (primary site server only)

➤ Solidifying its position in the SMS hierarchy

➤ Providing site status information

SMS Site Boundaries

In Chapter 3, we discussed in detail configuring site boundaries, which define what sites SMS clients belong to. You configure them using Internet Protocol (IP) network IDs and Internetwork Packet Exchange (IPX) network numbers. The site boundaries are defined in the Site Properties dialog box, shown in Figure 4.5.

You can define site boundaries by using multiple IP network IDs (pure class A, B, and C segments), as well as subnetted and supernetted segments. You can also enter multiple IPX network numbers.

You can add and delete site boundaries at any time. You should be particularly careful not to extend the site boundaries to include network segments that are separated from your site by slow wide area network (WAN) links. You also do not want to remove from the site boundaries network segments that host your SMS clients.

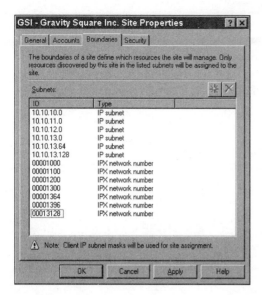

Figure 4.5 Defining site boundaries in the SMS Administrator console.

Note: Orphaned SMS clients deinstall SMS client software after 60 days of inactivity.

SMS Site Addresses

The SMS site uses addresses and senders—described in detail in the "Sender Servers (Component Servers)" section later in this chapter—to communicate with other sites in the hierarchy. You can use three primary types of addresses to communicate with other sites:

➤ **Standard Sender address** Used to transfer data between sites on established local area network (LAN) and WAN connections.

➤ **RAS address** Used to transfer data over dial-up connections. There are four different RAS Sender addresses: Asynchronous, ISDN, X.25, and SNA.

➤ **Courier Sender address** Used to transfer software distribution packages using a removable media.

A Courier Sender address must be used in conjunction with another address type. You can use Courier Sender only to transfer software distribution packages. You must use another type of sender to communicate between sites.

A single site can have multiple addresses to another site provided that each address is of a different type. For example, a primary site with the site code NYC might have two different addresses with the site code of CHI: an ISDN RAS sender address and an Asynchronous RAS sender address. The Asynchronous RAS sender address can be used only during business hours, although both addresses might be available at night and on weekends.

Configuring Addresses

To create and configure an address, go to the Address node in the SMS Administrator console.

You must have Modify access rights to an SMS site to create or modify an address.

You can configure each address, except for a Courier Sender address, through the three tabs on the Address Properties dialog box: General, Schedule, and Rate Limits. The Courier Sender Address Properties dialog box is composed of one tab only—the General tab.

The General tab allows you to specify the destination site and access properties. A Courier Sender address is simply the destination's site code. A Standard Sender address has more fields: a destination site code, a destination server NetBIOS name, and an account and password used to access the destination site's SMS_SITE Share. Finally, a RAS sender has additional fields for configuring a RAS phone book entry and a RAS access account.

The two more interesting address configuration options are available through the Schedule and the Rate Limit tabs. The Schedule tab is shown in Figure 4.6.

The Schedule tab allows you to specify times of the day and week when the address is available for any of the four priority settings:

➤ All priorities

➤ Medium and high priorities

➤ High-priority only

➤ Closed (not available)

In addition, you can specify whether the address is available as a substitute for an inoperative address. You should use this setting to add fault-tolerance to inter-site data transfer.

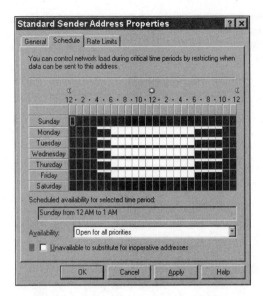

Figure 4.6   The Schedule tab of Address Properties.

The Rate Limits tab allows you to throttle the data transfer to a specific percentage of the connection bandwidth. You can specify throttling by the hour of day only; you cannot set different rate limits for specific days of the week. You should use this setting to minimize the effects of SMS inter-site communication on your day-to-day business activities. You need to be sure that you allow for enough bandwidth to transfer all SMS data during each SMS cycle. For instance, daily software inventory of 150K from each of your 2,000 SMS clients creates approximately 300MB of data that needs to be sent up to the parent site every day; your address rate needs to allow for all of this data to be sent each day.

The last address setting is available from the right pane of the SMS Administrator console. In situations where you have two or more addresses created for communication with a single site, you might want to modify their priorities. Figure 4.7 shows a Standard Sender address that has higher priority (a lower number) than the Asynchronous RAS Sender address.

You can prioritize addresses to inform SMS which one it should use first when connecting to another site. In the example shown in Figure 4.7, the Standard Sender address will always be used as the first address when communicating with site GS1. If this address is unavailable (scheduled to be closed or limited to 0 percent bandwidth), the Asynchronous RAS address will be used. You can change the address priority in increments of one by right-clicking on it and either choosing Increment Priority or Decrement Priority.

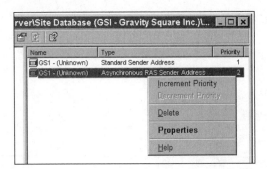

Figure 4.7 Assigning address priorities.

 Remember that you need addresses between direct child sites and their parent sites only. No addresses to other sites in the hierarchy are necessary. SMS uses fan-out technology, which allows for efficient data routing between subsites. You might want to create an address to a site other than your child site if you want to distribute packages there directly (without other sites being involved in the package distribution). This configuration might decrease the length of time required for package distribution and may lighten some of the load on your child site server(s).

Parent-Child Site Relationships

You can connect SMS sites together to form an SMS hierarchy. A single SMS site can have only one parent site, but it can have many child sites. To define the parent-child relationship of SMS sites, use the General tab of the Site Properties dialog box, shown in Figure 4.8, on the child site computer. As shown in the inset, when you click on the Set Parent Site option, you will see a screen that allows you to choose which site will be the parent site.

A primary site can be a central site, or it can report to a parent site. Prior to attaching your site to the new parent, you must create an address to the parent site. To specify the parent site, select its site code. Only the site codes of the sites to which you already have configured addresses will be available in the drop-down list (refer to Figure 4.8).

You can also detach a primary site from its parent site and attach it to a different one. However, you cannot change the parent site of a secondary site because a secondary site is attached to its parent only during the secondary site installation process. The only method of changing a secondary site's parent is to reinstall the secondary site.

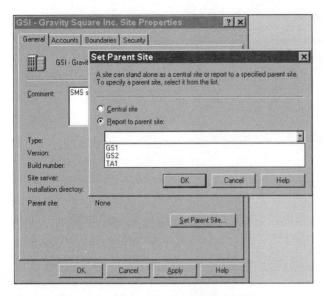

Figure 4.8   Attaching a site to a parent site.

 You can assign a new parent site to a primary site only. Once a primary site is attached to a new parent, it uploads all of its data and configuration settings to the new parent. A parent site can manage and configure its child site only after you create and configure addresses between the two sites.

Logon Points

You create logon points by enabling either the Windows Networking Logon Discovery method or the Windows Networking Logon Client Installation method. These two SMS features create logon points for either logon-script driven or manual client discovery and/or client installation (see Chapter 5 for more information on creating logon points). You can enable these methods from the Discovery Methods and the Client Installation Methods console nodes, respectively. Both methods have identical properties dialog boxes and configuration settings, and each works on a per-NT domain basis. All NT domain controllers in each domain that any of the enabled Windows Networking discovery or installation methods enumerates are configured as logon points. Figure 4.9 shows configuration of the logon discovery method for creating and controlling logon points on three domains.

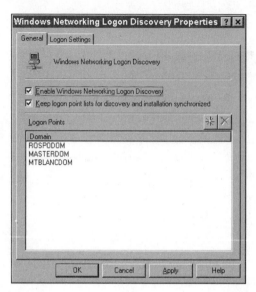

Figure 4.9 Logon Discovery Properties dialog box.

You cannot isolate specific domain controllers to become logon points. After you enable either the logon discovery or logon installation method for a domain, all domain controllers in that domain are configured as SMS logon points.

You can enable both logon discovery and logon installation methods and then manage the list of the domains they enumerate from the dialog boxes of any logon discovery method and any logon client installation method. You can do this if you enable the Keep logon point lists for discovery and installation synchronized option. The synchronization mechanism also synchronizes configuration settings for logon points and logon script updates. Alternately, you can keep the two domain lists, the logon points, and the logon script update options independent by disabling the above-described option. A similar option is available for both types of NetWare discovery and installation methods.

NT Logon Manager, a thread of the SMS Executive service, manages both the discovery and the installation methods. This thread does the following:

➤ Updates the domain controllers that are installed as logon points with the appropriate file content

➤ Makes sure that the logon points are functional and healthy

➤ Enumerates the NT account database (if logon script modification is enabled)

➤ Updates new users' logon scripts (if configured to do so)

You can configure the update interval of logon points through a setting in the Logon Settings tab of either method's properties page.

Both NetWare Bindery and NDS Discovery and Client Installation methods function very similarly to the Windows Networking methods. You configure them by bindery server or NDS volume. The Bindery Logon Manager and the NDS Logon Manager threads manage these logon points.

 SMS data required on SMS logon points is stored in the SMSLOGON directory. On Windows NT logon points, the SMSLOGON directory is shared, whereas on NetWare servers, you access it by using the standard bindery or NDS access methods. In addition, the Windows Networking Logon Discovery method creates and starts an NT Logon Discovery Agent, which forwards all received Discovery Data Records (DDRs) to all SMS sites enumerating the Windows NT domain.

CAPs

CAPs are the main points of contact between SMS clients and SMS site servers. You can configure CAPs on any of the following:

➤ A NetWare Bindery Server

➤ A NetWare NDS Volume

➤ A Windows NT Server

➤ A Windows NT Share

You use the Site Systems node under Site Settings for a specific SMS site to create CAPs, as shown in Figure 4.10.

The main difference between a CAP created on the Windows NT Server and a CAP created on a Windows NT Share is that by selecting a Windows NT Share, you can place a CAP on a specific drive. When you configure a CAP on a Windows NT Server, the CAP_*<sitecode>* Share is created on the NTFS partition with the most available drive space. If you specify a Windows NT Share, the CAP_*<sitecode>* directory is created under the specified NT Share.

A CAP_*<sitecode>* directory contains client configuration files, client agent files, and files that contain information about any distributed software. Inbox Manager (a thread running on the SMS site server) updates these files on an hourly schedule. Inbox Manager also reacts to certain directory change notification events. As soon as new software distribution instruction files or client

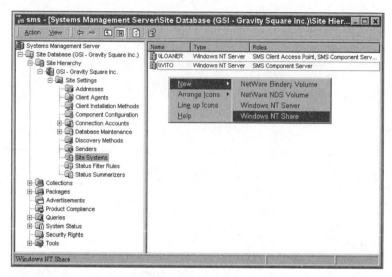

Figure 4.10 Creating CAPs, distribution points, and software-metering servers.

settings are configured on the site server, Inbox Manager synchronizes all CAPs with the new file content.

In addition, the CAP_<*sitecode*> directory contains inbox directories that SMS clients use to upload discovery records, inventory files, and status messages. Inbox Manager Assistant (a thread running on each CAP) monitors these inbox directories and forwards all files uploaded from client machines to the appropriate inboxes on the SMS site server.

CAPs created on NetWare servers work similarly with one exception—no SMS processes or services are running on the NetWare servers. Inbox Manager, which runs on the SMS site server, both uploads and downloads files from NetWare CAPs. SMS client objects that are uploaded to CAPs, except discovery data records are downloaded to the site server on an hourly cycle. You can configure the upload interval for discovery data records for both types of NetWare logon discovery.

Distribution Points

Distribution points serve only one purpose: They store distributed software made available for clients to run. As with CAPs, you can automatically create distribution points based on the NTFS logical drive with the most available drive space, or you can configure them to use a specific pre-created NT Share. Distribution Manager, a thread of the SMS Executive service, creates distribution package directories and configures them with the permissions that the SMS administrator has specified.

Note: *For more information about distributing packages, see Chapter 8.*

You can create distribution points on the same type of site systems as CAPs. These are:

➤ A Windows NT Server

➤ A Windows NT Share

➤ A NetWare Bindery Server

➤ A NetWare NDS Volume

As with CAPs, you use the Site Systems node under Site Settings for a specific SMS site to create distribution points, as you saw in Figure 4.10.

Software-Metering Servers

Software-metering functionality is built into three site system roles: the software-metering server, the software-metering database server, and the site server. The site server replicates metering data between the software-metering server(s) and the software-metering database. It also forwards metering data down and up the hierarchy to other SMS sites.

When you install software metering, the software-metering database server is configured and functional by default, whereas the metering server role is not assigned to any site system. To meter application usage, an SMS site must have at least one software-metering server configured.

To configure software-metering servers, use the Site Systems node under Site Settings in the SMS Administrator console. You may use either an existing SMS site system to host the metering role or any other Windows NT server. Only x86 and compatible machines that run the supported Windows NT Server operating system are eligible for the software-metering server role. Secondary sites can have a metering server as well. This is possible only if the secondary site's parent has been installed with the software-metering feature. A secondary SMS site uploads data collected on its metering server to the software-metering database server at its parent site.

 Alpha machines are not supported as software metering servers. SMS site servers running on Alpha machines cannot forward or receive software metering data from other sites in the hierarchy.

After you enable the software-metering server role on a Windows NT machine, you need to specify the following:

➤ Local file cache location

➤ Time zone of the metering server

➤ Account and password that the metering service will use

➤ Number of connection retries to use in attempting to connect to the software-metering database

➤ Connection retry delay in milliseconds (the time between attempts to connect to the metering database)

➤ Number of client connection points (number of threads available to intercept client requests)

Figure 4.11 shows the configurable properties of a software-metering server.

 If your software-metering server has trouble connecting to the software-metering database server, you might want to increase the number of connection retries as well as the connection retry delay. By increasing these two parameters, you will give the software-metering server a larger time window to connect to the database.

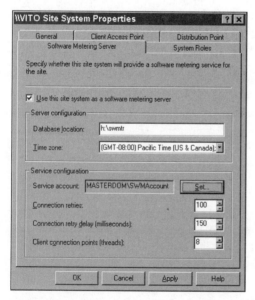

Figure 4.11   SMS software-metering server properties.

Note: See Chapter 7 for more information on software-metering functionality.

Sender Servers (Component Servers)

A single SMS site might have hundreds of child sites. There can be only one sender of each type set up on a single site system, so you might want to configure additional Windows NT servers with senders to decrease transfer times, for network load balancing, or for any other performance-related reason.

 You might increase the overall inter-site communication through-put by creating additional senders. Remember that configuring additional senders will improve network-related performance only if each sender server uses a different network route to the destination site.

You can create a new sender server by creating a new sender and configuring it with the desired Windows NT machine name. You can create and configure a sender site system from the Senders node under Site Settings for a specific SMS site, as shown in Figure 4.12.

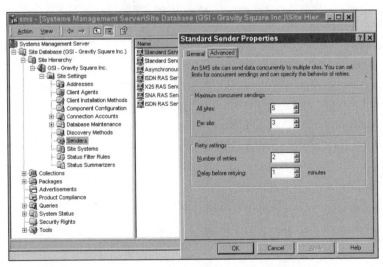

Figure 4.12   Modifying parameters for a Standard Sender.

You cannot configure Courier Sender. It is installed on SMS site systems by default. You can access Courier Sender from the Start menu under the Systems Management Server program group.

Each sender, except for Courier Sender, has a standard set of parameters. These are:

➤ **Maximum concurrent sendings for all sites** Use this setting to set the maximum number of concurrent sender connections (processing threads)

➤ **Maximum concurrent sendings per site** Use this setting to configure the maximum number of sender connections (processing threads) to a single site (available on Standard Sender only because the other senders can have only one session to a single site)

➤ **Number of retries** Use this setting to specify the number of retries to a single site that SMS should use when a communication failure occurs

➤ **Delay before retrying** Use this setting to change the delay between communication retries

 Increasing the number of concurrent sendings for all sites might actually increase overall transmission time per site (if the network bandwidth is limited). Assuming unlimited network bandwidth, an increase in the number of threads per all sites should improve overall data transmission, provided your system can handle multiple active sender threads.

Practice Questions

Question 1

> You want to install a primary site server on a Windows NT member server. You want to use a remote SQL Server 6.5 for the SMS site database. What must you do prior to installation? [Choose all correct answers]
>
> ❏ a. Create an SMS Service account on both the site server and the SQL Server computers.
>
> ❏ b. Create an SMS Service account on the SQL Server and give it Logon as a service advanced user rights.
>
> ❏ c. Configure the SQL Server default network library to TCP/IP.
>
> ❏ d. Create an SMS site database on the SQL Server.
>
> ❏ e. Create SMS data and transaction log devices on the SQL Server.

Answers b and e are correct. When you install a remote SQL Server, you must create an SMS Service account and grant it Logon as a service advanced user rights to the SQL server computer (answer b). You must also create the data and transaction log devices manually (answer e). Answer a is incorrect because SMS setup automatically creates the SMS Service account on the site server. Answer c is incorrect because SQL Server operates using named pipes or the multiprotocol network library. Answer d is incorrect because SMS creates the site database.

Question 2

> You plan to install a primary SMS site server with a local SQL Server. You anticipate that the server will operate under a heavy load, so you decide to separate the SMS data and transaction log devices onto separate physical disk drives. Which method should you use?
>
> ○ a. Run SMS Express setup and then specify different disk drives for the SMS data and log devices.
>
> ○ b. Create the SMS data and log devices on separate disk drives and then run SMS Express setup.
>
> ○ c. Run Custom setup and then specify different disk drives for the SMS data and log devices.
>
> ○ d. Create SMS data and transaction log devices on separate disk drives and then run SMS Custom setup.

Answer d is correct. To separate SQL devices on different drives, you must create them prior to the SMS setup. You can create them only if the SQL Server is already installed. Answers a and c are incorrect because neither Express nor Custom setup allows you to specify different locations for the SMS database devices. Answer b is incorrect because the Express setup option is not available if SQL Server is already installed.

Question 3

Your Windows NT domain includes a primary domain controller (PDC), three backup domain controllers (BDCs), and a Windows NT member server. All NT Servers, except for the PDC, are on a single IP segment. You installed a primary site server on the Windows NT member server. By default, which Windows NT Server computer will be configured as a CAP?

- O a. Only the Windows NT member server
- O b. The PDC and all of the BDCs
- O c. All of the Windows NT Servers except for the PDC
- O d. Only the PDC

Answer a is correct. Only the site server is configured as a CAP by default. This is true regardless of the site server's domain role and the installation type. Therefore, answers b and d are incorrect. Answer c is thrown into the list to confuse you: The combination of servers and a PDC has no relevance for any site system in SMS.

Question 4

You are planning to install a primary site server with a remote SQL Server 7. Your site will be managing 500 Windows NT 4 Workstations and 2,000 Windows 98 machines. You need to create the SMS database prior to installing SMS. What minimum size should you use for the data and transaction log files?

- O a. Data file of 50MB and log file of 5MB
- O b. Data file of 500MB and log file of 100MB
- O c. Data file of 250MB and log file of 50MB
- O d. Data file of 250MB and log file of 25MB

Answer c is correct. You should plan on 100K for each client. When you multiply the total number of clients (2,500) by 100K, you get an answer of approximately 250MB. You should then create your log file to be 20 percent of the data file, giving you a minimum size of 50MB. Note that the question asks for the minimum size and that answer c gives the exact minimum size. Answer a is incorrect because 50MB is not large enough for the data file. Answer b is incorrect because it provides enough space, but provides devices much larger than the minimum required. Answer d is incorrect because its log file is only 10 percent of the data file, not 20 percent.

Question 5

Your Windows NT domain includes a PDC, three BDCs, and two Windows NT member servers. You used Express setup to install a primary site server on one of the BDCs, and you configured your site boundaries to include the whole domain. Which Windows NT servers will automatically be configured as SMS logon points?

○ a. Only the BDC with SMS installed

○ b. All of the BDCs

○ c. Both of the Windows NT member servers

○ d. Only the PDC

○ e. All of the DCs

Answer e is correct. When you install an SMS site using Express setup on a domain controller, SMS configures all of the domain controllers within the domain as logon points. Answer e is correct because it includes the PDC and all of the BDCs in the domain. Answer a is incorrect because it lists only one of the BDCs. Answer b is incorrect because it includes all of the BDCs, but excludes the PDC. Answer c is incorrect because none of the member servers will be installed as logon points. Answer d is incorrect because it includes the PDC, but excludes the BDCs.

Question 6

You need to install 10 secondary site servers in remote offices that connect to the central site server through 56K analog phone lines. You want to use an unattended install without utilizing the already heavily loaded analog line connections. Which of the following options is the best choice for accomplishing your task?

○ a. Advertise the SMS setup program to all 10 secondary sites and send the installation files using Courier Sender.

○ b. Burn 10 copies of the SMS CD-ROM, send them to the remote locations via mail, have an individual at the local site insert the CD-ROMs, and initialize the setup from the primary site for each secondary site using the Secondary Site Creation Wizard. Then, specify that the installation files are on the secondary site server.

○ c. Burn 10 copies of the SMS CD-ROM, send them to the secondary sites via mail, and advertise an unattended installation program to all 10 secondary sites.

○ d. Burn 10 copies of the SMS CD-ROM, send them to the secondary sites via mail, and have someone at each of the remote sites run the setup program of the CD-ROM.

Answer b is correct. The process described in answer b allows you to minimize load on the 56K analog connection because you send SMS installation source files via mail. The solutions given in the answer also allow you to successfully accomplish an unattended install. In a real-world situation, you would still need human intervention at the secondary site; however, you would not need an administrator, so it is still considered unattended. Answers a and c are incorrect because the software distribution advertisement feature is not a method for installing secondary site servers. Answer d will allow you to successfully install the secondary sites, but it is not unattended. Therefore, answer d is incorrect.

Question 7

You are installing a primary site server on a Windows NT member server. You would like to use your existing dual processor SQL Server 6.5 as an SMS SQL Server. You have also decided to install the SMS Provider on the SQL Server machine. Your SQL Server is dedicated to SMS functionality; it does not store any other databases. How should you configure SQL Server 6.5 to work with the site server? [Choose all correct answers]

❑ a. Synchronize the SQL Server's time with that of the SMS site server.

❑ b. Set SQL Executive service to start automatically on system startup.

❑ c. Set the value of SQL Open Objects to 1,000 or greater.

❑ d. Set the processor affinity to 2.

Answers a and c are correct. For SMS to function properly, it is essential to have the time synchronized on all SMS site systems, including the SQL Server. A SQL Server should also be configured with at least 1,000 Open Objects for interoperability with SMS. You might need additional Open Objects if other applications are using SQL Server, but this is not the case here. Answer b is incorrect because SMS does not require the SQL Executive service to be running at all. Answer d is incorrect because processor affinity does not need to be set on SQL Server machines that are also running other applications.

Question 8

You installed a primary site server on a BDC in your master domain using Express setup. What shares and services will be created on other domain controllers in the master domain?

○ a. None

○ b. The SMSLOGON share

○ c. The NT Logon Discovery Agent service and the SMSLOGON share

○ d. The NT Logon Discovery Agent service

○ e. The NT Logon Installation service

Answer c is correct. SMS Express setup enables the Windows Networking Logon and Discovery methods. Once these methods are enabled, they are automatically configured to enumerate the NT domain to which the BDC belongs. The logon installation method creates an SMSLOGON Share, whereas the discovery method creates the share and installs the NT Logon Discovery Agent service. Answer a is incorrect because shares and services are created on the domain controllers. Answers b and d are partially correct because each one contains a part of the correct answer. However, they are incorrect because they do not contain both parts of the correct answer. Answer e is incorrect because there is no NT Logon Installation service.

Question 9

A primary server has six secondary sites connected to it using one Asynchronous RAS Sender. You want to send two packages to each site simultaneously and service all six sites at once. What maximum concurrent sendings setting should you use for the Asynchronous RAS Sender?

- ○ a. Configure the maximum number of threads to all sites to 6 and per site to 3.

- ○ b. Configure the maximum number of threads to all sites to 3 and per site to 6.

- ○ c. Configure the maximum number of threads to all sites to 6 and per site to 6.

- ○ d. You cannot send more than one package at a time to a single site using one Asynchronous RAS sender.

Answer d is correct. Only Standard Sender supports simultaneously sending multiple packages to a single site. It is not possible to send more than one package at a time to one site using a single Asynchronous RAS Sender. Therefore, answers a, b, and c are incorrect.

Question 10

You are planning to configure a parent site and a child site to communicate using the Standard Sender and the ISDN RAS Sender. You want to control the site communication by using the ISDN RAS Sender during business hours and the Standard Sender during nonbusiness hours. You want to use all available throughput of each link and avoid any send queue. How should you configure each SMS site?

- ○ a. Create one site address for each sender and then modify the schedules and priorities for each address.
- ○ b. Create one site address for each sender and then modify the rate limits and priorities for each address.
- ○ c. Create one site address for each sender and then modify the schedules for each address.
- ○ d. Create one site address for each sender and then modify the schedules and rate limits for each address.

Answer c is correct. You want to use each sender during specific times of the day and week. You need to configure two senders (Standard and ISDN RAS), create two addresses (one for each sender), and configure the schedules for the addresses (so that they work during the specified hours—refer back to Figure 4.6). Answer a is incorrect because you do need to modify the priority of each address; two addresses will never be available at the same time. Answers b and d are incorrect because you need to configure address schedules, not rates and priorities; you want to have both addresses operational at 100 percent of the available bandwidth within the specific hours.

Need To Know More?

 Garms, Jason. *Windows NT 4.0 Server Unleashed.* Sams Publishing, Indianapolis, IN, 1996. ISBN 0-672-30933-5. Chapter 16 is dedicated to Windows NT user administration. It explains domain accounts, global and local groups, and trust relationships. Understanding these important topics can make preparation for SMS installation easier.

 Microsoft Corporation. *Microsoft Systems Management Server Administrator's Guide, version 2.0.* Microsoft Corporation, Redmond, WA, 1999. Chapter 6 contains more detail about installing SMS. Chapter 8 discusses configuring addresses and senders.

 www.microsoft.com/smsmgmt/ Go to the Microsoft Systems Management Server Web page for the latest information about SMS 2, supported operating systems, upgrades, interoperability, white papers, and deployment case studies.

Resource Discovery And Client Installation

. . . .

Terms you'll need to understand:

√ Resource

√ Discovery Data Record (DDR)

√ Discovery hop count

√ Network Discovery

√ Logon discovery

√ Manual discovery

√ Windows NT User Account Discovery

√ Windows NT User Group Discovery

√ Heartbeat Discovery

√ Server Discovery

√ Logon scripts

√ Logon installation

√ Manual installation

√ Windows NT Remote Client Installation

Techniques you'll need to master:

√ Understanding when to use the various types of discovery

√ Learning the relationship between logon points and logon scripts

√ Configuring the site for SMS client installation using different methods and targeting different operating systems

√ Installing SMS clients manually

√ Determining the best circumstances for using the various combinations of discovery and client installation

Discovery is an important part of the process involved in analyzing your network environment and installing clients. Discovery allows you to gather information about resources in use in your site. SMS creates a Discovery Data Record (DDR) for each discovered resource. DDRs contain relevant information about each discovered resource and are stored in the SMS site database. You can create reports based on this information as well as use the discovery data as a prerequisite to client installation.

The discovery process also assigns clients to specific SMS sites. Site assignment is based on each client's Internet Protocol (IP) or Internetwork Packet Exchange (IPX) network location and the site boundaries. A client has to be discovered and assigned before it can be installed.

 Even though a client needs to be discovered and assigned before it is installed, you do not necessarily have to run a discovery method before running a client installation method. If client installation does not find a DDR for a particular computer, it creates one prior to installing SMS client software.

SMS provides several methods for installing clients. You can choose a combination of methods that will work best for your organization. We will discuss each discovery and client installation method in this chapter.

 It is possible to configure multiple SMS sites within a single NT domain and still have clients join their appropriate sites automatically. Site assignment is entirely dependent on the SMS administrators and the way they configure SMS site boundaries. For more information on site boundaries, refer to Chapter 3.

Discovery Types And Their Uses

SMS provides several different types of discovery. When you enable a discovery method or multiple discovery methods, SMS gathers information about *resources* in your site. SMS identifies three types of resources:

➤ Any networked object with an IP address (these can include computers, routers, hubs, gateways, communication servers, mainframes, or printers)

➤ Windows NT user accounts

➤ Windows NT user groups

SMS provides the following discovery types, which you can configure from the Discovery Methods node in the SMS Administrator console, shown in Figure 5.1:

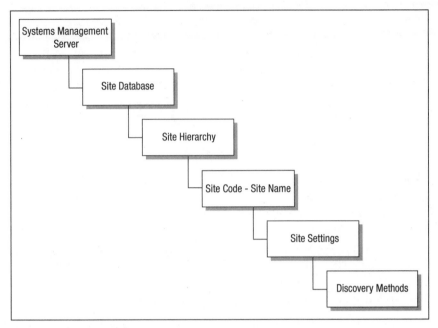

Figure 5.1   Navigating to discovery methods in the SMS
Administrator console.

➤ Network Discovery

➤ Logon discovery

➤ Manual discovery

➤ Windows NT User Account Discovery

➤ Windows NT User Group Discovery

➤ Heartbeat Discovery

➤ Server Discovery (not configurable)

Network Discovery

Network Discovery allows you to discover any object on your network that
contains an IP address. If you want to find computers, printers, routers, Simple
Network Management Protocol (SNMP) devices, subnets, or other network
devices, Network Discovery is an ideal option. A unique aspect of this discovery method is that it is not limited by your site boundaries; you configure
Network Discovery to find items on your network. At the scheduled time,
Network Discovery searches for resources, creates a DDR for each discovered
resource, and then forwards the DDRs to the SMS site database of the site
that runs discovery—regardless of your SMS site boundaries.

Many organizations use Network Discovery to create and update network maps. You will also find Network Discovery useful if you want to install SMS client software silently so that your users are unaware it is being installed. By pairing Network Discovery with Windows NT Remote Client Installation (which we cover later in this chapter), you can install SMS client software on computers that are running Windows NT 4 or higher operating systems with or without users logged on. If the users are logged on, they will not be aware that the installation is occurring.

Types Of Network Discovery

You configure Network Discovery to discover specific data about resources on your network, and then you configure the range where the discovery will occur. The configuration settings you specify in each of the tabs in the Network Discovery Properties dialog box (shown in Figure 5.2) work together to determine which objects will be discovered and how the discovery will be performed. Once you set up a configuration and a schedule, that configuration of Network Discovery will run on your network and create DDRs.

To determine how deep into the network your discovery will occur and what types of resource information will be gathered, configure the type and range of the discovery. Then, you need to schedule each discovery. You can select one of three types of Network Discovery on the General tab of the Network Discovery Properties dialog box. The method you select depends on the type of objects you would like to discover and your goals. Here is a brief description of each:

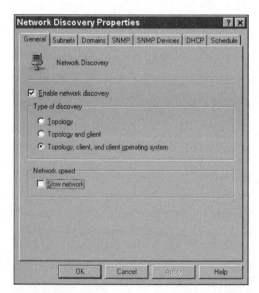

Figure 5.2 Network Discovery Properties dialog box.

➤ **Topology discovery** Returns information on subnets and routers on your network. It also reports how each of the found objects is connected. For example, you may want to find all the IP subnets defined in your Dynamic Host Configuration Protocol (DHCP) server scopes.

➤ **Topology and client discovery** Finds the same items as topology discovery, but also attempts to discover as many other IP devices as possible. The range of IP addresses it finds is limited by the subnets you specify and enable. For example, you may want to use this discovery type to learn which client machines are connected to a specific IP segment on your network. This information allows you to properly configure your site boundaries (IP boundaries) and can provide information that helps you design your hierarchy or place your site servers more optimally.

➤ **Topology, client, and client operating system discovery** Searches for the same items as topology and client discovery, but also includes information about the type of operating system detected on the resources. It does this by making a LAN Manager call to each computer. You can use this type of discovery to learn where clients with different types of operating systems are located on your network before you install SMS client software. The information then becomes useful for site planning.

Network Discovery is the only discovery method that does not copy any SMS files to the discovered client machines. The other discovery methods copy approximately 5MB of files and store them in the %*WINDIR*%\MS\SMS directory.

Network Discovery of Windows 95 and 98 computers will not generate client operating system information unless File Sharing is enabled.

The General tab of the Network Discovery Properties dialog box also allows you to specify whether or not you are operating on a slow network. If the Slow Network option is enabled, Network Discovery adjusts its settings to accommodate slower response times, doubles SNMP time-outs, and reduces the number of discovery threads used.

Ranges Of Discovery

The Network Discovery Properties dialog box has several tabs that allow you to choose various ranges of discovery. Here's a look at your configuration options:

➤ **Subnets tab** Use this tab to specify which subnets you want Network Discovery to search as it looks for resources. You specify a subnet by entering its IP network ID and subnet mask and then enabling it. After you complete a discovery, Network Discovery also lists all of the IP subnets found through any of the other discovery methods (for example, subnets found in DHCP scopes and routing tables). These subnets are listed in the Subnets tab, but they are disabled by default.

➤ **Domains tab** Use this tab to list the domains—or rather the domain browsing lists—that Network Discovery should attempt to access. By default, Network Discovery attempts to enumerate the computers on the local domain of the computer that is running discovery.

 If you plan to use Network Discovery and Windows NT Remote Client Installation to install SMS client software on Windows NT machines in your site, each NT computer you want to configure as a client must have a DDR in the SMS site database. In order to create a DDR, Network Discovery needs the client's IP address and its subnet mask. You can obtain this information with the help of the domain browsing list only if the NT machine has an SNMP agent running and the SNMP properties of Network Discovery are configured appropriately.

➤ **SNMP tab** Use this tab to specify the community names of SNMP devices from which Network Discovery will try to gather information. On this tab, you can also set the maximum hop count for Network Discovery to use while penetrating the network as it attempts to read information from the routing tables. If you specify 0 hops (the default setting), Network Discovery accesses only the routers connected to the site server's IP segment. If you specify 1 hop, Network Discovery tries to access all of the routers separated from your local subnet by no more than 1 router hop. This pattern continues as you increase the hop count; you can specify up to 10 hops.

➤ **SNMP Devices tab** Use this tab to specify from which SNMP devices Network Discovery should try to access and retrieve discovery data. You also must specify the SNMP community names that Network Discovery can use to access each device as well as the distance from the local IP subnet (see the SNMP tab bullet above for more information on configuring the distance). This method of gathering discovery data is not the most efficient because the routing tables are often flushed and don't hold client IP information for a long time.

➤ **DHCP tab** Use this tab to gather data from Microsoft DHCP servers. To configure Network Discovery to do this, type each DHCP server's IP address in this tab. Your site server's DHCP server is scanned by default if your site server is also a DHCP client. If your network clients are primarily using leased IP addresses, this is by far the most efficient method of gathering discovery information.

➤ **Schedule tab** Use this tab to specify the date, time, and frequency with which Network Discovery runs. You can also specify the maximum time discovery will run (discovery duration).

The combination of items you have configured in all of the tabs at the time the discovery runs will be used as the configuration for that session. You can configure and schedule additional sessions, but remember that it is always the combination of items in all of the tabs that determines the nature of the discovery.

 Network Discovery is multithreaded, and depending on its configuration and the size of your network, it might utilize all the processors on your site server for a long time. You should take this into account when configuring and scheduling Network Discovery.

Logon Discovery

Logon discovery is the process of discovering clients as users log on to the network. Logon discovery is the preferred method of discovery for all clients that are running Windows NT or NetWare logon scripts or for clients who are selected for discovery. In the latter case, you can ask users at the selected client computers to run the manual discovery process (described later in this chapter).

SMS provides three types of logon discovery, which work in a similar manner:

➤ **Windows Networking Logon Discovery** Used for discovering computers that participate in Windows NT domain(s)

➤ **NetWare Bindery Logon Discovery** Used for clients operating on NetWare networks

➤ **NetWare NDS Logon Discovery** Used for clients operating on NetWare NDS networks

When you use any of the logon discovery methods, SMS copies the discovery files to the specified Windows NT domain controllers or NetWare servers. SMS then makes them available for clients to run manually or automatically through logon scripts. Any client that logs onto the network and successfully runs discovery causes a DDR to be created. This DDR is then stored in the SMS site database of the site that is conducting logon discovery as well as the site databases of all the sites above it in the hierarchy.

Then, if the computer's IP address is within the defined boundaries for the site(s), SMS also assigns the client to the appropriate SMS site(s), even though the client does not yet have SMS client software installed.

The first step in configuring logon discovery is defining logon points. The next is enabling discovery to run automatically through logon scripts, or initiating discovery manually. We will discuss these three steps in detail in the following sections.

Defining Logon Points

You define logon points by enabling any of the logon discovery methods and specifying the working environment from a specific Logon Discovery Method Properties dialog box located in the SMS Administrator console.

The Windows Networking Logon Discovery method allows you to specify any number of Windows NT domains to be included in the discovery process (as shown in Figure 5.3). SMS configures all of the domain controllers in each specified domain as logon points.

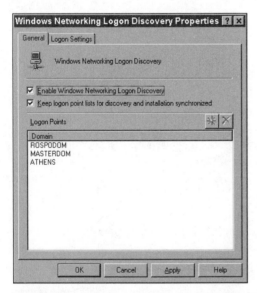

Figure 5.3 Windows Networking Logon Discovery Properties dialog box.

Windows NT Logon Manager creates an SMSLOGON share, creates and starts a Windows NT Logon Discovery Agent service, and copies SMS logon scripts and discovery initialization files to the NETLOGON directory of each domain controller of each specified domain. Within a domain, you cannot select which domain controllers are to become logon points. You can only configure all or none of them. You should remember that an SMS site installed using Express setup on a domain controller configures all of the domain controllers in its NT domain as logon points. If you install SMS on a member server, the logon points are not automatically created.

When you use any of the two NetWare logon discovery methods, you specify a NetWare Bindery server or an NDS volume for SMS to configure as a logon point. SMS creates the SMSLOGON directory on NetWare servers and copies logon scripts to their volumes. In Windows NT domains, you can specify multiple NetWare Bindery servers and NDS volumes as logon points.

DDR files passed from Windows computers to NetWare servers are downloaded to the site server by the NetWare Logon Manager threads (described in more detail in Chapter 11).

DDR files passed from Windows computers to Windows NT domain controllers are automatically passed to all SMS sites that enumerate the NT domain. The Windows NT Logon Discovery Agent service is responsible for moving the DDRs to the SMS sites.

Table 5.1 shows how you can create the SMS logon point site systems by enabling any of the logon discovery methods and specifying the appropriate NT domains, NetWare Bindery servers, or NDS volumes.

Table 5.1 SMS logon point site systems.	
Enabled Client Discovery Method	**Created SMS Logon Point Site Systems**
Windows Networking Logon Discovery	All domain controllers in each specified NT domain
NetWare Bindery Logon Discovery	Specified NetWare Bindery servers
NetWare NDS Logon Discovery	NetWare servers that contain the specified NDS volumes

To configure Windows NT and NetWare servers as SMS logon points, you need to have the appropriate access rights to them. You also need Administrator-level permissions to each enumerated Windows NT domain and the specific Site System Connection Accounts to NetWare Bindery servers and NDS objects. (See the "Need To Know More?" section later in this chapter for references where you can learn more about NetWare security settings.)

Once you have defined logon points, you can:

➤ Discover computers manually

➤ Modify NT or NetWare logon scripts manually

➤ Configure SMS to modify and manage NT or NetWare logon scripts automatically

Any of these actions allows for the discovery of computers.

You can select an option that synchronizes each discovery method with its paired client installation method. If you select this option, any changes made to the discovery method will be automatically applied to the paired installation method and vice versa.

Modifying Logon Scripts

SMS automatically modifies your logon scripts if you select the Modify Login Scripts option (available on the Logon Settings tab of the NetWare Bindery Logon Discovery Properties dialog box, shown in Figure 5.4). After you enable this option, SMS modifies the logon scripts and user account profiles so that they will run the SMSLS.BAT file, which initiates the discovery process. On the same tab, you can specify how often logon scripts will be updated (the default is every day). Both NetWare Logon Discovery methods have additional settings you can use to specify how often DDRs should be pulled from the NetWare servers (the default is every 12 hours).

Windows NT and NetWare users process logon scripts differently, so SMS configures them differently. Table 5.2 lists the modifications that SMS makes to Windows NT logon scripts.

SMS modifies NetWare Bindery and NDS scripts by inserting a call to the SMSLS.BAT file on the appropriate Bindery or NDS container scripts.

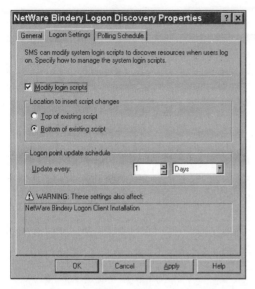

Figure 5.4 Enabling automatic logon script modification for NetWare Bindery Logon Discovery.

Table 5.2 SMS automatic NT logon script updates.	
Existing Script In The User Profile	**SMS Modifications**
No existing script	Adds SMSLS.BAT to user profiles (except for the Administrator and Guest user accounts)
Script exists and is listed with the file extension (.BAT or .CMD); i.e., SCRIPT1.BAT	Adds a call to the SMSLS.BAT file at the top or bottom of the listed logon script (except for the administrator and guest user accounts)
Script exists and is listed without a file extension or with a file extension that is different from .BAT or .CMD; i.e., KIX32 kixscript	No modification

If you already use logon scripts in your company, you can also modify them manually with an entry initiating SMS discovery and/or client installation:

```
call %\..\smsls.bat
```

This is a useful practice if you want to select which specific users, user groups, or machines will be discovered (rather than having SMS discover all computers that belong to users who logon to the network).

Manual Discovery

Manual discovery requires logon points to function. Once you have enabled a logon discovery method, you can use the Systems Management [Client] Installation Wizard; use SMSMAN.EXE to discover computers that are running 32-bit operating systems and SMSMAN16.EXE to discover computers that are running 16-bit operating systems. You need to execute either of these files on each client you would like discovered.

 Using SMSMAN.EXE, SMS can discover the computer and install the SMS client software. If you have enabled a discovery method but no client installation method, the client will be discovered only (not installed). If you have enabled both a discovery and a client installation method or a client installation method only, the client will be discovered and installed if it fits in the SMS site boundaries.

The SMSMAN.EXE and SMSMAN16.EXE files also support unattended installation through the use of command-line switches. The syntax for SMSMAN.EXE is as follows:

```
SMSMAN.EXE [Installation Mode] [/Q]
```

Table 5.3 lists the command-line switches.

Table 5.3 Command-line switches for SMSMAN.EXE.	
Options	**Description**
Installation Mode	Specifies one of the following: /S, /D, /B, /C, /A, or /U. If no installation mode is specified, the wizard opens.
/S <server_name>	Specifies a Windows NT Server discovery/installation location.
/D <domain_name>	Specifies a Windows NT domain discovery/installation location.

(continued)

Table 5.3　Command-line switches for SMSMAN.EXE (continued).	
Options	**Description**
/B <*server**volume*>	Specifies a NetWare Bindery discovery/installation location.
/C <*tree.org.orgunit*>	Specifies a NetWare NDS context discovery/ installation location.
/A	Automatically selects the discovery/installation location (based on the client location).
/U	Uninstalls all SMS client components.
/Q	Specifies quiet or silent discovery/installation. If no discovery/installation mode is specified, the /A option is assumed.
/H or /?	Displays help screen.

You can initiate manual discovery from the logon point, or you can distribute SMSMAN.EXE and SMSMAN16.EXE via email, provide it on the intranet, or use any other method your company uses for distributing files to users.

User Account And User Group Discovery

You can use the User Account and User Group Discovery methods to create DDRs for each user account and user group that exists in specified NT domain(s). You must use these discovery methods if you plan to distribute software to users and/or user groups. You can create a collection based on the discovery data you gather using these methods and then distribute software to the specific collection.

> *Note:　Refer to Chapter 8 for more information about distributing software to users and user groups.*

You configure the User Account and User Group Discovery methods from the Discovery Methods node in the SMS Administrator console (refer back to Figure 5.1). When you enable any of these methods, you have to specify an NT domain or a set of domains where you want discovery to occur. You can also specify if the discovery is to run on a schedule. After you have enabled and configured Windows NT User or User Group Discovery, SMS scans the security database located on the primary domain controller (PDC) of each specified domain to find all of the domain user or global (not local) user group accounts created in that domain.

The User Account and User Group Discovery methods are enabled by default on SMS sites created using Express setup. Both methods are also configured to enumerate the account database of the Windows NT domain to which the SMS site server belongs. This happens regardless of whether the site server is installed on the domain controller or on a member server. Remember that when you use Express setup, the Windows NT Logon Discovery method does not automatically enumerate the domain controllers when the site is installed on the member server.

Heartbeat Discovery

Heartbeat Discovery is a method for refreshing SMS client computer discovery data that already exists in the SMS site database. Heartbeat Discovery is enabled by default on SMS sites installed using any of the installation methods. Using this method, SMS clients refresh their discovery data by creating DDRs on a configurable schedule and passing them to the SMS site server, where they are processed and then inserted into the SMS site database. This method allows for automatic and continuous updates to older discovery data. You can configure the Heartbeat Discovery properties from the Discovery Methods node in the SMS Administrator console (again, refer back to Figure 5.1). The only two settings that you can configure for Heartbeat Discovery are:

➤ Enabled or disabled

➤ Schedule (simple hourly, daily, or weekly schedule with an option to specify the numeric frequency interval; the default is one week)

Server Discovery

The purpose of the Server Discovery methods is to make sure that SMS maintains the most current discovery data for site systems in your SMS sites. SMS provides two types of server discovery:

➤ Windows NT SMS Server Discovery

➤ NetWare Bindery SMS Server Discovery

You cannot view properties of either of these methods in the SMS Administrator console because you cannot configure either method. Both of them are enabled by default and work on a preset schedule. Using these methods, SMS initializes installation of SMS client software on Windows NT Servers within the site boundaries that are acting as site systems. SMS discovers only NetWare Bindery servers. SMS cannot discover NetWare NDS servers. SMS also does not install client software on any NetWare servers because they are not supported as SMS clients.

Note: *See Chapter 3 for a list of supported client operating systems.*

Inside DDRs

SMS creates a DDR for each discovered resource. The information contained in the DDR depends on the type of discovered object. For example, a DDR for a discovered user group has different properties than a DDR for a discovered computer.

You can access the properties of discovered resources using the SMS Collections node (as described in Chapter 7) to view both collected and site-generated discovery data. Table 5.4 lists all of the discovery properties and the discovery record types where they appear.

Table 5.4 Discovery data properties.	
Discovered Resource	**Discovery Record Property**
System	SMS Unique Identifier
System	NetBIOS name
System	IP addresses
System	IP subnets
System	IPX addresses
System	IPX network numbers
System	Media Access Control (MAC) addresses
System	Resource domain or workgroup
System	Operating system name and version
System	Last logon user name
System	Last logon user domain
System	Client version
System, User Group, User	Discovery agent name
System, User Group, User	Discovery agent site
System, User Group, User	Discovery agent time
System	SMS client
System, User Group, User	Name
System, User Group, User	SMS assigned sites

(continued)

Table 5.4 Discovery data properties (continued).

Discovered Resource	Discovery Record Property
System	SMS installed sites
System	SNMP community name
System	System roles
System, User Group, User	Resource ID
System	Resource name
System, User Group, User	Resource type
User Group	Unique user group name
User Group, User	Windows NT domain
User Group	User Group name
User Group, User	Network operating system
User	Full user name
User	Unique user name
User	User name

You can query against an individual property or a set of DDR properties listed in Table 5.4. You can create collections (groups of resources) based on discovery properties and distribute software to them. You can also create reports or write applications using the SMS Toolkit to improve business use of the data contained in DDRs.

Note: Chapter 7 explains the differences between queries and collections and provides details on how to create and use them.

Client Logon Installation

After a client computer is discovered and assigned to a single site or multiple SMS sites, it is ready for SMS client software installation. SMS client software can be installed only if the client machine is a Windows NT SMS site system (and was discovered by Server Discovery) or if an appropriate SMS Client Installation method is enabled and configured.

SMS provides different installation methods that accommodate different client operating systems and networking environments. You can install SMS client software automatically or manually, and you can initiate client installation from either Windows NT or NetWare servers. The Windows NT and NetWare client installation methods are similar except for the type of networking environment in which the installation is initiated.

You can also install SMS client software silently on any Windows NT computer located on the network. SMS can install the software automatically without any user actions at the Windows NT client computer; the user might not even be logged on to the NT computer, or the NT computer can be locked. This installation method requires communication between the Windows NT site server and the Windows NT client computers. We describe each Windows NT and NetWare installation method in the following sections. Windows NT and NetWare have paired installation methods, so we discuss them together. Figure 5.5 shows how you can access the client installation methods by navigating to the Client Installation Method node in the SMS Administrator console.

Logon Installation

Logon installation is probably the most popular client installation method. SMS provides three logon installation methods:

➤ Windows NT Networking

➤ NetWare Bindery

➤ NetWare NDS

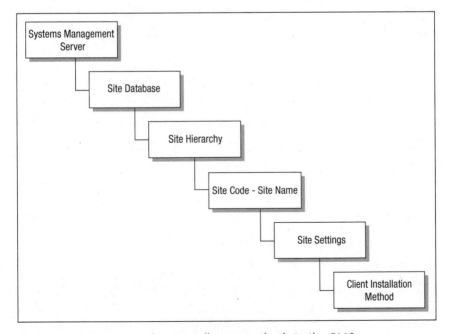

Figure 5.5   Accessing client installation methods in the SMS Administrator console.

The one you choose depends on the type of networking environment you have. Each of these methods operates on the same principles. SMS client files are made available to the machines that log on to the network at their first point of contact with the network server. In a Windows NT domain, the first point of contact is a domain controller. In a NetWare environment, the first point of contact is either the NetWare Bindery or NDS container object and volume.

Figure 5.6 shows the General tab of the NetWare NDS Logon Installation Properties dialog box, as well as its location in the SMS Administrator console.

SMS does not impose a limit on the type and number of any of the above networking environments. Each logon installation method is enabled per Windows NT domain, NetWare Bindery server, and NetWare NDS container and volume. A single SMS site can make SMS client files available to multiple NT domains or NetWare servers and volumes.

You can configure one Windows NT domain to use a Windows Networking Logon Client Installation method at multiple SMS site servers. For example, you can configure each of the SMS sites located in the Windows NT resource domains with the Windows Networking Logon Client Installation method and enumerate a single master NT domain. In this case, all of the domain

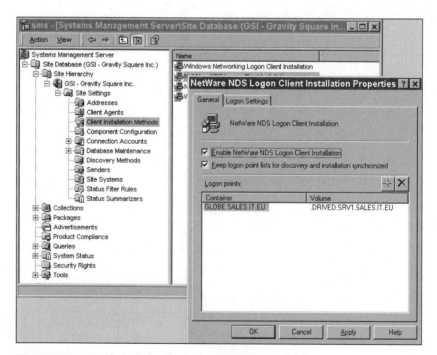

Figure 5.6 Configuring a logon installation method.

controllers in the master NT domain contain a single set of client installation files and several sets of site configuration files (the number of sets equals the number of SMS sites that enumerate the master domain). Each set of site configuration files contains the following information:

➤ A list of the client access points (CAPs) defined at each SMS site

➤ Site boundary data for each SMS site

The information available in the site configuration files is essential for a new client to recognize its site assignment (based on the SMS site boundaries) and to connect to a CAP at each assigned site. Clients need to connect to a CAP to complete SMS client software installation.

After you enable the logon installation method appropriate for your networking environment and specify the set of SMS logon points to be enumerated, you can configure SMS to modify the logon scripts automatically, or you can do it manually.

SMS 2 does not require the Directory Replicator service to be running on any domain controllers in order for you to use logon scripts. The Windows NT Logon Server Manager component replicates logon scripts throughout the entire NT domain.

When you enable any of the logon client installation methods, the only installation method you make available to clients is manual installation. To have clients install automatically, you must also select the Modify User Logon Scripts option or you must manually create or rewrite your client logon scripts. Refer to Figures 5.4 and 5.7 for information on where to change the Modify User Logon Scripts option.

Logon Script-Based Installation

To enable SMS logon script modification, go to the Logon Settings tab of each of the logon installation methods' dialog boxes. Refer back to Table 5.2 to see what criteria the Windows Networking Logon Client Installation method uses to modify logon scripts.

The logon installation methods can also modify user logon scripts of multiple NT domains, NetWare Bindery servers, and NDS objects. The logon scripts are automatically updated based on a schedule that you can configure through the Windows Networking Logon Client Installation Properties dialog box, shown in Figure 5.7.

Alternatively, you might add a call to the SMS installation batch file from your existing logon script(s). Doing so allows you to control which users and user

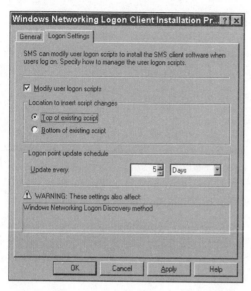

Figure 5.7 Enabling automatic modification of user logon scripts.

groups install the SMS client software and which ones do not. If you manually modify user logon scripts, you must add the following entry to initiate SMS client installation:

```
call %\..\SMSLS.BAT
```

Manual Installation

You don't have to run a logon script to install the SMS client software using the logon installation methods. You don't even have to run the SMSLS.BAT batch file at all. A different SMS installation file allows you to install SMS client software without connecting to the logon point. As we mentioned earlier, SMSMAN.EXE and SMSMAN16.EXE launch the Systems Management [Client] Installation Wizard on 32-bit and 16-bit operating system machines, respectively. You can execute these files from the SMS logon point(s), your machine drive, or a Web site. Alternatively, you can distribute them in email messages, on floppy disks, or by many other methods. Refer back to Table 5.3 for the syntax for SMSMAN.EXE.

SMS client installation creates the %*WINDIR*%\MS\SMS directory on client machines. If the client machine does not have Windows Management Instrumentation (WMI) installed prior to SMS client installation, WMI is installed on all 32-bit operating system machines together with the client software. Note that WMI was previously called Web-Based Enterprise Management (WBEM). The Hardware Inventory Agent does not have to be enabled for WMI to be installed.

Windows NT Remote Client Installation

SMS 2 can also silently install SMS client software on any supported Windows NT computer and configure it as an SMS client with no user intervention—logon script processing is not even required. This installation method is called Windows NT Remote Client Installation. You can enable and configure it from the Client Installation Method node in the SMS Administrator console (refer back to Figure 5.6).

Using this method, you can select whether Windows NT Servers, Windows NT Workstations, or Domain controllers are to be automatically configured as SMS clients. You can select all three or any combination you desire. To configure the types of computers that will install software, use the Windows NT Remote Client Installation Properties dialog box, shown in Figure 5.8.

Installation Accounts

The Windows NT Remote Client Installation method bases its functionality on client DDRs and Windows NT security. Once an NT machine is discovered, SMS has its NetBIOS name and IP address and can locate it on the

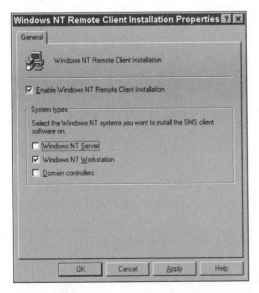

Figure 5.8 Configuring the Windows NT Remote Client Installation method.

network. Assuming that either the SMS Service account or the SMS Client Remote Installation account has Administrative rights to the discovered NT machine, Client Configuration Manager (CCM) can attach to it over the network, copy the necessary SMS client installation files, and start the installation process. For more information on CCM, see Chapter 11.

 The SMS Client Remote Installation account is optional in Windows NT environments. If no account is specified, SMS uses the SMS Service account to install the client software. The SMS Client Software Installation account is required in NetWare environments because by default, the SMS Service account does not have access to Windows NT client computers that are not participating in a Windows NT domain.

You can configure the SMS Client Remote Installation account from the Site Properties dialog box. CCM uses this account in the following ways:

➤ As entered in the Site Properties dialog box (*domain_name\user_name*)

➤ With the *domain_name* replaced with the name of the domain the user is logged on to

➤ With the *domain_name* replaced with the name of the domain the machine account is created in

➤ With the *domain_name* replaced with the name of each domain the machine has an open connection to

➤ With the *domain_name* replaced with the name of the NT machine

➤ With *user_name* only

If all of the access methods listed above fail, CCM uses the SMS Service account in one last attempt to install the client software.

This access algorithm allows for successful SMS client installation in multiple domain environments where machine accounts are created in the resource domains and users logon to the master domain with a single SMS site. Figure 5.9 illustrates such an example.

Machines located in resource domains have local domain machine accounts. Therefore (by default), only local Domain Admins groups have administrative access to them. Table 5.5 lists accounts that have access to the resource domains. If all domains have the same Administrator account (for example

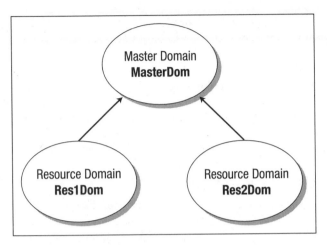

Figure 5.9 The SMS Client Remote Installation account in a trusted domain model.

Table 5.5 Accounts with access to Windows NT computers.	
Windows NT Computers Located In	**Full Account Name**
Master domain	MasterDom\DomAdmin
Resource domain 1	Res1Dom\DomAdmin
Resource domain 2	Res1Dom\DomAdmin

DomAdmin) with the same password, and this account is a member of global Domain Admins group of each domain, then accounts listed in the table have access to the Windows NT computers in the three domains shown in the table.

In the case listed in the table, you can configure the SMS Client Remote Installation account with any of these accounts:

➤ MasterDom\DomAdmin

➤ Res1Dom\DomAdmin

➤ Res2Dom\DomAdmin

➤ DomAdmin

DomAdmin does not have to be a member of the Domain Admins group as long as it has Administrative rights to the Windows NT computers where you want to install SMS client software.

The SMS Service account is defined at the master domain level, so the trust relations do not allow it to be a member of the Global Domain Admins groups in the resource domains. This is because the trusted accounts can be added only to the local groups, not to the global ones. You could use the SMS Service account to remotely install SMS clients if all domains had the same SMS Service account defined, if this account was a member of the Domain Admins global group on each domain, and if it had the same password across all domains.

Client Configuration Requests

As mentioned above, CCM installs the SMS client software based on DDR data. This information is passed to CCM in the form of Client Configuration Requests (CCR files). These request files contain information necessary for CCM to connect to NT machines that are ready for client installation and to initiate installation. Discovery Data Manager (DDM—which you'll learn more about in Chapter 10) creates CCRs under the conditions listed in Table 5.6.

Table 5.6 Conditions for CCR creation.	
System Event	**CCRS Are Created If**
New DDR arrives for processing	The DDR is from a non-SMS client machine that is within the site boundaries of the site **and** The Windows NT Remote Client Installation method is enabled and the DDR was created on the NT machine targeted for the remote installation (refer back to Figure 5.8) **and** The DDR is from an SMS site system
Site boundary change **or** Windows NT Remote Client Installation is being enabled **or** Windows NT Remote Client Installation configuration changes	The DDR stored in the database is from a non-SMS client machine that is within the site boundaries **and** The DDR was created on the NT machine enabled for remote installation (refer back to Figure 5.8) **or** The DDR is from an SMS site system

The Windows NT Remote Client Installation method is also used (without being enabled) when SMS client software is installed on an NT machine in situations where the logged-on user does not have the local Administrative rights required to install the client software. In such a case, the client installation procedure creates the CCR file and passes it to the CAP. The file is then forwarded to CCM for processing. SMS uses the Windows NT Remote Client Installation method to install SMS client software on Windows NT-based SMS site system machines within the site boundaries.

Practice Questions

Question 1

> Your network is composed of several Windows NT Servers, Windows NT Work-
> stations, and Windows 98 machines. Most of the Windows NT Workstation
> users don't have Administrative rights to their machines. You decide to deploy
> SMS 2 client software using unattended mode to all of the computers on your
> network. Which installation method(s) is the best to use?
>
> ○ a. Windows Networking Logon Client Installation
>
> ○ b. Windows Networking Logon Client Installation and Windows NT
>   Remote Client Installation
>
> ○ c. Windows NT Remote Client Installation
>
> ○ d. Systems Management Installation Wizard

Answer a is correct. When you use Windows Networking Logon Client Installation and the logon scripts, SMS client software is automatically installed
on all Windows 98 computers. On Windows NT machines, SMS first tries to
install SMS client software using the logged-on user account. If this account
does not have the proper administrative privileges, a CCR file is passed to the
site server, and SMS installs the client software using CCM's remote installation capability. Answer b contains part of the right answer, but there is no need
to include Windows NT Remote Client Installation. Therefore, answer b is
incorrect. Answer c works only for Windows NT clients; Windows NT Remote Client Installation does not install Windows 98 clients. Therefore, answer
c is incorrect. Answer d does not allow you to install in unattended mode because it requires user intervention to install using the installation wizard.
Therefore, answer d is incorrect.

Question 2

You've decided to start an SMS 2 pilot project and roll out SMS to just a few selected clients of a single NT domain on your multiple IP segment network. The selected clients are configured with a variety of Windows operating systems: Windows NT (with the default settings), Windows 95, and Windows 98. You will be installing the SMS 2 client software manually using the Systems Management Installation Wizard. What must you do prior to manually installing clients?

❑ a. Enable Windows Networking Logon Client Installation.

❑ b. Enable Windows Networking Logon Discovery.

❑ c. Enable Windows NT Remote Client Installation.

❑ d. Add the IP network IDs of your pilot clients to the site boundaries of your site.

❑ e. Create the SMS Client Remote Installation account.

Answers a and d are correct. You must enable Windows Networking Logon Client Installation (answer a) to create logon points and to allow SMS to install client software when you run the Systems Management [Client] Installation Wizard. For client software to install, each pilot client must first be assigned to the site; therefore, it has to fit within the site boundaries (answer d). Answer b provides a discovery method, which is not required to accomplish the goal stated in the question, so it is incorrect. Remember that you do not have to separately discover a computer before you can install SMS client software using logon installation. Answer c lists an unattended installation method for Windows NT clients only and you cannot use it to run the installation wizard. Therefore, answer c is incorrect. Answer e is incorrect because in a single domain, SMS can use the SMS Service account to install client software on low-rights NT machines.

Question 3

Most users of your NetWare 4.11 network don't have Administrative rights to their Windows NT workstations. These workstations are not participating in any Windows NT domain. What must you do to install SMS 2 client software on these machines?

○ a. Create a Client Connection Account and make it a member of each workstation's administrator group.

○ b. Create a Site System Account and make it a member of each workstation's administrative group.

○ c. Create an SMS Client Remote Installation Account and make it a member of each workstation's administrative group.

○ d. Install the TCP/IP protocol on all NetWare 4.11 servers configured as SMS site systems.

Answer c is correct. You must have an account that SMS can use to install client software on NT machines located on NetWare networks. The Client Remote Installation Account is the account you need to create, and it must be a member of each workstation's administrative group. CCM uses this account if logon installation is used and NT users have no Administrative rights, or if NT Remote Client Installation is used to push software to NT machines. Answers a and b are incorrect because they list accounts that are irrelevant for installing NT clients on NetWare networks. Answer d is incorrect because TCP/IP is not required for NetWare servers to function as SMS site systems.

Question 4

You used Custom setup to install a primary SMS site server on a Windows NT member server that participates in the Sales domain. You want to discover all computer systems logging into the Sales domain. What should you do?

❑ a. Enable Windows Networking Logon Discovery.

❑ b. Enable Windows Networking Logon Installation.

❑ c. Enable the Modify User Logon Scripts option.

❑ d. Enable Network Discovery.

❑ e. Enable Heartbeat Discovery.

Answers a and c are correct. Enabling logon discovery is a two-step process. First, you enable Windows Networking Logon Discovery (answer a), which causes SMS to configure all domain controllers as logon points. Then, you modify logon scripts (answer c) so that clients will be discovered when they logon to the network. If you do not enable logon scripts, no automatic discovery occurs. Answer b is a client installation method rather than a discovery method, so it is incorrect (the machines would be discovered, but they would also be set up as SMS clients). Network Discovery and Heartbeat Discovery do not discover computers as they log on to the network. Therefore, answers d and e are incorrect.

Question 5

Most SMS client computers on your multisegment network are configured with static IP addresses. Only Windows NT Servers have operational SNMP agents. Most users, including laptop users, lock their Windows NT workstations when they are away from their desks. You want to distribute daily software packages to all Windows NT SMS clients based on the IP segments where they are located; you therefore need the most current discovery information. Which discovery method and what settings should you use?

- ○ a. Network Discovery; schedule it to run every day.
- ○ b. Logon discovery; enable Modify User Logon Scripts.
- ○ c. Logon discovery; enable Modify User Logon Scripts and set the Logon Point Update Schedule to run every day.
- ○ d. Heartbeat Discovery; set the heartbeat schedule to every day.
- ○ e. Enable both Windows NT User Account and User Group Discovery; set their polling schedules to every day.

Answer d is correct. Heartbeat Discovery refreshes the discovery data for each SMS client on your network without any user intervention. Once SMS client software has been installed on a client, Heartbeat Discovery refreshes the discovery data regardless of the other conditions. Answer a, Network Discovery, is incorrect because you are using static IP addresses and you do not have SNMP agents installed on all of your Windows NT machines. Logon discovery does not work because not everyone logs onto the network every day. (When users lock their workstations and come back, they do not need to logoff and logon to the network.) Therefore, answers b and c are incorrect. Answer e is incorrect because User Account and User Group Discovery don't refresh IP information.

Question 6

You use three DHCP servers to assign dynamic IP addresses to clients located on 120 IP subnets. You use static IP addresses for your routers, switches, and printers. You want Network Discovery to list all 120 IP subnets so that you can gradually enable them and discover clients subnet by subnet. How should you configure Network Discovery so that it will discover all 120 IP subnets but will not discover the client machines?

○ a. Enter the SNMP community names of your routers and set the maximum number of hops to 120.

○ b. Manually enter all 120 subnets in the Subnets To Search table.

○ c. Enter the three IP addresses of your DHCP servers in the DHCP Servers table.

○ d. On the Domains tab, enter the names of all Windows NT domains located on your network.

Answer c is correct. By entering the IP addresses of your DHCP servers, you enable Network Discovery to access data located in DHCP server scopes. It discovers only the IP subnets from the defined IP scopes; no other resources are discovered. Answer a is incorrect because both the SNMP community names and the SNMP devices have to be specified to scan the routing tables; also, the hop count cannot exceed 10. Answer b is incorrect since Network Discovery can find IP subnets as indicated in answer c. Answer d is incorrect because entering domain names does not allow you to find subnets.

Question 7

All of the users in your three resource domains authenticate through the master domain. You have a central SMS site defined on the master domain, two secondary SMS sites defined on two of the three resource domains, and a primary SMS site located on the third resource domain. The primary site and both secondary sites are child sites of the central SMS site. You are the administrator of the central site, and prior to SMS client installation, you want to enable logon discovery to find all of the computer resources located on your network. You realize that a discovery process might consume a large amount of the network bandwidth, which you want to avoid. Which discovery method(s) should you enable and how should you configure it (them)?

- O a. Enable logon discovery at the central site and enumerate the master domain and all of the resource domains.

- O b. Enable logon discovery at the central site and enumerate the master domain only.

- O c. Enable logon discovery at the central site and enumerate all of the resource domains.

- O d. Enable logon discovery at all of the SMS child sites and configure each of them to enumerate the master domain.

Answer b is correct. This option discovers all of the machines that log onto the master domain and consumes a minimum amount of network bandwidth. Answer a is incorrect because no computers are authenticated throughout the resource domain. Not only is it unnecessary to enumerate the resource domains, but setting up this configuration requires SMS to unnecessarily consume network bandwidth. Answer c is incorrect because nobody authenticates through the resource domains. Answer d allows you to discover the computers, but it causes a lot of network traffic as the DDRs are sent from the SMSLOGON shares of the master domain to each child site. Therefore, answer d is incorrect.

Question 8

> You have installed a primary SMS site server on a Windows NT member server with a NetBIOS name of VITO. VITO is participating in the ENGINEERING Windows NT domain. You have enabled Windows NT User Group Discovery. Which user groups will be discovered?
>
> ○ a. VITO's global groups
>
> ○ b. VITO's local groups
>
> ○ c. ENGINEERING domain global groups
>
> ○ d. ENGINEERING domain local groups

Answer c is correct. User Group Discovery discovers only domain global groups. Answers a and b are incorrect because User Group Discovery does not enumerate each members server's machine groups; rather, it enumerates each domain group. Answer d is incorrect because User Group Discovery does not discover local groups.

Question 9

> All Windows 95 machines are located on a single IP segment and logon to a single Windows NT domain. Each user account is configured with the LOGON.BAT logon script. Your firm leases two Windows 95 computers from the bank to process your daily accounting figures. You always logon to these machines with the user account Bankonit, and you are prohibited from installing any software on them. The Bankonit account is not used to logon to any other machines. You want to manage your environment with SMS 2. How can you configure Windows Networking Logon Discovery to use logon script processing to discover all of the computers except the two leased from the bank?
>
> ○ a. Enable logon discovery and have all of your users except the Bankonit users run SMSMAN16.EXE.
>
> ○ b. Enable logon discovery and enable the Modify User Logon Scripts option.
>
> ○ c. Copy LOGON.BAT to a new file called BANKONIT.BAT, change the Bankonit user profile to run the BANKONIT logon script (do not specify the file extension), then enable logon discovery and enable the Modify User Logon Script option.
>
> ○ d. Modify the Bankonit user profile by removing the file name extension from the logon script file name. Then, enable logon discovery and enable the Modify User Logon Script option.

Trick! question

Answer c is correct. By creating a new logon script file for the Bankonit user and specifying it in the user profile without the file extension, you exclude this script file from being modified by SMS. The original script will be modified when the user profiles reference its name, including a file extension. Answer a is incorrect because running SMSMAN16.EXE is a manual, not logon script-based, installation method, and this file is intended for 16-bit clients only. Answer b is incorrect because by enabling logon discovery and modifying the user logon scripts, you cause all of the computers to be discovered, including the two leased from the bank. Answer d is incorrect because LOGON.BAT will be still modified as other user profiles are configured with this logon script file name.

Need To Know More?

 Microsoft Corporation. *Microsoft Systems Management Server 2.0 Administrator's Guide.* Microsoft Corporation, Redmond, WA, 1998. This book is shipped with SMS. Chapter 9, "Discovering Resources and Installing Clients," provides more information on each of the topics discussed in this chapter.

 Microsoft Corporation. *Microsoft Systems Management Server Resource Guide.* Microsoft Corporation, Redmond, WA, 1999. ISBN 0-7356-0583-1. This is one volume of the *Microsoft BackOffice 4.5 Resource Kit.* Chapter 12, "Upgrading Clients from SMS 1.2 to SMS 2.0," contains advanced information on the concepts discussed in this chapter. Chapter 8, "Using Network Discovery Architecture," describes detailed methods for configuring and using Network Discovery.

 Garms, Jason. *Windows NT Server 4 Unleashed.* Sams Publishing, Indianapolis, IN, 1996. ISBN 0-672-30933-5. Chapters 23 and 25 explain Windows NT security including multidomain configurations and give great examples of how to set them up properly.

 www.microsoft.com/smsmgmt/ is the Microsoft Systems Management Server Web page. This Web site contains the latest information about SMS 2, including a white paper on how to configure SMS on NetWare networks.

Client Configuration

Terms you'll need to understand:

- √ Hardware Inventory Client Agent
- √ Software Inventory Client Agent
- √ Remote Tools Client Agent
- √ Advertised Programs Client Agent (software distribution)
- √ Software Metering Client Agent
- √ Event To Trap Translator Client Agent
- √ Client Configuration Installation Manager (CCIM)
- √ SMS_DEF.MOF
- √ NOIDMIF
- √ IDMIF
- √ Remote Diagnostics
- √ Remote Control
- √ Event To Trap Translator application
- √ Principal site

Techniques you'll need to master:

- √ Enabling and configuring each client agent
- √ Modifying the SMS_DEF.MOF file to control inventory collection
- √ Understanding the difference between IDMIFs and NOIDMIFs
- √ Collecting files from SMS client computers
- √ Enabling SMS client mobile support
- √ Configuring NT systems to send NT events in the form of Simple Network Management Protocol (SNMP) traps to the management station
- √ Understanding client configuration in a multisite environment
- √ Configuring the Remote Tools Client Agent for optimum functionality on Windows NT client computers

Installing SMS client software is an important step in setting up your SMS site. Once clients are installed, you can begin to manage them with SMS. In Chapter 5, we described different client installation methods. The next step is for you to understand how to configure the SMS client agents. Using the client agents, you can collect hardware and software inventory, automate the distribution and installation of software applications, remotely control the clients, and meter software usage. This chapter explains how client agents are configured and installed to allow you to fully manage your Windows machines. Then, the last section of this chapter describes the Systems Management Control Panel applet that SMS installs on certain discovered computers.

Installing And Configuring Client Agents

Client agents are services and applications that run on client computers to provide SMS functionality. Each client agent, listed below, maps to an SMS feature:

➤ Hardware Inventory Client Agent

➤ Software Inventory Client Agent

➤ Remote Tools Client Agent

➤ Advertised Programs Client Agent (Software Distribution)

➤ Software Metering Client Agent

➤ [NT] Event To [SNMP] Trap Translator Client Agent

Before you can use a particular feature on your clients, you must first install the client agent for that feature. For example, before you can perform hardware inventory, you must first install the Hardware Inventory Client Agent on each of your clients. You need to enable only the client agent for the feature you wish to utilize. As a result, you can install and configure each client agent separately as you are ready to use each feature. Using this method, you can make sure that one feature is running properly before you enable another feature on your clients.

 Remember that you can install and configure client agents on a site-wide basis only. In other words, when you enable the Hardware Inventory Client Agent, the agent is installed on all clients in your SMS site. You cannot select specific groups of clients for client agent installation.

SMS client agents supplement the core SMS client components. SMS always installs the core client components that each client requires to run SMS properly;

these components are installed even if all of the client agents are disabled. Both Express and Custom setup automatically install the following core components on all SMS client machines:

➤ SMS Client Base Components

➤ Available Programs Manager

➤ Windows Management (WMI)

Note: See the "Systems Management Control Panel Applet" section later in this chapter for more information on verifying the version and status of these components.

When you install an SMS site using Express setup, SMS automatically installs each of the client agents during client installation. When you install an SMS site using Custom setup, you select which optional components you would like to install. Then, you need to enable each client agent individually for installation on all client machines in the site (Event To Trap Translator Client Agent is enabled by default).

You can enable, disable, or modify client agent configurations at any time. The clients then update their configuration during the next CCIM cycle.

 CCIM works on a 23-hour schedule and retrieves new client agent settings from the configuration files located on all client access points (CAPs). CCIM must have access to at least one CAP within an SMS site in order to synchronize clients' settings. If CCIM cannot connect to a CAP, it keeps retrying every 60 minutes for another 60 days. If it cannot reach a CAP in 60 days, the SMS client software is deinstalled.

The following sections describe the process of enabling and configuring each of the client agents. To do so, use the Client Agents node in the SMS Administrator console, as shown in Figure 6.1.

Hardware Inventory Client Agent

The Hardware Inventory Client Agent collects inventory on each client computer and forwards it to the site server to be stored in the SMS site database. SMS provides two configuration options for hardware inventory: client state (enabled or disabled) and runtime schedule. Table 6.1 lists the scheduling

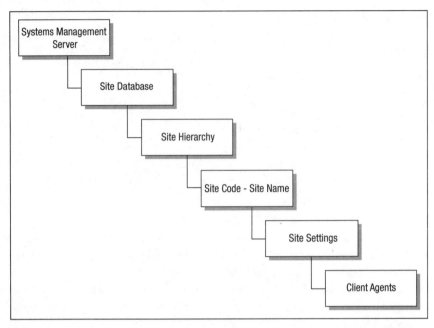

Figure 6.1 Configuring client agents using the SMS Administrator console.

Table 6.1 Hardware inventory schedule options.	
Schedule Type	**Schedule Frequency**
Simple	Hourly, daily, or weekly
Full frequency	Flexible schedule that allows you to specify days of the week or month, and when the agent will first be available

options for hardware inventory, and Figure 6.2 shows the Hardware Inventory Client Agent Properties dialog box.

You use the Hardware Inventory Client Agent Properties dialog box to enable client agents as well as to configure the schedule for collecting hardware inventory. When you create a schedule in this dialog box, you are scheduling hardware inventory frequency for your entire site.

Approximately 15 minutes after the 32-bit Hardware Inventory Client Agent (HINV32.EXE) is installed on a client machine, the agent collects inventory data using WMI (see Chapter 2 for more details on WMI). The inventory data is collected based on a template file called SMS_DEF.MOF. The default SMS_DEF.MOF file, which allows you to select which major computer and

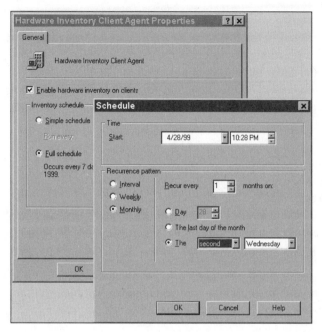

Figure 6.2   Hardware Inventory Client Agent configuration.

operating system data you would like SMS to inventory, includes many properties, such as:

➤ BIOS, motherboard, memory, keyboard, mice, and network card data

➤ Disk controller as well as physical and logical drive information

➤ Operating system name, version, and system directory

➤ Video and display configuration

After SMS conducts inventory on a client, Copy Queue Manager passes the inventory data file to the CAP (for more information on Copy Queue Manager, see Chapter 10). Then, the inventory data file is either uploaded (NT CAPs) or downloaded (NetWare CAPs) to the site server for processing. Each subsequent time the Hardware Inventory Client Agent collects inventory on 32-bit clients, it compares the new inventory with the previously collected inventory and creates a difference (or delta) file that is again passed to the CAP and to the site server. Hardware inventory history is also preserved on the site server (for more information on inventory management, see Chapter 7).

Sixteen-bit client computers don't use WMI for inventory collection, and they always send full inventory files to the site server.

If either a full or a delta inventory file is found to be corrupt or its contents don't match the data stored in the SMS site database, the site server requests an inventory resynchronization (per single client). The hardware inventory resynchronization starts a new full hardware inventory on the client. After the new full inventory file is created on the client, it is marked as a resynchronized file. The content of this file replaces the latest client information in the SMS site database.

Modifying Hardware Inventory Scope

You can change the inventory items about which SMS collects information from clients by using the SMS_DEF.MOF file. The SMS_DEF.MOF file contains a list of all hardware and operating system attributes currently available for the Hardware Inventory Client Agent to collect data about. By default, SMS collects inventory data about only a small number of the total possible hardware attributes.

The following list presents some of the hardware inventory classes that are disabled (their information is not collected) by default:

➤ Boot Configuration

➤ Directory Tree Structure

➤ Environment

➤ IRQ Table

➤ NT Event Log Content

➤ Printer Configuration

➤ Program Groups

➤ Serial Port

➤ User Accounts

An SMS administrator can modify the SMS_DEF.MOF file to collect more or less inventory data from clients. A sample section of the SMS_DEF.MOF file is shown in Listing 6.1; it corresponds to the Network Client class and lists six inventory attributes.

Listing 6.1   Sample section of the SMS_DEF.MOF file.

```
    [SMS_Report(TRUE),
    SMS_Group_Name("Network Client"),
    ResID(2600),ResDLL("SMS_RXPL.dll"),
    SMS_Class_ID("MICROSOFT|NETWORK_CLIENT|1.0")]
class Win32_NetworkClient : SMS_Class_Template
```

```
{
     [SMS_Report(FALSE)]
       string          Caption;
     [SMS_Report(TRUE)]
       string          Description;
     [SMS_Report(FALSE)]
       datetime        InstallDate;
     [SMS_Report(TRUE)]
       string          Manufacturer;
     [SMS_Report(TRUE),key]
       string          Name;
     [SMS_Report(TRUE)]
       string          Status;
};
```

Notice that this class and some of its attributes are enabled for inventory reporting (set to **TRUE**). SMS collects each parameter that is set to **SMS_Report(TRUE)**. Two out of six of the Network Client's attributes have the **SMS_Report** parameter set to **FALSE**, so their information is not reported to the SMS site server.

If an inventory class is enabled and all attributes are disabled, the inventory information is still collected for one or more attributes marked with the **key** qualifier. The Network Client's name is a key attribute of the Network Client class (see Listing 6.1 above).

You modify the SMS_DEF.MOF file on the site server. SMS then replicates it to all CAPs within the site. The clients then receive the file during the next client configuration update.

During the next inventory cycle, each client passes the file that contains the new and updated hardware inventory information to the CAP. The Inbox Manager Assistant that is running on the Windows NT CAP (or Inbox Manager running on the site server if CAPs are created on NetWare servers) then passes the inventory file to the site server for processing. After the inventory file is processed, its data is stored in the SMS site database.

Two SMS components are responsible for processing hardware inventory files: Inventory Processor and Inventory Data Loader. Inventory Processor collects the MIF files created by the client agent on each client and prepares them for Inventory Data Loader. Inventory Data Loader processes the hardware inventory files and adds their data to the SMS site database.

On a secondary site, the inventory file is not processed locally but is passed to the parent site for processing (the deltas of hardware inventory files produced on 16-bit clients are first calculated on the site server, which could be a secondary site server). All inventory files at both secondary and primary sites are passed to a site's parent site, if one exists. This process continues until the data reaches the central site. Each primary site processes all of the inventory files from all its clients and the clients for all of its subsites. In this way, SMS collects information about all subsites' client machines.

Collecting Custom Hardware Inventory

If you need to collect hardware inventory data that is not available by modifying the SMS_DEF.MOF file, you can use IDMIF or NOIDMIF files to modify or create new hardware classes and their attributes. Using IDMIFs, you can even create new system architectures (office supplies, office inventory, or your cafeteria lunch meals, for instance). A NOIDMIF can extend only an existing system architecture.

For example, your company might need to store information about non-Universal Serial Bus (USB) speakers connected to client computers. To collect the information, you might want to create a NOIDMIF that contains the speaker information. Similarly, you might want to collect the phone numbers of users that use particular computers. To keep this information dynamic, many SMS administrators build custom applications that periodically display pop-up boxes. These pop-up boxes ask users about the properties (attributes) of items (classes) of objects (architectures) that administrators want detailed information about.

You must place both IDMIFs and NOIDMIFs on your clients in the %*WINDIR*%\MS\SMS\IDMIF and %*WINDIR*%\MS\SMS\NOIDMIF directories, respectively. Then, the Hardware Inventory Client Agent evaluates the files and includes the data in the next inventory file.

The inventory agent checks IDMIFs and NOIDMIFs for their syntax before the agent creates the inventory file; data from custom MIFs with incorrect syntax is not included in the inventory file passed to the CAP.

Software Inventory Client Agent

The Software Inventory Client Agent is a client component that collects software inventory data from clients. You can fully configure software inventory from the SMS Administrator console. The Software Inventory Client Agent has all of the same settings as the Hardware Inventory Client Agent and more. In addition to the agent state (enabled or disabled) and schedule (configurable from the General tab of the Software Inventory Client Agent Properties dialog box), you can configure this agent to inventory files by file type and collect files by file name. You can also configure the Software Inventory Client Agent to collect inventory data of no more than a specified size (the default is 1MB).

Figure 6.3 shows the Inventory Collection tab of the Software Inventory Client Agent Properties dialog box.

In this tab, you configure the type of files you want SMS to inventory. You specify files for SMS to inventory by file extension; you can specify a file extension with or without a leading period. By default, only executable file (EXE) inventory collection is configured. Software inventory data is collected based on the file header information. In the Reporting Detail section, you specify whether to collect the data about the following (all are enabled by default):

➤ **Product Version Information** This is the information about file manufacturer, product name, and version numbers; SMS can identify a particular product by name and version, but not by file name. If you choose to collect the data about known products, you can also collect the

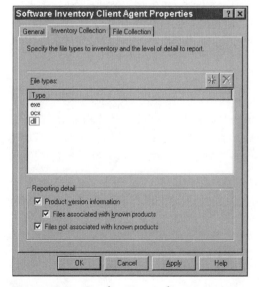

Figure 6.3 Configuring software inventory.

specific file name data by checking the Files Associated With Known Products option.

➤ **Files Not Associated With Known Products** These are files with unpopulated headers. In other words, the headers in these files do not contain information about the product manufacturer, version, etc.

The Software Inventory Client Agent can also collect files from client computers, making them available for viewing in the SMS Administrator console (for more information on software inventory management, see Chapter 7). The File Collection tab in the Software Inventory Client Agent Properties dialog box allows you to specify the files that are designated for collection. By default, no files are selected. You can specify files using file names including ? and * wildcard characters (except *.*).

About 30 minutes after the Software Inventory Client Agent is installed on a client computer, the agent collects its first inventory by scanning all local hard drives. As with hardware inventory on 32-bit computers, the Software Inventory Client Agent creates a full inventory file (with a SIC file extension for complete software inventory) the first time it runs. During subsequent inventory collection, it creates only a delta file (with a SID file extension for delta software inventory). These files are sent to the CAP, forwarded or uploaded to the site server (on secondary sites, they are forwarded up the hierarchy to the parent), and processed by the Software Inventory Processor.

The Software Inventory Client Agent does not use WMI. Still, on 32-bit clients, the agent calculates the delta on the client machine; on 16-bit clients, the agent passes the full inventory file to the CAP. No software inventory history is preserved in the SMS site database.

SMS clients receive a software resynchronization request if their software inventory files are corrupt or if they do not match the SMS inventory data (for example, the delta inventory reports removal of an application that has not been reported yet).

Remote Tools Client Agent

The Remote Tools feature of SMS is installed by default during Express setup or during Custom setup if it is selected. You must enable the Remote Tools Client Agent before you can use it. This feature is composed of two sets of utilities:

➤ **Remote Diagnostics** These allow SMS administrators to view the configuration of SMS client computers. This set of utilities is enabled by default for Windows NT clients regardless of whether or not the Remote Tools Client Agent is available. You can configure these utilities through the Remote Tools Client Agent for all other SMS clients.

➤ **Remote Control** These allow SMS administrators to view the computer screen as well as control mouse and keyboard actions. In addition, you can reboot, execute programs, chat with a user, and copy files to and from the client computer.

You can enable/disable and configure the Remote Tools Client Agent from the Client Agents node in the SMS Administrator console (refer back to Figure 6.1). The Remote Tools Client Agent Properties dialog box is composed of five tabs.

General Tab

This tab allows you to enable and disable the agent. You can also specify whether computer users are allowed to modify Remote Tools Client Agent settings locally or if the agent settings are configurable only from the SMS Administrator console.

Security Tab

This tab allows you to specify all users and user groups that are allowed to remotely control Windows NT SMS client machines. You should remember that the following security requirements are associated with the ability to remote control SMS client machines:

➤ Access to the SMS Administrator console

➤ Read, Read Resources, and Use Remote Tools security rights to SMS Administrator console collection(s)

➤ Membership in the Permitted Viewers List in the Security tab of the Remote Tools Client Agent Properties dialog box

The Permitted Viewers List is downloaded to the client on a 23-hour CCIM cycle. Prior to allowing or disallowing a remote control session, Windows NT clients check to see if the user attempting to initiate the remote session is listed in the Permitted Viewers List.

➤ Local Administrator rights to the Windows NT machine(s) you are remotely controlling

Policy Tab

This tab allows you to specify the level of access you will have to remotely controlled machines. There are three preset access levels: Full, Limited, and None. Full access allows you to perform all remote control functions on the client machines; None gives you no access. Limited access (the default setting) allows you varying configurable levels of access. You can change these settings according to your user or your company requirements. Figure 6.4 shows the list of remote control functions available for permission control.

 The View Client Computer Configuration option allows you to view configuration information for only non-Windows NT client computers. See Chapter 10 for detailed information on how to view this information on any SMS client.

The Policy tab also allows you to specify whether users at the client computers can grant or deny access to their computers via remote control sessions. Figure 6.5 illustrates the Remote Control Agent dialog box. This is displayed on the client computer when a Remote Tools session starts, and the user can control the remote control access from it. Remember that if you allow users to the modify the Remote Tools Client Agent settings from their client machines, they can configure the settings so that you may never be granted access to remote control their machines.

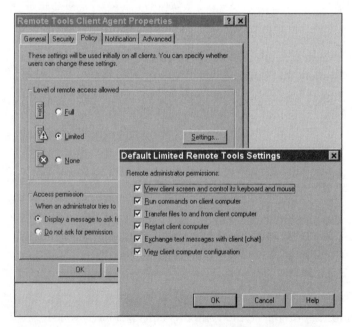

Figure 6.4 Policy settings for the Remote Tools Client Agent.

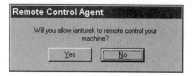

Figure 6.5   Asking for remote control permissions.

Notification Tab

This tab specifies visual and audio indicators for the active Remote Tools Client Agent during the remote session. The notification options are shown in Figure 6.6.

You can configure SMS clients with two visual indicators: a status icon on the taskbar and a high-security indicator on the desktop. There is really nothing different between the two indicators except that the status icon is located in the system tray (available on 32-bit Windows clients) and the high-security indicator appears on the desktop (available on all SMS clients).

Advanced Tab

This tab, shown in Figure 6.7, allows you to accomplish a number of tasks.

First, you can configure the remote control compression settings. SMS client computers that run the Windows NT operating system might gain additional performance benefits if you compress remote screen captures. There are two

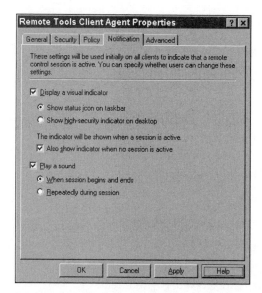

Figure 6.6   Remote Tools Client Agent notification settings.

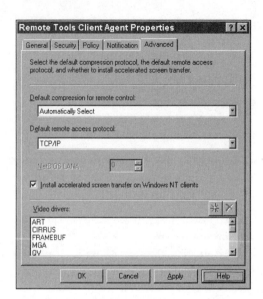

Figure 6.7 Remote Tools Client Agent advanced settings.

compression levels: Low (RLE) and High (LZ) compression. Automatic compression selection is based on the client machine's CPU speed: Machines with a Pentium 150MHz or higher processor are automatically set to LZ compression; all others are set to RLE. By default, compression is level set to automatic.

 LZ compression is available only to Windows NT clients with enabled and functional accelerated video drivers. The NT screen capture compression consumes additional CPU cycles, so you should use it with caution.

The next setting that you can configure in the Advanced tab is the connectivity method between the remote control management station and the remote control client. The options for the default protocol that SMS clients use to listen to the incoming remote session initiation signals are:

➤ **TCP/IP** For Windows IP sockets

➤ **NetBIOS** For any protocol that supports NetBIOS, including NetBEUI (you also need to configure a LANA number if you select NetBIOS)

➤ **IPX** To support clients located in NetWare environments

Last, you can configure acceleration settings available only to Windows NT clients. The default list of supported video card chipsets is specified (refer back to Figure 6.7). You can extend this list with additional chipset names.

 You should always test the functionality of accelerated drivers on a new chipset before making them available in accelerated form to SMS clients.

Advanced settings changes propagate to the SMS clients on the next CCIM update cycle, but they are not automatically applied to the agent's configuration. There are three methods of reconfiguring the Remote Tools Client Agent with the new advanced settings:

➤ Disable the agent and wait until all of the clients deinstall it; then enable it with the new advanced settings.

➤ Change the advanced settings and wait until they propagate to all SMS clients and run on each client's Remote Control Hardware Munger utility with an option to reinitiate the agent:

`%WINDIR%\MS\SMS\Clicomp\Remctrl\Rchwcfg install.`

You can advertise the above command as an assigned software distribution program.

➤ Repair installation of the Remote Tools Client Agent from the Systems Management Control Panel applet (discussed later in this chapter) on each SMS client.

Advertised Programs Client Agent

Before you can distribute software to SMS clients, you need to enable the Advertised Programs Client Agent. This agent is enabled by default on all SMS sites installed using Express setup; otherwise, it is disabled. You configure the Advertised Programs Client Agent from its properties dialog box available in the Client Agents node in the SMS Administrator console (refer back to Figure 6.1).

The Advertised Programs Client Agent Properties dialog box contains two tabs.

General Tab

This tab allows you to enable or disable the client agent, specify the frequency of connections required to check for new advertised programs, and lock Advertised Programs Client Agent settings on each client.

The Advertised Programs Client Agent has three Offer Data Providers: Systems, User, and User Groups. The Systems Offer Data Provider checks for distributed software made available to the SMS client machine (the Advertised Programs Client Agent runs on); User and User Groups providers check for the software advertisements made available to the NT user and user groups of the user logged onto the machine. This frequency of checking for advertised software is specified in minutes and can be changed to any number between 5 and 1,440. By default, each Offer Data Provider connects to the CAP every 60 minutes and checks for changes to advertised software.

As with the Remote Tools Client Agent, you can allow SMS users to modify the Advertised Programs Client Agent settings on their client machines. If the Clients Cannot Change Agent Settings option is disabled, SMS clients can change the agent's interval between connections to the CAP to check for new or modified advertisements as well as any settings on the Notification tab (described shortly). However, they cannot disable the agent on their machines.

Notification Tab

This tab, shown in Figure 6.8, allows you to modify how advertisements are displayed on SMS client machines.

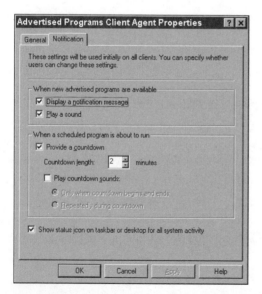

Figure 6.8   Notification properties of the Advertised Programs Client Agent.

You can enable visual and audio notifications for the following events:

➤ The agent learns of a newly available advertised program

➤ The agent is about to run the assigned (mandatory) program (you can configure the countdown time for this event)

You can also specify whether the Advertised Programs Client Agent status icon should be visible in the client's taskbar during all of the agent's activities.

Software Metering Client Agent

The Software Metering Client Agent is the client program required to meter software usage on clients in your site. After you configure a software metering server (see Chapter 4 for details on configuring a software metering server), you might want to enable and/or configure the Software Metering Client Agent. This agent is enabled by default on SMS sites installed using the Express setup method. It is disabled on primary sites installed using Custom setup and on all secondary SMS sites with the software metering feature installed.

You can configure the Software Metering Client Agent from the Client Agents node of the SMS Administrator console (refer back to Figure 6.1) by accessing the Software Metering Client Agent Properties dialog box, shown in Figure 6.9.

The Software Metering Client Agent Properties dialog box has multiple tabs and many configurable settings that can be divided into two groups: agent

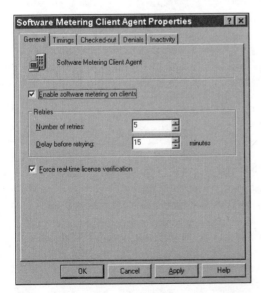

Figure 6.9   Software Metering Client Agent Properties dialog box.

configuration settings (the first two tabs) and client notification messages (the last three tabs).

Agent Configuration Settings

The General tab allows you to enable or disable the client agent. Here, you can specify whether the client agent is to function in online mode (real-time license verification) or offline mode (clients connect to the software metering server to periodically report license use data). In addition, this tab allows you to modify two important client parameters:

➤ **Number Of Retries** The number of times the agent retries to connect to a single metering server. After the last retry attempt, the agent tries connecting to a different metering server (if one is available in the SMS site). If the client is in online mode, after the last retry attempt to the last metering server in the site, the client switches to offline mode.

➤ **Delay Before Retrying** The number of minutes the agent waits before retrying to connect to the metering server.

The Timings tab presents the administrator with many additional numeric settings:

➤ **Configuration Polling Interval** This setting specifies the frequency with which the metering agent receives configuration updates from the software metering server.

➤ **Client-Timeout** These three settings specify how often clients should report live status to the software metering server, how often the metering server(s) should check for timed-out clients, and the length of client inactivity after which it is considered timed out.

➤ **Callback** These three settings specify how a client requests application seats in the callback queue, how long an application license should remain in the callback queue before the client retrieves it, and the interval with which the client checks for the available applications in the callback queue.

Client Notification Messages

The client notification tabs are the last three tabs in the Software Metering Client Agent Properties dialog box. They are Checked-Out, Denials, and Inactivity. Each of these tabs allows you to customize the messages that the metering clients see displayed on their screens when the following events occur, respectively:

➤ A license is about to expire

➤ An application runtime is denied (you can also specify the length of time the message is displayed)

➤ An application is inactive for a specified period of time (see Chapter 7 for more information about application inactivity settings)

NT Event To SNMP Trap Translator Client Agent

The NT Event To SNMP Trap Translator Client Agent converts specified Windows NT event messages to SNMP traps. The SNMP traps are then forwarded to the SNMP management station specified in the Windows NT SNMP Agent Properties dialog box. For example, you can use the Event To Trap Translator Client Agent to have all of your Windows NT servers and workstations, with the SMS client software installed, send important messages to a central management console that then alerts the administrators about the reported problems.

This client agent is installed on SMS clients by default. This is the only client agent that has only one configuration option: The client can be either enabled or disabled. By default, the Event To Trap Translator is enabled on all SMS sites. Although it's very simple to configure this client agent, some additional SNMP settings and event filtering make this feature's configuration much more complicated.

In order for SMS to be able to receive NT events in the form of SNMP traps, the following is required:

➤ An SMS NT client must have the SNMP services configured and running.

➤ The Event To Trap Translator Client Agent must be enabled.

➤ An SMS NT client has to be configured to translate specific NT events to SNMP traps. You do this using the Event To Trap Translator application (shown in Figure 6.10), available for launch by right-clicking on any Windows NT resource in the SMS Administrator console's Collection node.

Systems Management Control Panel Applet

The Systems Management Control Panel applet is automatically installed on all discovered computers in an SMS site (except for computers discovered using the Network Discovery method). You can view both the SMS core and

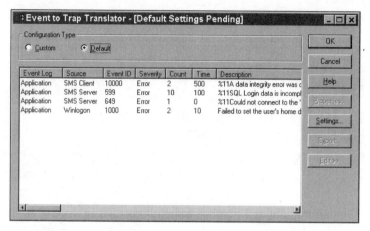

Figure 6.10 Configuring NT events for SNMP translation.

optional components in the Components tab of the Systems Management Properties dialog box, shown in Figure 6.11. This tab has three action buttons:

➤ **Repair Installation** Reinstalls each of the listed components

➤ **Refresh Status** Refreshes the list of components

➤ **Start Component** Starts the Hardware Inventory Client Agent or Software Inventory Client Agent so that an immediate inventory occurs on that client machine

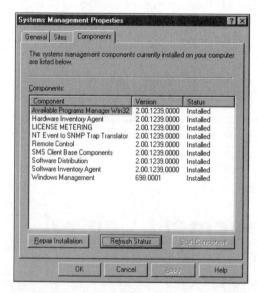

Figure 6.11 All SMS components listed in the Systems Management Control Panel applet.

In the General tab, the Systems Management Control Panel applet lists the client properties that are passed to the site server in a Data Discovery Record (DDR). In the Sites tab, all sites that the client is a member of are listed. If a client is a member of more than one site, the site listed at the top of the list is the client's *principal* site. You can change a client's principal site by shifting sites up or down in the Sites tab.

If an SMS client is a member of multiple sites, it uses the client agent configurations from its principal site. There is one exception to this rule: The client uses the most restrictive Remote Tools Client Agent settings of all sites it is a member of. For example, if one site allows for remote diagnostics and the other one doesn't, it doesn't matter which site is the client's principal site; the client is not enabled for Remote Diagnostics.

The Sites tab also allows you to update your SMS client configuration with the one stored on the CAP. By initiating an update of the site configuration, you are essentially launching the CCIM outside of its 23-hour cycle.

Mobile SMS Client Settings

The client is a member of multiple sites if its IP address is within their site boundaries. When a client machine moves from one site to another, it might change its membership. As a result, its client agent configuration may change as well, or the client software might even be completely deinstalled. If a client processes a logon installation method at a new site and is assigned, its configuration changes based on the new site's settings. If the client is not within the site boundaries (and therefore is not assigned), it deinstalls its SMS client software. You might want to prevent this from happening by enabling the This Computer Connects To The Network From Different Locations option (the mobile client option) located on the General tab of the Systems Management Properties dialog box.

While the mobile SMS client option is enabled, each SMS installation process that is not started from the original client's SMS site launches the dialog box that asks whether the client should become a member of the new site. The possible answers to this question and the corresponding results are listed in Table 6.2.

On Windows NT SMS clients, you need to have Administrative rights to enable or disable the mobile client option. However, you do not require Administrative privileges to answer the question about which site the client should belong to.

Table 6.2 Client options for multiple site installation.	
Is The Client To Join The New Site?	**Action Performed By The SMS Client**
No	The client configuration does not change, and the question is repeated 30 days later.
Yes	The SMS client software synchronizes with the new SMS site: Disabled agents are deinstalled, enabled agents are installed, and all agents are configured according to the new site's configuration.

Practice Questions

Question 1

> You installed the core SMS 2 client software on all computers on your network. Now you want to install the Hardware Inventory Client Agent and the Software Inventory Client Agent. You've configured both agents to run on a simple schedule—once a week. The Heartbeat Discovery schedule interval is set to two days. How soon should you see most of the inventory in the SMS Administrator console?
>
> ○ a. In one week
>
> ○ b. In half a week
>
> ○ c. In one day
>
> ○ d. In two days

Answer c is correct. The client configuration is updated by the CCIM, which works on a 23-hour cycle. Both components should be installed on all computers within the 23-hour period. Then it takes 15 and 30 minutes to collect hardware and software inventory, respectively. As a result, you should be able to view all of your inventory data in the SMS Administrator console within 24 hours (one day). If you have to wait one week, half a week, or two days, there is something wrong at your site. Therefore, answers a, b, and d are incorrect.

Question 2

> You need to collect a file named NUMBER1.BCP from all client computers. Your clients have several other BCP files: NUMBER2.BCP, NUMBER3.BCP, and so on. You also want to learn how many BCP files each client has. What is the best action to take?
>
> ○ a. Collect *.BCP files and inventory BCP files.
>
> ○ b. Collect NUMBER*.BCP files and inventory BCP files.
>
> ○ c. Collect *R1.BCP files and inventory BCP files.
>
> ○ d. Collect NUMBER*.* files and inventory BCP files.

Answer c is correct. Collecting *R1.BCP files and inventorying BCP files properly isolates collecting just the NUMBER1.BCP file and counts the number of BCP files installed on each client as it conducts an inventory. Answers a, b, and c are all incorrect because they collect all of the BCP files rather than just the NUMBER1.BCP file.

Question 3

> You want to find all of the network connections and the share names mapped to your SMS clients' network drives. What should you do?
>
> ○ a. Write a custom application that asks the user to enter requested data and create an IDMIF.
>
> ○ b. Collect software inventory with the information of the path of each reported file.
>
> ○ c. Modify the SMS_DEF.MOF file.
>
> ○ d. Run the HINV32.EXE on each client.

Answer c is correct. If you want to collect more information about the hardware in use at your clients, you should modify the SMS_DEF.MOF file. Share names happen to be one of the hardware inventory classes you can enable. Answer a is incorrect because you use an IDMIF to create a new architecture that reports on objects not related to computers, making this method inefficient for collecting this type of data. Answer b is incorrect because you need to collect hardware inventory rather than software inventory; software inventory does not provide network connection and share name information. Finally, answer d is incorrect because running HINV32.EXE collects only the data mapped through the SMS_DEF.MOF file, and it is not a supported method of initiating hardware inventory (to initiate hardware inventory, you should use the Systems Management Control Panel applet or wait for the scheduled inventory cycle).

Question 4

> Two of your sites share the same site boundaries. Clients of site WAW check for new advertised programs every six hours. Clients of site KRK check for new advertised programs every day. Clients are not allowed to change Advertised Programs Client Agent settings. After your computer was set up with the SMS client software, you verified, in the Advertised Programs Monitor, that your computer checks for new distributed software every day. You just received your computer back from the repair shop and noticed that your computer is checking for new programs every six hours. Where would you change your Advertised Programs Client Agent settings back to checking for advertisements every day?
>
> ○ a. Modify the SMS.INI file.
>
> ○ b. Use the Advertised Program Monitor Control Panel applet.
>
> ○ c. Use the Systems Management Control Panel applet.
>
> ○ d. Use the Advertised Programs Control Panel applet.

Answer c is correct. Your principal site must have been changed to WAW, and you need to adjust it back to KRK. You can correct the problem by using the Systems Management Control Panel applet. Answer a is incorrect because SMS 2 clients don't use the SMS.INI file (only SMS 1.2 clients do). Answer b could be correct if the clients were allowed to modify the Advertised Programs Client Agent settings (see Chapter 8 for details on this Control Panel applet). However, answer b is incorrect because in this question, clients are not allowed to modify agent settings. Answer d is incorrect because you cannot make configuration changes using the Advertised Programs Control Panel applet.

Question 5

> You have no Administrative rights to your laptop running Windows NT 4 Workstation. Every time you use your computer in the New York office, you see a Remote Tools icon on your desktop. You never see this icon in your home office in Philadelphia. You tried to modify the Remote Tools Policy and Notification settings, but you could not change them. What can you do to prevent this icon from coming and going?
>
> ○ a. Enable Mobile (traveling) mode.
>
> ○ b. Disable Mobile (traveling) mode.
>
> ○ c. Have your domain administrator enable Mobile (traveling) mode.
>
> ○ d. Have your domain administrator disable Mobile (traveling) mode.

Answer c is correct. You are moving your site membership from site to site as you connect to the network from different cities, so your laptop is showing the configured settings for whichever site you are currently a member of. You do not have Administrative rights to your computer, so you cannot enable Mobile (traveling) mode, which would allow your computer to retain the rights of your original site. As a result, you need to ask your domain administrator (who does have Administrative rights to your computer) to enable Mobile (traveling) mode for you. Answers a and b are incorrect because you do not have Administrative rights to your computer and you cannot change the settings. Answer d is incorrect because Mobile (traveling) mode is disabled on your computer; otherwise, you would be asked if you want to change the site membership when connecting to the network in the New York office.

Question 6

Your network clients are running the Windows NT 3.51 Workstation (SP3) operating system and Windows 95 OSR1. You want to monitor application usage. You also want to ensure that a valid license is available for each started application. What can you do?

○ a. Upgrade your Windows NT 3.51 clients to Windows NT 4, install SMS 2 client software, and enable the Software Metering Client Agent in offline mode.

○ b. Install SMS 2 client software and enable the Software Metering Client Agent in online mode.

○ c. Install SMS 2 client software and enable the Software Metering Client Agent in offline mode.

○ d. Upgrade your Windows NT 3.51 clients to SP5a, install SMS 2 client software, and enable the Software Metering Client Agent in online mode.

Answer d is correct. Windows 3.51 clients are supported by SMS 2 if they are running SP5a. You also must be running software metering in online mode for real-time license verification to work (verifying an application when a client computer launches it). Answer a suggests upgrading all of your client computers to Windows NT 4. Although this will allow you to configure your machines with SMS client software, you still must have software metering configured in online mode for real-time license verification. Therefore, answer a is incorrect. Answers b and c suggest installing SMS client software with no upgrades to your client computers. Windows 3.51 clients with SP3 are not supported as SMS clients. Therefore, answers b and c are incorrect.

Need To Know More?

 Microsoft Corporation. *Microsoft Systems Management Server 2.0 Administrator's Guide*. Microsoft Corporation, Redmond, WA, 1998. You can find more information on each client agent in the chapter about each feature. For example, the software metering chapter contains more information on the Software Metering Client Agent.

 Microsoft Corporation. *Microsoft Systems Management Server Resource Guide*. Microsoft Corporation, Redmond, WA, 1999. ISBN 0-7356-0583-1. This is one volume of the *Microsoft BackOffice 4.5 Resource Kit*. Chapter 9 discusses various Remote Tools Client Agent settings. Chapter 10 discusses how to customize hardware inventory and includes information on how to use NOIDMIFs and IDMIFs. Part 8 contains flowcharts that illustrate many SMS processes, including client installation and various features. In addition, Appendix C lists all of the hardware inventory classes and attributes.

 www.microsoft.com/smsmgmt is the Microsoft Systems Management Server Web page. This Web site contains the latest information about SMS 2, including best practices documents, white papers, and deployment case studies. You can use these resources to find out more about SMS client agents and their configuration

  Microsoft TechNet available on CDs or on the Web at **www. microsoft.com/technet** is a great source on detailed information related to Microsoft products. Searching for "NOIDMIF" and "IDMIF" will point you to the sources of information on the correct syntax of these files and common business scenarios where they are used.

Inventory Management With SMS

Terms you'll need to understand:

- √ Query
- √ SMS Query Builder
- √ WBEM Query Language (WQL)
- √ Query criterion type
- √ Relational operator
- √ Logical operator
- √ WQL wildcard characters
- √ Collection
- √ Subcollection
- √ Collection membership rule
- √ Query-based collection
- √ Direct collection
- √ Resource Explorer
- √ Software Metering tool
- √ License balancing
- √ Resource Manager

Techniques you'll need to master:

- √ Creating and modifying queries using SMS Query Builder
- √ Creating queries based on other queries
- √ Creating and modifying query-based collections
- √ Creating and modifying direct collections
- √ Viewing inventory data using Resource Explorer
- √ Configuring the software metering component
- √ Excluding programs from being managed by software metering
- √ Registering programs to manage their usage
- √ Configuring programs and application suites for license enforcement
- √ Creating software metering reports and graphs

Systems Management Server (SMS) not only allows you to collect valuable data from the client computers in your site, but it also enables you to view, manipulate, and use the data as a basis for additional management tasks like software distribution. SMS queries and collections are the two basic SMS Administrator console objects that give you access to collected data.

SMS queries and collections allow you to view computer resources based on their hardware and software inventory attributes, whereas the Software Metering tool allows you to register and control the applications being run on client machines and associated information. This chapter explains how you can manage SMS resources by using queries, collections, and the Software Metering tool. In addition, this chapter introduces you to a sample Windows Management Instrumentation (WMI) application—the Crystal Reports tool, which is included with SMS 2.

Resource Management

Many companies deploy SMS because it helps them gather and access data about their networked computers. Data obtained from discovery as well as software and hardware inventory is available for you to view through two nodes in the SMS Administrator console: Queries and Collections.

Queries and collections are both preconfigured by default with a number of sample instances. You can create new instances from scratch, or you can create new instances based on the sample ones. Queries allow you to manually initiate a real-time search through the SMS site database. Collections can be evaluated and updated on a schedule that you can configure. This feature allows for dynamic software distribution because collections define the targets for software distribution (see Chapter 8 for more information on software distribution), and every time collections are updated, their members are refreshed according to the user-defined collection rules.

Queries

Queries define and store the search criteria for specific objects in the SMS site database; queries do not store the result set of the search. For example, a query can search for all systems that are running the Windows NT Server operating system with Microsoft SQL Server 7 installed. Once the query runs, the result set is displayed in the SMS Administrator console, but it is not stored in the database. You can use queries to retrieve current result sets as well as to define collection membership.

Some queries can return a large number of objects, so you can specify the size of the result set. You can limit the result set by running a special query (from the All Tasks Action menu item) and then limiting the number of returned result items.

SMS 2 Queries

You can query the SMS site database against the discovery data, hardware and software inventory, sites, packages, programs, and advertisements tables.

> *Note: Packages, programs, and advertisements are important software distribution objects. See Chapter 8 for more information on each of these items.*

SMS queries are similar to Structured Query Language (SQL) queries. You define a query using WBEM Query Language (WQL).

SMS supports a superset of WQL known as Extended WQL. Extended WQL includes the JOIN statement to retrieve data from multiple classes, as well as ORDER BY, COUNT, and DISTINCT. Extended WQL supports elements from both American National Standards Institute (ANSI) 89 and ANSI 92 SQL.

SMS queries have multiple configuration settings that you can specify or modify in the Query Properties dialog box for the new query. You can also use this dialog box to modify an already-defined query. Figure 7.1 shows the Query Properties dialog box with its two tabs.

The General tab lists the query name, comments, the query object type, and the query scope. The Security tab allows you to specify users and user groups that are allowed to run and manage the query.

Using the Security tab, you can limit a query to a collection to make it available to SMS administrators or help desk personnel with limited access to SMS collections. You can run queries only against data you have permission to; therefore, some queries need to be limited to specific collections—query scope.

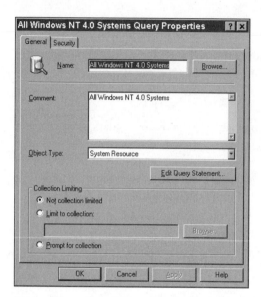

Figure 7.1 The All Windows NT 4.0 Systems Query Properties dialog box.

You can create queries by using the SMS Query Builder graphical user inter-face, available in the SMS Administrator console, or by writing WQL statements. SMS Query Builder looks like a standard SMS Administrator con-sole dialog box, but it has many properties, action buttons, and nested dialog boxes. You can launch the SMS Query Builder, which we cover in detail shortly, from the General tab of the Query Properties dialog box (refer back to Figure 7.1) by clicking the Edit Query Statement button.

You can also copy the WQL statements from any other SMS query stored in the SMS site database by selecting a query using the Browse button from the General tab of the Query Properties dialog box (refer back to Figure 7.1). The displayed list of queries includes the ones available in the SMS Administrator console's Queries node as well as many others. The selected query statements are available for use as they are, or you can modify them by editing their WQL statements manually or by using the SMS Query Builder. The following de-fault queries are available through the SMS Administrator console:

➤ All Client Systems

➤ All Non-Client Systems

➤ All Systems

➤ All Systems with Hardware Inventory Collected

➤ All Systems with Microsoft Word 97

- ➤ All Systems with Specified Software File Name and File Size

- ➤ All Systems with Specified Software Product Name and Version

- ➤ All User Groups

- ➤ All Users

- ➤ All Windows 3.1 Systems

- ➤ All Windows 95 Systems

- ➤ All Windows 98 Systems

- ➤ All Windows for Workgroups Systems

- ➤ All Windows NT 3.51 Systems

- ➤ All Windows NT 4.0 Systems

- ➤ All Windows NT 4.0 Systems with Service Pack 3

- ➤ All Windows NT Server 4.0 Systems (>64MB)

- ➤ All Windows NT Systems

- ➤ All Windows NT Workstation 4.0 Systems (>32MB)

- ➤ Systems by Last Logged On User

- ➤ This Site and Its Subsites

- ➤ Y2K All Compliant Software by System in This Site and Its Subsites

- ➤ Y2K All Compliant Software in This Site and Its Subsites

- ➤ Y2K All Compliant Software on Specified System

- ➤ Y2K All Non Compliant Software by System in This Site and Its Subsites

- ➤ Y2K All Non Compliant Software in This Site and Its Subsites

- ➤ Y2K All Non Compliant Software on Specified System

All queries created at a parent site are automatically replicated to all primary child sites. You can run these queries on all sites, but you cannot modify or delete them from the subsites. You can create other queries based on the locked queries by copying them as described above.

SMS Query Builder

The SMS Query Builder, shown in Figure 7.2, is a graphical user interface that assists you in writing WQL query statements. The Query Builder lists most of the available WQL query properties and assists you in putting the elements together to create custom queries.

There are three tabs in the SMS Query Builder dialog box: General, Criteria, and Joins. Each tab allows you to switch between query language and query design mode. In query language mode, you can view WQL statements and write WQL query expressions manually. While in design mode, you can build the query statements using the graphical interface. Most of the time, you use only the first two tabs because query joins are almost always entered automatically.

 A query searching for all computers with a modified amount of physical memory within some period of time is an example of a query where you should specify a join manually.

The General tab allows you to specify class attributes to be retrieved and displayed in the SMS Administrator console. This tab also allows you to specify the sort order of the displayed result set as well as to filter only the distinct results.

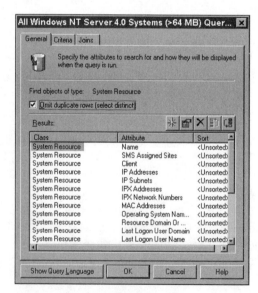

Figure 7.2 SMS Query Builder.

The Criteria tab has many more options. Here, you can specify the selection criteria by selecting any of the criterion types listed in Table 7.1 and specifying the comparison parameters.

After you specify the query criterion type, you need to specify the attribute; the relational operator; and the comparison value, values, another attribute, or another query.

You can choose from several relational operators, and their types depend on the data type of the attribute you select for comparison. For example, to find computers with at least 32MB of physical memory, you would query for memory size, which is a numerical value, and only the numerical relational operators would be available. Table 7.2 lists some of the relational operators available for different data type attributes.

You can use wildcard characters, presented in Table 7.3, in WQL statements with the LIKE relational operator.

You can also combine multiple query expressions to form larger and more complex queries. There are three logical operators that allow you to join expressions:

➤ **AND** Joins expressions and returns the results that satisfy all of them

➤ **OR** Joins expressions and returns the results that satisfy either of them

Table 7.1 SMS criterion types.	
Criterion Type	**Description**
Null value	Queries for NULL and NOT NULL attributes
Simple value	Compares the query attribute to the constant value entered in the SMS Query Builder dialog box
Prompted value	Compares the query attribute to the constant value that you supply when you run the query
Attribute reference	Compares the query attribute to another attribute entered in the SMS Query Builder dialog box
Subselected values	Compares the query attribute to the results of another query specified in the SMS Query Builder dialog box
List of values	Compares the query attribute to a list of constant values entered in the SMS Query Builder dialog box

Table 7.2 Sample relational operators grouped by data type.	
Data Type	**Relational Operator**
Numerical	Is equal to
	Is not equal to
	Is greater than
	Is greater than or equal to
	Is less than
Date and time	Day is equal to
	Hour is greater than
	Is equal to
	Minute is less than or equal to
	Week of year is not equal to
String	Is equal to
	Is like
	Lowercase is greater than
	Uppercase is less than or equal to

Table 7.3 WQL wildcard characters.	
Wildcard Character	**Description**
%	Any string of zero or more characters
_ (underscore)	Any single character
[ ]	Any single character within the range or set (for example, [k-m] or [klm])
[^]	Any single character not within the range or set (for example, [^k-m] or [^klm])

➤ **NOT** Operates on a single expression and returns the results that do not satisfy this expression

For example, the query shown in Figure 7.3 returns all Windows NT and Windows 9x computers with at least 64MB RAM of physical memory.

As you can see, it is important to properly group query expressions. The expressions are evaluated from top to bottom except for expressions in parentheses and expressions preceded by NOT, which are always evaluated first. If the query expressions shown in Figure 7.3 were not enclosed in parentheses, the returned results would be different than intended—the results would return all NT machines with at least 64MB of physical memory and all Windows 9x machines.

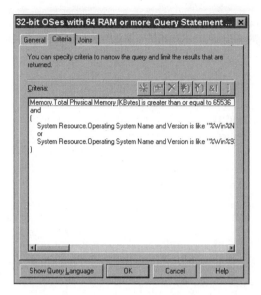

Figure 7.3   Multiple expression query.

Collections

Collections are sets of resources grouped together based on defined membership rules. You use collections to organize resources for distributing software,
viewing inventory, partitioning resources into groups for security delegation,
and so on.

Collections can contain only discovered resources, and they always display a
fixed set of attributes: name, resource class, NT domain, sitecode, SMS client
status, and site assignment status. Unlike queries, collections store both membership rules and result sets in the SMS site database.

 Collections can contain subcollections. A *subcollection* is a
collection that is a member of another collection. The membership rules of both the parent collection and its subcollections
are not linked; their result sets are independent. Subcollections
allow for better management in a high-security environment
and allow administrators to target more than one collection for
a particular software distribution. Administrators who have
access only to a single collection can still create subcollections
(limited to the members of the collection).

As with SMS queries, collections propagate down the hierarchy as a set of rules
and are evaluated locally at each site. Secondary SMS sites are an exception.
They cannot evaluate collections because they do not have a local database; they
receive collection result set files that contain local resources only. For example,

a primary site with the All Windows 95 Systems collection sends files that list Windows 95 machines to all secondary sites; the files contain resources filtered by sitecode so each secondary site is aware of only its own Windows 95 machines. This functionality preserves computing resources and allows for faster data replication.

As with SMS queries, you cannot modify collections created on the parent site from subsites; this also applies to the following default SMS collections:

➤ All Systems

➤ All User Groups

➤ All Users

➤ All Windows 3.1 Systems

➤ All Windows 95 Systems

➤ All Windows 98 Systems

➤ All Windows for Workgroups Systems

➤ All Windows NT Server Systems

➤ All Windows NT Systems

➤ All Windows NT Workstation 3.51 Systems

➤ All Windows NT Workstation 4.0 Systems

➤ All Windows NT Workstation Systems

Each defined collection has a Collection Properties dialog box that you can access from the action menu or by right-clicking on the collection and then selecting Properties. The Collection Properties dialog boxes contain four tabs:

➤ **General tab** Includes collection name, comments, and the information about the latest update and membership changes

➤ **Membership Rules tab** Allows you to view and modify collection membership criteria

➤ **Advertisements tab** Lists all of the software advertisements currently targeted for distribution at that particular collection

➤ **Security tab** Lists the security privileges that users and user groups have to this collection and allows you to change them

There are two types of collection membership rules: query-based and direct. *Query-based* collections contain resources that satisfy a WQL query. *Direct* collections target individual resources or groups of resources.

A single collection can have both query-based and direct membership rules. For example, you might want to distribute a software application to all machines within your European branch (a query that searches for machines assigned to the SMS site with a sitecode EUR) and everyone in the Spanish Language NT user group (a direct rule that targets the Spanish Language NT user group).

Query-Based Collections

You can build a query-based collection using an already existing SMS query, as shown in Figure 7.4.

 A query-based collection is not linked to the SMS query; the WQL expressions are copied from the query properties to the collection properties. Any changes made to the query that the collection is based on do not affect the collection at all. In order for the changes to be applied to the collection, you would either have to modify the collection manually or re-create it based on the changed query.

You can specify multiple membership rules in the Membership Rules tab of the Collection Properties dialog box, but they can be joined only with the OR

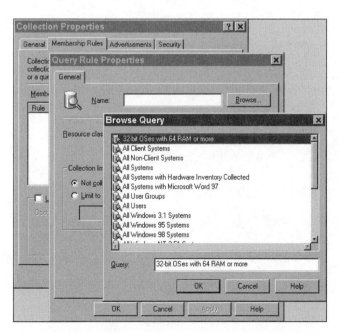

Figure 7.4   Creating a collection based on an existing query.

logical operator. To create a collection that targets resources identified by more than one criterion joined with the AND logical operator, you first have to create a multi-expression query and then base the collection on that query. Alternatively, you might want to write the WQL statements yourself and include the AND operator(s).

You can enable query-based collections for unattended scheduled evaluation. This SMS feature allows you to always maintain current collection membership grouping, which, in effect, allows for more accurate management.

You can enable the Update collection on a schedule feature from the Membership Rules tab of the Collection Properties dialog box. The scheduling options are the same as the options available in the inventory agent properties dialog boxes (refer back to Figure 6.2 in Chapter 6).

Direct Collections

Direct collection membership rules allow you to create collections that contain specific system resources or specific users or user groups. A collection can have multiple direct membership rules. As with query-based collections, these rules are joined with the OR logical operator and include resources that satisfy either of the membership rules.

You create membership rules by running the Create Direct Membership Rule Wizard, shown in Figure 7.5. This wizard allows you to locate and select specific resources that you want as direct members of the collection.

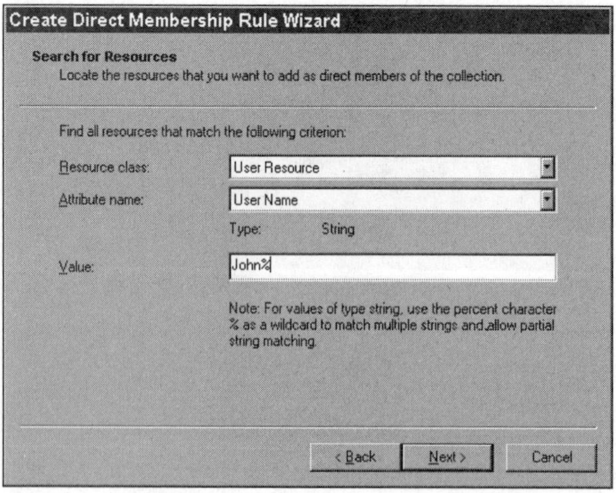

Figure 7.5 Adding direct members to a collection.

All SMS 1.2 machine groups are converted to SMS 2 direct collections when you upgrade the SMS 1.2 site server. SMS 1.2 queries are not converted to SMS 2 queries or collections because the two SMS versions use different query languages. In order to move SMS 1.2 queries to SMS 2, you need to document them prior to the upgrade and then re-create them manually in the SMS Administrator console.

You can update direct collections on a schedule, although their result set changes only if some or all of the direct members are no longer SMS resources.

You can update any or all collections manually by selecting the Update Collection Membership task from the Action|All Tasks menu or by right-clicking on the menu of the collection class or instance. You should always refresh (by using the Action menu or the F5 key) a collection after the update to display the most current result set in the SMS Administrator console.

Viewing Discovery And Inventory Data

SMS collections display only a predefined set of discovery attributes in the SMS Administrator console, as described in the "Collections" section of this chapter. SMS queries allow you to view selected sets of discovery and inventory data in the right pane of the SMS Administrator console. This view is limited by the size of your screen and the computer resources required to transfer data sets from the SMS site database to the SMS Administrator console. The preferred way of viewing resource discovery and client inventory information is by using the Resource Properties dialog box and the SMS Resource Explorer.

The discovery information of an SMS resource is easily accessible from the Resource's Properties dialog box, shown in Figure 7.6. You can open this dialog box from any collection by selecting the Properties menu item from the Action menu (when the resource is highlighted) or by right-clicking on the resource. Alternatively, you can double-click on a resource object to display its Properties dialog box.

In addition to the discovery data, the Resource Properties dialog box also displays the advertisements made available to the resource; this information is available in the Advertisements tab of the Properties dialog box.

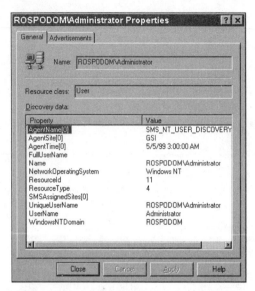

Figure 7.6 Discovery data of a resource.

You can view SMS client inventory data from any of the system resource collection nodes by highlighting the SMS client and launching Resource Explorer from the right-click or Action|All Tasks menu. Resource Explorer is a Microsoft Management Console (MMC) interface that displays hardware and software inventory for a specific SMS client. Resource Explorer is shown in Figure 7.7.

Here, you can find the most current hardware and software inventory data as well as any available hardware inventory history. SQL triggers calculate hardware inventory history automatically as soon as updated client inventory data is received. The inventory history remains in the database for 90 days (this default setting is configurable) or until you delete the SMS client manually.

 You can delete an SMS client or an SMS resource from the Collections node. You can also delete a group of clients by running the Delete Special task from an SMS collection action menu. When SMS deletes the resource, it also deletes all of the data associated with it, including discovery and inventory data.

From Resource Explorer, you can also view the collected software files. These are accessible in the Software, Collected Files node, shown in Figure 7.8. The following information associated with the collected files is available in Resource Explorer:

➤ File name

➤ File path

Figure 7.7   Hardware inventory displayed in Resource Explorer.

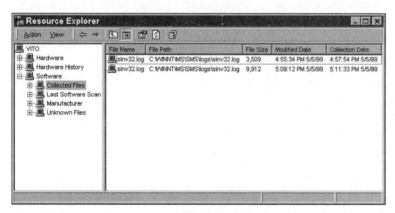

Figure 7.8   Viewing collected software files.

➤ File description

➤ File version

➤ File size

➤ File count

➤ Creation date

➤ Collection date

You cannot view the collected files directly from the site server's hard drive as they are being renamed from their original names (SMS keeps the reference of the original file names as well as collection dates and times and relates them to the SMS created file names). Due to this feature, SMS can save collected file history (see Figure 7.8) and make all versions of the collected file available for viewing and saving. You can save the collected files to any location by running the Save task from Resource Explorer (Action|All Tasks menu item). By default, the five latest versions of the collected file are saved.

Software Metering

Software metering and licensing is considered another method of managing computer inventory—software licenses. We described Software Metering Server role configuration in Chapter 3 and Software Metering Client Agent configuration in Chapter 5. This section of the chapter is dedicated to license management, licensing data summarization, and software usage reporting.

There is one configurable Software Metering component that we have not yet discussed. This item allows you to configure information regarding the software you want to meter. You can configure this component by traversing the SMS Administrator console objects from the SMS Site node, through Site Settings, and finally to the Component Configuration node, as shown in Figure 7.9.

You can configure the Software Metering component through the Software Metering Properties dialog box, which is composed of four tabs: General, Local, Intersite, and Data Summarization. Through these tabs, you can configure the following metering options and settings:

➤ **Product Version Policy (General tab)** Specifies the policy that identifies products by their version. Full policy requires an exact specification of product version. For example, an application with version 5.1 registered for metering monitors only this exact version of the product. On the other hand, a Partial version policy allows you to specify only the leading version numbers or letters. For example, an application with version 5.1 registered for metering monitors usage of versions 5.1, 5.11, 5.1a, and any other version of this application that starts with 5.1.

➤ **Program Name Policy (General tab)** Specifies whether the metering agent should report the application with the file name visible in Windows Explorer (Standard Program Name Policy) or with the file name accessible from the file header (Original Program Name Policy).

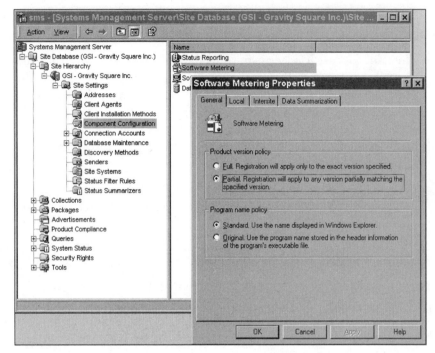

Figure 7.9 Software Metering component configuration.

To prevent usage of applications whose executable files could have been renamed, you should use Original Program Name Policy.

➤ **License Balancing (Local tab)** Specifies how often software licenses should be transferred between the metering servers within an SMS site. By default, this setting is configured to four hours. You should decrease this interval if your site is configured with multiple metering servers and your application licenses are scarce. You can disable inter-site balancing by setting the interval to none.

➤ **Site Management (Local tab)** Specifies how often data should be moved from the site server to the metering servers; this includes all licensing information entered through the Software Metering tool (discussed shortly). The default setting is one hour. You can decrease this setting if all of your application licenses are defined and their configuration does not change very often.

➤ **Data Collation (Local tab)** Specifies how often the data should be uploaded from the metering servers to the site server and the Software Metering Database server. This data is moved and not copied. As soon as the License Metering thread retrieves the data from each metering server, the local data cache on each metering server is emptied.

➤ **Intersite License Management (Intersite tab)** Allows you to enable and schedule movement of unused software licenses between SMS sites. The Intersite tab has an additional setting, Receipt Time Period, which specifies the number of days within which the recipient of the transfer licenses should acknowledge the license arrival. If the receipt for sent licenses is not received within this time, the licenses are considered lost and they can be reused on the originating site.

➤ **Data Summarization (Data Summarization tab)** Allows you to create summaries of software usage. Here, you can enable and schedule licensing data summarization as well as define summarization rules. The summarization rules are configured through the Summarization Rule Properties dialog box, shown in Figure 7.10.

You can specify the type of metering data you want to summarize:

➤ Programs defined in SMS for metering (licensed products)

➤ Programs not defined in SMS but registered by the metering servers (unlicensed programs)

You can also specify the age of the data to be summarized and the granularity of summarization. For example, you might want to summarize metering data

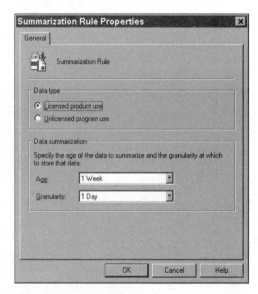

Figure 7.10 Defining license metering summarization rules.

on a weekly basis (age of one week) and be able to recognize daily usage trends (granularity of one day).

Software Metering Tool

With all of the server and client metering components configured, you can now register applications to be metered or licensed. You do this using the Software Metering tool (shown in Figure 7.11), which is available from the Tools node in the SMS Administrator console.

You can perform four major tasks from the Software Metering tool:

➤ Exclude programs you are not interested in monitoring or licensing

➤ Register programs to monitor in a controlled way or license their usage

➤ Configure registered programs for licensing

➤ View software usage data through reports or graphs

Excluding Programs

Many programs that run on SMS client computers do not need to be monitored or licensed; you can exclude these programs from the software metering registering process. Excluding programs allows you to lighten the load on the

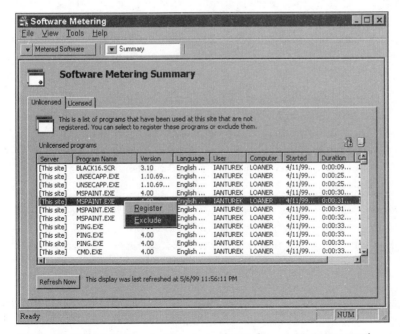

Figure 7.11   Excluding programs in the Software Metering tool.

SMS client machines and the software metering servers. You should exclude only programs that are unimportant or uninteresting to you, for example: CMD.EXE, NET.EXE, or MSPAINT.EXE. Excluding metered programs decreases the disk space used on the metering servers and the Software Metering Database Server as well as preserves some valuable network bandwidth.

To exclude a program from the Software Metering tool, right-click on any of the already registered programs in the Summary window and select the Exclude menu item (refer back to Figure 7.11). There are many excluded programs by default. You can view the list in the Excluded Programs dialog box by selecting the Excluded Programs item from the Tools menu. You can also add new excluded programs (ones that have not been reported to the Software Metering tool) or delete the programs you would like to start managing.

After a program is excluded and the new exclude list is downloaded to the SMS client, the metering client agent ignores events associated with this excluded program. No information about this program is reported to the metering server(s). You can configure the frequency of new excluded lists being downloaded via the Configuration Polling Interval setting of the Software Metering Client Agent, described in Chapter 6.

Registering Programs

If you want to meter the usage of applications and programs, you first need to register them. You should also register the programs if you want to manage who can use them on which machines, and when. By registering a program, even ones that do not have any specific licensing limitations, you might limit its usage by NT user, NT user group, and time of day.

You can register a program in two ways. You can right-click on any of the programs listed in the Summary window (similar to the method you use to exclude the program). Alternatively, you can right-click on the empty space of the Licensed Software pane in the Metered Software window of the Metering tool (shown in Figure 7.12) and then select the New menu item.

You can specify which machines the program can be run from, by which users or user groups, and during what times of day. You can configure these options from the Registered Program Properties dialog box. This dialog box has five tabs and several settings, the first two of which are described here (we'll discuss the other three shortly):

➤ **Identification tab** Specifies a program's product name, the number of available licenses, the serial number, the purchase date, and product notes.

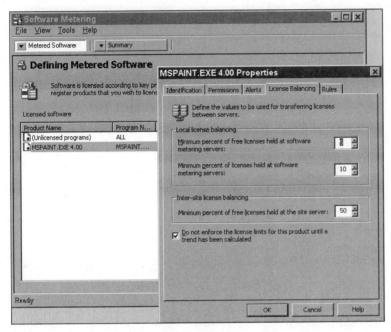

Figure 7.12   Properties of the registered program.

➤ **Permissions tab** Allows you to specify NT users, NT user groups, and
SMS client computers allowed to run this program. You can also specify
the program access time limitations.

By default, each registered program is set with zero available
licensees; disabled license enforcement; and access to the
program set to everyone, all machines, and for 24 hours a day.
By default, no users or user groups are defined in the Software
Metering tool; the tool recognizes only machines that have
reported software usage. You can add users, user groups, and
machine names to the Software Metering tool via Resource
Manager, available in the Tools menu. You can also import
users and user groups from the Windows NT domain SAM
database.

Licensing Programs

You can configure and enforce product licensing from the last three tabs of the
Program Properties dialog box. Several settings control licensing of the programs, applications, and application suites. This section explains some of the
available settings and the basic steps required to configure licensing.

You can register a program as an application suite and then add to it one or more programs. You can license an application suite per suite or per program. For example, you might have 10 licenses for Microsoft Office 97 but 50 additional licenses for Microsoft Excel. In this case, you would configure the Office suite with 10 licenses, Excel with 50 licenses, and all other MS Office programs with 0 licenses (they use suite licensing restrictions).

To complete configuration of a program, you can use the three remaining tabs. The remaining three tabs of the Registered Programs Properties dialog box are described below:

➤ **Alerts tab** Allows you to specify the administrative alerts triggered in case of extreme licensing conditions: Low licenses, Out of licenses, and Access denied. You can also enable inactivity monitoring and specify the client inactivity time and events. Available options are: Generate event, Show warning dialog, and Shut down the application.

➤ **License Balancing tab** (shown in Figure 7.12) Allows you to specify the threshold settings for local and inter-site license balancing (used only if license balancing is enabled in the Registered Programs Properties dialog box, described earlier in this chapter). You can also specify whether the license limits can be enforced before the usage trends are calculated.

The trend analysis feature calculates license usage on each of the metering servers for a period of 7 days for an individual program and 14 days for an application suite. After this period, the appropriate number of licenses is distributed to each of the metering servers. If trend analysis is not enabled, the licenses are moved from the SMS site to the metering servers based on demand. As a shortage of licenses is reported on the metering server, the license(s) are moved there. This might be the source of numerous help desk calls as users are temporarily denied software usage due to lack of licenses.

➤ **Rules tab** Allows you to enforce the licensing for the product. This is perhaps the most important licensing setting of all. With the Enforce license limits for this product option disabled, the licenses are registered and summarized, but their usage is not enforced. This tab also allows you to configure a licensed program as being available for checkout—the ability to move a license to mobile computers. You can also enable concurrent licensing (multiple copies of the program being run on one computer are counted as one), license extensions (multiple copies of the program running nonsimultaneously on different computers under the same user context are counted as one), and license expiration date.

 You should remember that in order to license the usage of programs, the Software Metering Client Agent has to be configured to work in online mode (Force real-time license verification is enabled). If the client agent is configured to work in offline mode, you cannot meter software usage, but you can still deny usage by setting the time limitation of the program (Permissions tab) to be unavailable 24 hours a day.

Creating Software Usage Reports And Graphs

The Software Metering tool can create reports and graphs that describe software usage on your site and its subsites. A sample Web page report is shown in Figure 7.13. You can create reports and graphs using the wizards available from the Tools menu. There are several predefined graphs and report templates you can use to learn the details and summaries of active license use, denials, callbacks, checked-out licenses, and many other activities as well as metering historical data.

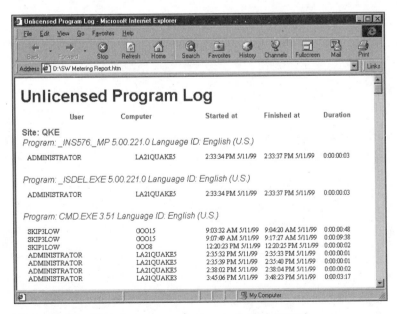

Figure 7.13 Web browser software metering report.

Crystal Reports

Another important part of managing inventory is creating management reports from the data you have collected. From the reports, you can determine how many computers you have running a particular operating system, how many require a specific hardware upgrade, or myriad other reports that are important in your organization. Crystal Reports provides reporting capability for SMS.

Crystal Info for SMS, an optional SMS component, is a limited smaller version of Crystal Info 6 from Seagate Software. Crystal Info for SMS uses WMI and WBEM open database connectivity (ODBC) to access SMS site database data. This reporting tool allows you to modify precreated sample reports, create new reports, and schedule any reports to be generated at any time and on a repetitive basis. However, this tool is limited and should be used only in SMS hierarchies with 500 clients or fewer.

 Crystal Info for SMS is a sample product that demonstrates the capabilities of WMI and shows how third-party products can be incorporated into SMS 2.

Practice Questions

Question 1

You want to create a collection that lists all Windows 95 computers that have more than 32MB of physical memory. What should you do?

- ○ a. Create a new collection with the following two criteria: all Windows 95 systems and all systems with 32MB physical memory or more.

- ○ b. Create a new collection with the following criterion: all Windows 95 systems. Then, create a subcollection with the following criterion: all systems with 32MB physical memory or more.

- ○ c. Create a collection based on two queries: all Windows 95 systems and all systems with 32MB physical memory and more.

- ○ d. Create a collection based on a query with two criteria joined with the AND operator: all Windows 95 systems and all systems with 32MB physical memory or more.

Answer d is correct. To create a collection that gathers specific resources from the SMS site database based on two criteria joined with an AND operator, you must first create a query. The query has to include the two criteria and the AND operator. Answers a and c are incorrect because they will create a result set based on either of the two criteria rather than on both—they will display all Windows 95 machines (with any amount of memory) and all machines with at least 32MB of memory (including machines other than Windows 95). Answer b is incorrect because it will list one set of data in the collection and the other set of data in the subcollection. Each collection and subcollection returns its own result set, so you will have two separate collections, one with Windows 95 systems and one with all systems that have 32MB or more of physical memory.

Question 2

> You are the administrator of a central SMS site server that uses a remote SQL Server configured with the SMS Provider. You want your assistant, Andrew, to manage only members of the secondary site with the GDA sitecode. What should you do? [Choose all correct answers]
>
> ❑ a. Add Andrew to the SMS Admins group on the computer that hosts the GDA secondary site.
>
> ❑ b. Give Andrew File and Directory permissions to the SMS_GDA share.
>
> ❑ c. Create a collection with all members of the GDA site and give Andrew Instance rights to this collection.
>
> ❑ d. Add Andrew to the SMS Admins group on the central SMS Server.
>
> ❑ e. Add Andrew to the SMS Admins group on the remote SQL Server.

Answers c and e are correct. To allow Andrew to manage only members of the secondary site GDA, you need to create a collection that contains members of the GDA site and give Andrew appropriate rights to the collection. The SMS Provider is stored on a remote SQL Server, so you also have to be sure Andrew has rights to WMI on that server (refer to Chapter 3 for security access requirements). You do this by adding Andrew to the SMS Admins group on the remote SQL Server. Answers a and d are incorrect because neither the secondary site nor the central site server guards access to the SMS site database through WMI and the SMS Provider. Answer b is incorrect because giving Andrew rights to a share does not allow him to manage items using the SMS Administrator console.

Question 3

> You have created a direct collection that lists the only two Windows 2000 Professional computers on your network and named it Win2KPro. Last night, you installed another Windows 2000 Professional system and set it up with the SMS 2 client software. The following morning, you opened the Win2KPro collection and noticed that your new machine is not listed there. What is the cause of the problem?
>
> ○ a. The collection has not updated yet.
>
> ○ b. The direct collection is not based on a query.
>
> ○ c. The Data Discovery Record (DDR) of the new Windows 2000 Professional workstation has not been processed yet.
>
> ○ d. You did not enable the Hardware Inventory Client Agent.

Answer b is correct. A direct collection is not based on a query, so it is not automatically updated with the new members. Answers a, c, and d are incorrect because a direct query is based on a specific result set, not on any attributes of a resource. Updating the query (answer a) or waiting for discovery (answer c) or inventory data (answer d) does not add new resources to the result set of a previously created direct collection.

Question 4

Your network had several hundred Windows for Workgroups 3.11 clients running on Intel 386 computers. You have replaced these computers with new Pentium III machines running Windows NT 4 Workstation. What is the best way to delete the Windows for Workgroups 3.11 resource data, including their inventory, from the SMS site database?

○ a. Delete each Windows for Workgroups resource by using the Delete button in the SMS Administrator console.

○ b. Delete each Windows for Workgroups resource by using the Delete button in the SMS Administrator console to delete the orphan inventory by using DBCLEAN.EXE.

○ c. Delete all Windows for Workgroups 3.11 computers by using the Delete Special task in the SMS Administrator console.

○ d. Use SQL Enterprise Administrator to remove all Windows for Workgroups 3.11 data from the SQL database.

Answer c is correct. By deleting the entire contents of the Windows for Workgroups 3.11 collection, you delete all of the data for each of the computers running Windows for Workgroups 3.11. Answer a also allows you to delete the data of each Windows for Workgroups 3.11 computer, but it could be quite time consuming, depending on the number of computers you have to delete. Answer a is not the *best* answer, so it is incorrect. Answer b is incorrect because you do not need to run DBCLEAN.EXE to delete specific computers (this utility was used in SMS 1.2 to delete orphaned database records). Answer d is incorrect because direct operations on the SMS SQL database are not supported.

Question 5

> You have created a number of complex queries on your SMS test site. You would like to use these queries on your SMS production site. How should you move them?
>
> ○ a. Restore the test site database onto the production site.
>
> ○ b. Make your production site the parent of the test site.
>
> ○ c. Copy the WQL statements from the SQL database of the test site and paste them into the Query Properties dialog box of the production site.
>
> ○ d. Copy the WQL statements from the Query Properties dialog box of the test site and paste them into the Query Properties dialog box of the production site.

Answer d is correct. In order to move queries from one site to another site so that you can edit and use them, you have to copy their WQL statements from one site and paste them into the appropriate Query Properties dialog box of the other site. Answer a is incorrect because although you might get the queries by restoring the test site's site database to the production site, you will end up with unwanted data in your database (not to mention that the backup and restore procedures have additional strict requirements, described in Chapter 9). Answer b is incorrect because it makes the child site receive its parent's queries and collections, not the other way around. Answer c is incorrect because direct access to the SMS SQL database is not supported.

Question 6

Your computing environment is composed of computers running several operating systems. The three computers used at your help desk center are running Windows NT 4 Workstation. Your help desk operators often logon to other client computers remotely when troubleshooting the reported problems; their logon names are: helpd1, helpd2, and helpd3. How can you create a collection that lists only the three computers used by your help desk operators?

○ a. Create a collection that queries for the Windows NT 4 Workstation operating system.

○ b. Create a collection that queries for the Windows NT 4 Workstation operating system and the last logged-on user (helpd1 or helpd2 or helpd3).

○ c. Create a collection that queries for the Windows NT 4 Workstation operating system and last logged-on user of helpd1 and helpd2 and helpd3.

○ d. Create a direct collection that lists all three help desk computers.

Answer d is correct. To specifically get the three computers you want, you should create a direct collection. Answer a is incorrect because it gives you all of the computers in your site that are running the Windows NT 4 Workstation operating system. Answer b is incorrect because it gives you all three computers, but it may contain additional computers (Windows NT 4 Workstation computers to which help desk operators recently logged on). Answer c is incorrect because the last logged-on-user attribute cannot include three user names at the same time. If you use the AND operator, all three have to be true.

Question 7

You have noticed that a number of your employees play a distributed game called Buddy Boy. You want to deny usage of this application on your network, but are afraid that some employees might rename the startup executable file. What is the best way to achieve your goal?

○ a. Enable full product version policy.

○ b. Enable original program name policy.

○ c. Enable inactivity monitoring.

○ d. Set the live status acknowledgment interval to one minute.

Answer b is correct. By setting original program name policy, you cause software metering to evaluate the data included in the file headers when making application usage decisions. So, a name change to the executable file does not cause it to be hidden from software metering. Answer a is incorrect because file version recognition does not allow you to capture the usage of renamed executables. Answers c and d are both incorrect because they are not related to the proper recognition of the file name of the executed program.

Question 8

You purchased three licenses for a custom VB application composed of three modules. Each module can be run independently, but counts as a usage of one license. How should you set up licensing for this application?

- ○ a. Register each module independently and set the number of available licenses of each module to three.

- ○ b. Register the VB application using the name of one of the modules and set its number of available licenses to three.

- ○ c. Register each module and the application independently; specify that the application is a suite parent and that it has three available licenses; set the number of available licenses for each module to zero.

- ○ d. Register each module and the application independently; specify that the application is a suite parent and that it has one available license; set the number of available licenses for each module to one.

Answer c is correct. You have three modules and three licenses, so you want to allow more than one user to use the same module if a license is available. By registering each module independently and specifying that the module and the application are members of an application suite, you allow three licenses in any combination of modules to be in use at any one time. Answer a is incorrect because it puts you in violation of your licensing agreement by allowing each application to be used by three users simultaneously (a total of nine possible license uses at one time). Answer b is incorrect because it licenses only one module (allow for three copies to be run simultaneously) and it does not license usage of the other two modules at all. Answer d is incorrect because it allows for a total of two instances of each module to be used at any given time. Under these circumstances, six instances could be open at any given time, which exceeds your limit of three licenses.

Question 9

You configured the Software Metering Client Agent to run in offline mode. You want to deny usage of the application with the executable file name BINGO22.EXE. What should you do?

- ○ a. Register BINGO22.EXE, enforce the license limits for this product, and set the number of available licenses to zero.

- ○ b. Register BINGO22.EXE and set the number of available licenses to zero.

- ○ c. Register BINGO22.EXE and set its access time to unavailable 24 hours per day.

- ○ d. Add this product to the Excluded Programs list.

Answer c is correct. To deny usage of an application in offline mode, you have to register the application and then make it unavailable during the desired hours of the day. Answer a is incorrect because you can enforce license limits only in online mode. Answer b is incorrect because it does not prevent BINGO22.EXE from being executed in either online or offline mode. Answer d is incorrect because it excludes BINGO22.EXE from the software metering operations.

Question 10

You are the administrator of an SMS central site. You want to view a summary of an application usage in two of three SMS child sites with 700 clients each. How can you do it?

- ○ a. Use Crystal Info for SMS to create a report that summarizes product usage in the two sites.

- ○ b. Launch the Report Summary task from the Software Metering component object in the SMS Administrator console.

- ○ c. Launch the Report Summary task from the Software Metering Site Server object.

- ○ d. Use the Report Wizard in the Software Metering tool.

Answer d is correct. The Report Wizard in the Software Metering tool creates report summaries of product usage for any set of the specified SMS sites. Answer a is incorrect because the Crystal Info tool is limited for use in SMS hierarchies of 500 or fewer SMS clients. Answers b and c are incorrect because you cannot create any summary reports from either the Software Metering component object or the Software Metering Site Server object.

Question 11

You have installed a primary SMS site server using Express setup and you have enabled logon script modification. Your parent site is actively monitoring software usage. What should you do to be able to meter software usage on your network and exchange the licenses with the parent site every 12 hours? [Choose all correct answers]

❑ a. Enable the Software Metering Client Agent.

❑ b. Create at least one software metering site system.

❑ c. Enable local license balancing and set it to 12 hours.

❑ d. Enable intersite license balancing and set it to 12 hours.

Answers b and d are correct. After Express setup is complete, you must create a software metering site system before you can meter and license software usage. Then, to exchange licenses with other sites in the hierarchy every 12 hours, you need to enable intersite license balancing and set its frequency to 12 hours. Answer a is incorrect because Express setup automatically enables the Software Metering Client Agent. Answer c is incorrect because enabling local license balancing allows for license balancing between the metering servers within the site, not for exchanging licenses with other SMS sites.

Need To Know More?

 Microsoft Corporation. *Microsoft Systems Management Server Administrator's Guide, version 2.0.* Microsoft Corporation, Redmond, WA, 1999. Chapter 10 has a short discussion about using Resource Explorer. Chapter 11 contains more detailed information about creating and using SMS collections and queries. Chapter 14 contains a detailed explanation of software metering and licensing.

 Microsoft Corporation. *Systems Management Server 2.0 Resource Guide, Microsoft BackOffice Resource Kit.* Microsoft Corporation, Redmond, WA, 1999. Chapter 15 describes the tools you can use to view the contents of collections and the results queries using Microsoft Access and Excel.

 www.microsoft.com/smsmgmt/ is the Microsoft Systems Management Server Web page. This Web site contains the latest information about SMS 2, including supported operating systems, upgrade and interoperability information, white papers, and deployment case studies.

Distributing Software To SMS Clients

Terms you'll need to understand:

- √ Y2K compliance
- √ Product Compliance Database
- √ Package
- √ Package Definition Files (PDFs) and SMS files
- √ Compressed package source
- √ Status Management Information Format (MIF) file
- √ Package access accounts
- √ Generic account
- √ Program
- √ Dependent program
- √ Advertised Programs Control Panel applet
- √ Advertisement
- √ Instruction file
- √ Advertisement Start Time
- √ Advertisement Expiration Date
- √ Mandatory assignment
- √ Advertised Programs Monitor
- √ Advertised Programs Wizard
- √ SMS Installer
- √ Installation Expert
- √ Script Editor
- √ Repackage Installation Wizard
- √ Watch Application Wizard

Techniques you'll need to master:

- √ Understanding how to create, configure, and manage packages
- √ Learning how to create and configure programs
- √ Becoming familiar with package access accounts
- √ Knowing where to view available advertisements on the client
- √ Becoming familiar with the process of creating SMS Installer scripts and executables
- √ Understanding the difference between uninstall and roll-back

Once you have learned how you configure SMS to gather the data about the computers in your SMS hierarchy (discovery, inventory, and metering), you are ready to continue learning about the remaining SMS features. These features allow you to manage your clients and identify their compliance status. This chapter explains the process of identifying Y2K and Euro noncompliant software in use in your company as well as the computers where this software is installed. It also explains how to distribute software to SMS clients from a centralized location as well as the process of creating customizable installation files using SMS Installer.

Y2K And Euro Compliance Analysis

The optional Product Compliance feature of SMS assists you in determining software products that are not compatible with the date and time format past the year 2000 and the new European currency—the Euro. Based on the software inventory data that SMS collects from your SMS client computers and the data contained in your Product Compliance Database, you can quickly recognize not only noncompliant software products, but also machines where these products are installed. You can use the default Y2K queries and Crystal Info reports to help you identify software that is not compliant.

In addition, hardware inventory allows you to gather details about the system Basic Input/Output System (BIOS) installed on each client computer. You can then check with the BIOS manufacturers to find out the compliance status.

Product Compliance is installed on primary sites by default during Express setup. Product Compliance is an optional SMS feature (available only on primary sites) if you use Custom setup. Or, you can add it at any time after initial installation by rerunning Custom setup and modifying the existing installation. The SMS Administrator console on primary sites with Product Compliance installed includes the Product Compliance node, shown in Figure 8.1, and the following Y2K compliance queries:

➤ Y2K All Compliant Software by System in This Site and its Subsites

➤ Y2K All Compliant Software in This Site and its Subsites

➤ Y2K All Compliant Software on Specified Systems

➤ Y2K All Non Compliant Software by System in This Site and its Subsites

➤ Y2K All Non Compliant Software in This Site and its Subsites

➤ Y2K All Non Compliant Software on Specified Systems

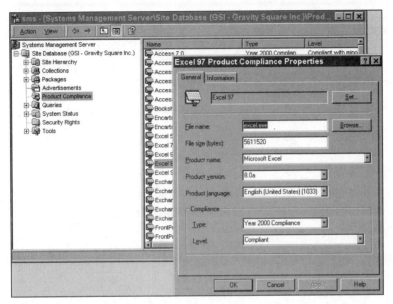

Figure 8.1   Viewing properties of products listed in the Product Compliance Database.

The preinstalled Product Compliance Database, which you can modify and extend, includes over 80 Microsoft products with their compliance status. You can change the Y2K data of any product by changing its properties (refer back to Figure 8.1). In addition, you can add new products to the Product Compliance Database manually or in batches by using a tab-delimited ASCII file—the compliance file.

 Microsoft provides continuously updated compliance files on its Web page at **www.microsoft.com/technet/year2k/product/ prodcomp.txt**.

You can import the Y2K compliance file downloaded from the Web site through the right-click or All Tasks|Action menu on the Product Compliance node. After you have collected software inventory from your clients and compared the data with the data in the Product Compliance Database using precreated queries, you can use software distribution to upgrade noncompliant software with patches or new versions.

Electronic Software Distribution

The Software Distribution feature of SMS 2 allows SMS administrators to distribute software applications or single files, or run commands on client computers selectively and based on a schedule.

Before you can distribute software, you have to ensure the following:

➤ There is at least one accessible distribution point in each site with clients targeted for distribution (see Chapter 4 for more information on creating distribution points).

➤ There is at least one accessible client access point (CAP) in each site with clients targeted for distribution (see Chapter 4 for the steps required to create a distribution point).

➤ The Advertised Programs Client Agent must be enabled and configured on each site with the targeted machines, users, or user groups (see Chapter 6 for the details on client agent configuration).

➤ If targeted machines are selected based on inventory, then the Hardware Inventory and/or Software Inventory Client Agents must be enabled and configured (see Chapter 6 for more information on client agent configuration).

➤ If the software distribution targets users or user groups, then User Account or User Group Discovery method must be enabled on each primary site with the targeted users or user groups (see Chapter 5 for the details on discovery methods).

Discovery data is necessary information for software distribution. You may distribute software to SMS resources only if their discovery data exists in the SMS site database, and if the targeted resources have SMS client software installed and running.

 You cannot distribute software to discovered machines that do not have SMS client software running. You also cannot distribute software to users or user groups who are logged on to machines that do not have SMS client software installed and running.

The software distribution process contains three stages: package creation and distribution, program creation and configuration, and creation of program advertisements that target a collection of SMS resources.

Package Creation And Distribution

To advertise software to SMS clients, you must first create a *package*. A package contains the files and/or instructions that SMS uses to distribute software to a distribution point. Clients then access the distribution point to obtain the package.

Software packages contain the files that SMS clients need to execute, copy, read, and so on. These files have to be copied to the distribution points in each SMS site where the targeted clients are located. If a package is not placed on a distribution point at a particular site, no clients in that site will be aware of the advertised software.

You have to create a software package even if no files need to be sent to the distribution points. For example, you might want to synchronize the time on all of your client computers by advertising a command-line executable called NET.EXE. NET.EXE is present on all client machines, so you don't have to provide this executable to them; however, you still have to create a software package.

You create a package from the Packages node in the SMS Administrator console by selecting New|Action or the right-click menu, as shown in Figure 8.2.

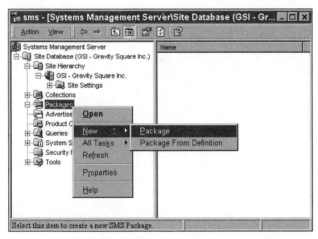

Figure 8.2   Creating a new package for distribution.

Packages created on a parent site are visible on all subsites and can be locally downloaded to the subsites by assigning new distribution points. For example, a package created on a central site and distributed only to the central site's distribution points can be assigned to the child site's distribution points by its local administrator. If the child site's distribution points are assigned by the central site's administrator, only that administrator can modify them.

You can create a package manually or from a package definition template in either the PDF or SMS format. When you install a site using Express setup, SMS installs sample PDFs. If you install a site using Custom setup, the sample PDFs are optional. Many current software applications are sold with PDF or SMS files for easy distribution using SMS.

 SMS files are enhanced versions of the PDFs that were used in SMS 1.2. Both types of definition files contain information about the package and different programs available to advertise. For example, a package created using the Office 97 SMS file automatically creates SMS program objects for Custom, Typical, and Manual installation.

A package has several settings that you can configure using the six tabs of the Package Properties dialog box, shown in Figure 8.3.

General Tab

This tab allows you to provide package description information, including name, version, publisher, and the package icon.

Data Source Tab

This tab specifies whether the package has source files, and if so, their location: network path or the path on the local site server's drive. You can also specify if Distribution Manager (an SMS Executive service thread) should compress the source files locally and use them as a master distribution source or if it should always obtain the files from the source location. If you select to always obtain the files from the source location, you can configure a schedule that Distribution Manager uses when updating distribution points containing that particular package.

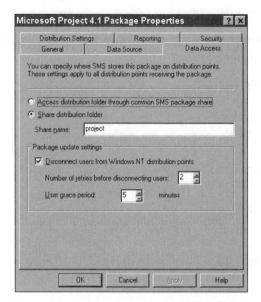

Figure 8.3   Configuring a software distribution package.

 If you specify a network location as a source for distribution files, make sure that the SMS Service account has Access privileges to that location. If you create the package using an SMS Administrator console that is not running on the site server, you cannot browse through the site server's local directory structure. However, you can still specify the location of source files on the site server using the full path with the drive letter. Alternately, you can point to this location using the Universal Naming Convention (UNC) network path.

Data Access Tab

This tab (refer back to Figure 8.3) allows you to specify the location of the distributed files on the distribution point(s) and the Package Update Settings. By default, SMS packages are stored in the common shares (Windows NT distribution points) named with the package ID, for example, GSI00001. You may specify that the package is to be shared with a given share name (each share name must be unique within all packages) or a given share name and a path (the path has to be unique within all packages).

The Data Access tab does not allow you to specify on which drive the share is to be created. In order to do that, you should create a distribution point on the Windows NT share site system rather than on the Windows NT Server system.

If a distribution point is created on a Windows NT share, the package with a specified share name is created beneath the distribution point share. Table 8.1 shows examples of these package share names.

When Distribution Manager updates a package, Distribution Manager deletes its directory and re-creates the directory with the new content. If any clients are connected to the distribution share and have open files, Distribution Manager cannot update the package. To resolve this situation, you might configure Distribution Manager to disconnect users from distribution points after a specified number of retries and a given grace period. These options are disabled by default.

Distribution Settings Tab

This tab allows you to set the priority of the package distribution (by default, all packages are sent with their priority set to Medium) and the preferred sender. For example, you can specify that the package is to be sent using Courier Sender. By default, each package is sent with the first available address defined to a child site or a subsite.

Reporting Tab

This tab allows you to specify information about the Management Information Format (MIF) status files that the distributed program creates. These status files are the ones that will be reported to the SMS Status System as it reports progress about the distributed program. By default, SMS uses information entered in the General tab of the package (the name of the package will be the name of the properties dialog box) to create status messages that report the installation status of the advertisement based on this package. Some installation procedures create their own status MIF files that might be more informative. You can specify their names in the Reporting tab. For example, SMS reports as successfully installed a program that gracefully fails its installation due to low available disk space conditions. If your package uses status MIFs, the above installation can be reported as being unsuccessful, and the detail reason for the failure will be reported.

Table 8.1   Distributed package locations.

Site System	Package Share Name	Resulting Package Path
\\SERVER	SQL	\\SERVER\SQL
\\SERVER	SQL\SQL70	\\SERVER\SQL\SQL70
\\SERVER\SHARE	SQL	\\SERVER\SHARE\SQL
\\SERVER\SHARE	SQL\SQL70	\\SERVER\SHARE\SQL\SQL70

Security Tab

You use the Security tab to configure who has access to the package object. As explained in Chapter 3, this tab allows you to specify the operators and managers as well as their permissions to all packages or to each separate package.

Using Package Objects

Once you have finished creating a package, a node for that package appears in the SMS Administrator console. Each package object has three nodes: Access Accounts, Distribution Points, and Programs. The Access Accounts and Distribution Points nodes are discussed below. For information about the Programs node, see the "Creating And Configuring Advertised Programs" section later in this chapter.

Access Account Management

You use the Access Accounts node to specify which users or user groups have access to the distribution directory on the distribution points. By default, Administrators have Full Control permissions, and users and guests have Read Access rights. You can configure four account types: Windows NT, NetWare Bindery, NetWare NDS, and generic. The generic accounts (administrators, guests, and users) are mapped to the appropriate NT or NetWare accounts and permissions.

Distribution Point Management

A package has to be distributed to a distribution point or points in a site containing clients that will receive an advertisement. You can use either the New Distribution Point Wizard or the Manage Distribution Points Wizard to distribute the software to selected distribution points. Using the Manage Distribution Points Wizard, you can also do the following:

➤ Refresh the package on selected distribution points

➤ Update all distribution points with new source files

➤ Remove the package from all distribution points

Both wizards are available from the Distribution Points node's Action or right-click menu.

Every time you send a package to a distribution point located at a subsite, Distribution Manager first compresses the package source files locally and then sends the compressed file to the subsite. Each site can receive packages from its parent or any other site higher in the hierarchy. You can achieve the latter by creating direct addresses between sites that are not in parent/child relationships. Each site stores a compressed copy of the package locally and sends decompressed files to the designated distribution point site server or servers.

When you refresh a package, you synchronize the package with a local compressed file. When you update the package, SMS synchronizes all of the compressed packages with the source files located on the originating site; a refresh is a second phase of an update.

You can configure additional package distribution settings from the Software Distribution Properties dialog box, which is available from the Component Configuration node (refer back to Figure 7.9). This dialog box allows you to specify the following:

➤ The number of Distribution Manager processing threads (more threads allow you to perform more tasks at a time, but might utilize all the processing power of your site server)

➤ The drive where the compressed packages are to be stored

➤ The retry settings for the distribution point updates and refreshes

From this dialog box, you can also configure the Windows NT Client Software Installation account.

Creating And Configuring Advertised Programs

Before you can advertise a package, it must have at least one *program*. A program is a set of instructions that controls how distributed software is executed on client machines. A program's properties dialog box contains a command line to the program or file to be executed and attributes that control the execution.

> *Note: The actual distributed software made available to clients is called an advertisement. Physically, advertisements are instruction files that cause SMS clients to run the advertised or distributed software programs.*

A package can have multiple programs, as shown in Figure 8.4. Each program must have a name and a command line that references the full path to the program, batch, or data file you wish your clients to execute or open.

The program properties dialog box has four tabs; they are described in the following sections.

General Tab

This tab lists the program name, command line, starting directory, and comments. It also allows for configuration of two parameters: Run and After Running. Run specifies the program run mode: Normal, Minimized, Maximized, or Hidden. After Running specifies what happens or should happen

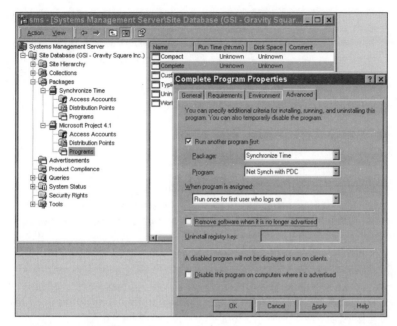

Figure 8.4   Modifying the properties of a program in the Complete
Program Properties dialog box.

after the program runtime completes. The options are: No action required,
SMS restarts computer, Program restarts computer, and SMS logs user off.
These options are required for the correct reporting of a program's success or
failure. For example, a complete execution of software that requires a restart is
not reported if the After Running option is not set properly.

Requirements Tab

This tab allows you to specify informative data about both the estimated disk
space required for the advertised software to complete and the estimated
runtime. You can also specify what platforms (processor platform and operating system) the program can run on.

If a program you are distributing is intended for a specific platform, you might advertise it to a collection based on a computer platform and/or operating system, or you might set the
platform option in the Program Properties dialog box. You often
use the latter choice if a single application has different command-line syntax for different computer platforms. In this situation, you need to create only one package, create one program
for each specific platform, and advertise the package to a single

collection. When you advertise the package, include all platforms multiple times, each time pointing to a different program. A client that receives an advertisement not intended for its platform disregards that advertisement.

Environment Tab

This tab allows you to specify the context under which the program runs: Administrative context for NT users or context of a logged on user. You can also choose whether the program should run when a user is logged on, logged off, or at any time. In addition, you can specify whether the program requires a specific mapped drive to run, any mapped drive to run, or a whether it can run with a UNC path.

When marking a program to run without the user logged on, make sure that the Windows NT Client Software Installation Account is configured and has access rights to all of the network resources it requires to successfully execute the program.

Advanced Tab

The Advanced tab allows you to select the Run Another Program First option (refer back to Figure 8.4). You can use this option to specify a dependent package and a program to be executed first. That program does not have to be advertised separately. This option is ideal for creating package dependencies. For example, Service Release 2 (SR-2) for Microsoft Office 97 can be applied to Office 97 SR-1 only. If you upgrade the released version of Office 97 to SR-2, you create two packages: SR-1 and SR-2 (one program for each package) and then make the SR-2 program dependent on SR-1.

The Remove software when it is no longer advertised option allows you to specify the Uninstall Registry key (not all software titles support the Uninstall Registry key) and remove the software from client computers on deletion of the advertisement. This option provides similar functionality to the Program Group Control feature in SMS 1.2.

From the Advanced tab, you can also disable the program from being executed on the target computers. This option is particularly useful if the program has already been advertised, but you want to delay its runtime. For example, you might want to disable the advertisement of a batch file that copies a financial figures data file to the accounting group after you discover that the stock figures being sent are incorrect. You can enable the program again after you update the distribution points with the corrected data file.

Advertising Programs

After you have distributed packages and created programs, you can advertise their contents to selected clients. You can advertise a program to a single collection or to a collection and its subcollections. SMS comes with several preconfigured collections, so you don't always have to create a new collection for a new advertisement. If your software distribution target computers are to be selected based on their specific discovery data (not covered by the default collections), software inventory, or hardware inventory, you must create new collections.

You can create advertisements from the Advertisements node in the SMS Administrator console, shown in Figure 8.5.

An advertisement must reference a package, a program, and a collection. In addition, an advertisement can have specific security rights, which you configure through the Security tab, and scheduling settings, which you set in the Schedule tab:

➤ **Advertisement Start Time** Specifies the time the advertisement can be made available to clients. By default, it is the local time of the site server where the advertisement is created.

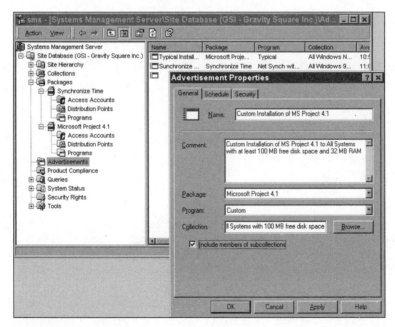

Figure 8.5 Creating a new advertisement.

➤ **Mandatory Assignments** Lists the times and the frequency with which the advertisement starts on client machines without user intervention. The assignments can be based on specific events: logon; logoff; or on the time of day, week, month, or year. You can also schedule an advertisement to be executed on client computers immediately after the client agents retrieve it. In addition, you can schedule advertisements to reoccur on a specified timetable.

If the advertisement does not have any mandatory assignments, it can be run at any time between the Advertisement Start Time and the Advertisement Expiration Date. You can also configure mandatory advertisements to be available for independent execution. Mandatory advertisements can also be configured to not run if the client connection is too slow (by default 40Kbps or less).

For advertisements to function properly, you must synchronize the times of your SMS site servers and clients. You may schedule mandatory advertisements to run based on either local time or Greenwich Mean Time (GMT). If the advertisement is scheduled with the local time, it runs at different times across the time zones. If the advertisement is scheduled with GMT, it runs everywhere at the same time (provided the dates, times, and time zones of the targeted computers are set correctly). Time synchronization is also important when you are setting the advertisement start and expiration times.

Retrieving And Running Advertised Programs

After you create advertisements, Offer Manager (an SMS Executive service component) makes instruction files that inform the client machines of available advertisements. Every time collections are updated, Offer Manager updates the instruction files based on the new collection result sets. The instruction files are replicated to the CAP(s), where they are made available to SMS client services to be read.

Instruction files, created for each targeted user, user group, and SMS client computer, contain information about advertisements and the targeted collection. Additional information required to run the advertisement (package name, program name and path, schedule, and the distribution point path[s]) is supplied to clients in additional files that are located on CAP(s); all files related to advertisements are located in the \OFFERINF.BOX and the \PKGINFO.BOX directories on CAP(s).

The Advertised Programs Monitor is an application accessible through the Control Panel applet named after the application. Users at client computers can use this applet to detect new advertisements and to see all of the currently available and previously run advertisements.

The Advertised Programs Client Agent is configured to check for advertisements on a schedule. When the agent finds new advertisements, it reports them to the Advertised Programs Monitor. You can force the agent to check for advertisements by refreshing its data list from the View menu of the Advertised Programs Monitor, shown in Figure 8.6.

Remember that advertisements that target users and user groups are compared to the logged-on user data when the advertisement is checked. Windows NT does not update group membership in real time but rather at logon time. If your user group membership was modified after you logged on to the NT domain, these changes are not in effect before you log off and log on again.

The Advertised Programs Monitor allows you to change the Advertised Programs Client Agent settings; however, you can change the settings only if the SMS administrator sets the agent to allow clients to make changes. To make these changes on the client, go to the System|Options item menu of the Advertised Programs Monitor.

The Advertised Programs Monitor lists only programs that are assigned (mandatory programs) and have not run yet, as well as all of the previously executed programs (both assigned and not assigned). The Advertised Programs Monitor does not list programs that are available to run but that are not assigned. You can view and run these programs from the Advertised Programs Wizard, shown in Figure 8.7.

```
Advertised Programs Monitor                                        _ □ ×
System  Program  View  Help
Name                                    Scheduled to Run      Assigned  Last Run                        Expires
Microsoft Project 4.1 - Custom          Unscheduled           No        Sat 5/15/99 12:10 PM (Completed) Never
Synchronize Time - Net Synch with PDC   Unscheduled           No        Sat 5/15/99 12:59 PM (Completed) Never
Synchronize Time - Run Y2K PC Analyzer  Sat 5/15/99 1:30 PM   Yes       Never                           Never
Synchronize Time - Update Virus Signature File  Thu 5/20/99 12:55 PM  Yes  Never                        Never


4 program(s)
```

Figure 8.6   Viewing assigned and executed programs in the Advertised Programs Monitor.

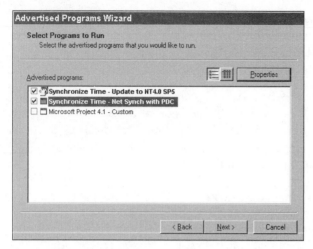

Figure 8.7 Selecting an unassigned program to run.

Programs that are both assigned and available to execute by users independent of assignment are available in the Advertised Programs Wizard and in the Advertised Programs Monitor. The wizard, as well as the Advertised Programs Monitor, are Control Panel applets and are available on all clients that have the Advertised Programs Client Agent installed and running. The Control Panel applet that starts the wizard is called Advertised Programs.

All assigned programs will display a Countdown dialog box just before the program executes (if the Advertised Programs Client Agent is configured to do so). When the dialog box (shown in Figure 8.8) is displayed, you can start executing the program immediately. You can also acknowledge the assigned program and close the Countdown dialog box, view the details of the program, launch the Advertised Programs Monitor to view all scheduled programs, and launch the associated Help file.

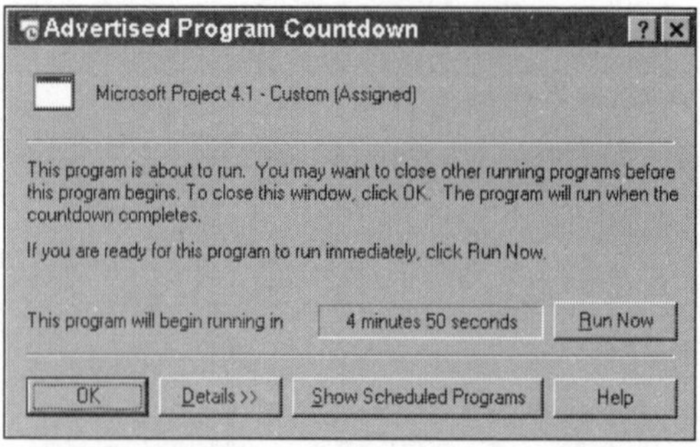

Figure 8.8 Advertised Program Countdown dialog box.

Every time the Advertised Programs Client Agent receives, runs, and completes a program execution, it generates a status message that indicates the action performed and its success or failure.

> *Note:* *See Chapter 9 for details on software distribution monitoring and status system configuration.*

Automating Software Installation With SMS Installer

Many software installations require manual procedures and complex configuration choices that are unfamiliar to many users. These software titles are not designed for unattended or silent installation, and although they are not the ideal candidates for electronic software distribution using SMS, you can still distribute them electronically. SMS Installer eliminates the need for you to manually install most of these titles by generating a self-extracting file or a set of files that can be installed unattended or with just a few user prompts.

Many SMS components are installed using SMS Installer-generated unattended installation files. The core SMS client components are an example of SMS Installer functionality. You can install software prepared for installation using SMS Installer in unattended mode by using the /s switch. You can also pass a number of parameters to the Installer executable.

SMS Installer is not installed by default on any site server or SMS Administrator console machine. You can install SMS Installer only on x86 computers running either the 16- or 32-bit version of Windows by executing the SMSINSTL.EXE file (available in the SMS_INSTI\I386 directory of the SMS_<*sitecode*> share).

After you install SMS Installer, you start it from the Microsoft SMS Installer program group of the Start menu. The initial SMS Installer screen is shown in Figure 8.9.

SMS Installer is a complex application and can be described only briefly here. We offer enough information for you to familiarize yourself with SMS Installer's features as well as to create and distribute simple Installer executable files.

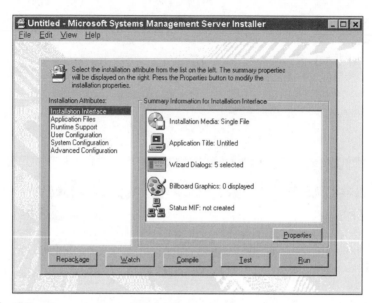

Figure 8.9 Using SMS Installer.

SMS Installer Overview

SMS Installer allows you to create an executable file based on Installer-generated editable script. You can generate the Installer script in a number of ways:

➤ By specifying application files, directories, environmental parameters, and related information through the graphical interface (Installation Expert)

➤ By manually writing or enhancing script generated by other methods (Script Editor)

➤ By "watching" the original application installation process (the Repackage feature)

The main features of SMS Installer are presented in Table 8.2.

Table 8.2 SMS Installer features.	
Feature	**Description**
Installation Expert	Automatically creates the installation script by having the author fill out basic dialog boxes.
Script Editor	Allows the executable's author to edit the pregenerated script or create a script manually.

(continued)

Table 8.2   SMS Installer features (continued).

Feature	Description
Repackage Installation Wizard	Creates a script by "watching" changes made to the system after the application installs. This is the easiest method of creating Installer scripts; unfortunately, you can use this method only on machines with the same hardware and/or software configuration. For example, you cannot use this method to create a script on a machine with a system directory on C: drive, and then run the Installer executable file on a machine with a system directory on D: drive.
Watch Application Wizard	Adds files not installed by the application setup process but required by the application to run. These files are included based on the files used during application runtime.
Software Patching	Allows you to create an incremental upgrade executable installation file. For example, using the Patching feature, you might create a small installation file that upgrades the application from one version to another instead of re-installing a new version of the application that is potentially quite large.
Uninstall	Allows for removal of the software installed using an Installer executable file.
Roll back	Allows for the removal of the software installed using an Installer executable file and a restore of overwritten files, Registry keys, icons, and so on.
16- and 32-bit support	Enables Installer to generate executables for both 16- and 32-bit platforms.
Media Selection	Enables Installer to compile a single executable file or a set of files to be distributed on floppy disks.
Full SMS support	Creates SMS PDFs and status MIF files.
Open database connectivity (ODBC) and Visual Basic (VB) support	Adds files necessary to support ODBC and VB applications.
Test	Allows for the testing of customized installation scripts before actual installation.

Creating SMS Installer Distribution Files

You can create an Installer script using some of the methods described in Table 8.2. Although not all applications or utilities can be installed using the Repackage feature, it is the easiest method of doing so. For instance, software that requires installation of the NT service and specific Registry entries might be suitable for installation using the Repackage feature. You might want to repackage the software and then manually edit the generated script. You may even want to write the script from the beginning if the software to be installed does not have a setup procedure.

 You should always use a reference computer to generate Installer scripts and executable files. A reference computer should be identical to the client computers on which the Installer-generated executable file will run. Any dissimilarities might affect the success of the software installation.

Once the Installer's script is created, you should compile it and then test it on a client machine—or on a few of them. You can also test the Installer script (without compiling it) from the SMS Installer interface (refer back to Figure 8.9). This test does not install any files, but it presents you with all of the dialog boxes and screens the actual user will see.

Table 8.3 shows the files that are created after you compile an Installer script.

The only file you need to distribute to your client machines is the executable file. You might want to preserve the script file in case you ever need to modify the script.

Table 8.3   Files created when you compile an Installer script.

File Name	Description
APPNAME.IPF	Saved script file
APPNAME.EXE	Executable file
APPNAME.PDF	PDF (only if the Create Package Definition File option is selected)
APPNAME.WSM	Working file used by the script

Practice Questions

Question 1

You want to advertise a program to all of your Windows 98 machines with 32MB or more of memory. Which of the following do you have to create? [Choose all correct answers]

❑ a. Package with the source files

❑ b. Program

❑ c. PDF

❑ d. Collection

❑ e. Status MIF file

Answers b and d are correct. To distribute software, you must have a package (with or without files), a program, and a collection. Although there is a default collection for all Windows 98 machines, you must create a collection to get the Windows 98 machines with 32MB or more of RAM. You can use source files, but they are not always required. Therefore, answer a is incorrect. Likewise, you can use a PDF, but you don't have to. Therefore, answer c is incorrect. Finally, a status MIF file is not required either. Therefore, answer e is incorrect.

Question 2

You want to install an off-the-shelf application that has uninstall functionality, supports unattended installation, and comes with the PDF. You created a package and a program using the PDF. You want to be able to uninstall this application when it is no longer needed. How can you accomplish this?

○ a. Enable Roll back support.

○ b. Check the Disable this program on computers where it is advertised option.

○ c. Specify the Uninstall Registry Key.

○ d. Create a patching installation file.

Answer c is correct. To use uninstall functionality, you have to specify the Uninstall Registry Key in the Advanced tab of the Program Properties dialog box. Answers a and d are incorrect because Roll back support and patch installation files are SMS Installer features, and you do not need to use SMS Installer for this software distribution. Answer b is incorrect because checking this option simply disables the program; it does not remove it.

Question 3

Your hierarchy is composed of a central SMS site (sitecode 048), and three direct primary child sites (sitecodes 039, 061, and 062). You created a package at the central site and distributed it to site 039. How can the administrator at site 062 advertise this package to the clients in the 062 site? [Choose all correct answers]

❑ a. Decompress the package and copy it to all of site 062's distribution points.

❑ b. Distribute the package to any distribution points in site 062.

❑ c. Ask the administrator at site 039 to distribute this package to all of the distribution points in site 062.

❑ d. Ask the administrator at site 048 to distribute this package to all of the distribution points in site 062.

Answers b and d are correct. A package created on the parent site is visible on all of its subsites. An administrator of any of these sites can distribute this package to its distribution points and those of its subsites. Therefore, the administrators of sites 048 and 062 can place the package on any distribution point in site 062. Answer a is incorrect because SMS does not support manual decompression and manual copying of packages. Answer c is incorrect because site 039 is not even aware of site 062; neither site reports to the other.

Question 4

You want to distribute software to all Windows 95 clients. What could you do?

○ a. Advertise the software to the All Systems collection and specify that the program can run only on the Windows 95 platform.

○ b. Advertise the software to the All Windows 95 Systems query.

○ c. Distribute the software to all distribution points in your site and have all Windows 95 users run the program from the Advertised Programs Monitor Control Panel applet.

○ d. Distribute the software to all distribution points in your site and have all Windows 95 users run the program from the Advertised Programs Control Panel applet.

Answer a is correct. Of the available choices, only answer a accomplishes the task because it is the only answer that specifies advertising to a collection; for successful software distribution, you have to advertise to a collection. Answer b is incorrect because you cannot advertise programs to a query. Answers c and d are incorrect because you have to create an advertisement before clients can run it using the Advertised Programs Control Panel applet, and these answers do not include a step to create a package that is advertised to a collection.

Question 5

You want to change the time of your new Windows NT 4 Workstation user's machine using the **NET TIME** command. The user does not have Administrative rights to her NT Workstation, and you've decided to use software distribution. What could you do? [Choose all correct answers]

❑ a. Create an advertisement and set the program run mode to Hidden.

❑ b. Create an advertisement and set it to run when the user is logged off.

❑ c. Create an advertisement and distribute it to a machine instead of a user.

❑ d. Create an advertisement and set the program to run with Administrative rights.

Answers b and d are correct. To use software distribution, you must create an advertisement with the appropriate program. In this situation, the **NET TIME** command, which changes the time on a computer, is the program. You must have Administrative privileges to change the time on an NT machine; therefore, you have to advertise the **NET TIME** command and configure it to run with Administrative rights. All programs advertised to machines with users logged off run under administrative privileges. Therefore, answer b is correct. Answers a and c have advertisements, but the second half of the answer does not make the advertisement run under the context that allows for the system time change. Running the program in Hidden mode or when the user is logged off does not satisfy the Administrative rights requirement. Finally, whether you distribute the software to a machine or to a user is irrelevant to the outcome.

Question 6

You have advertised a software program to a collection including the Accountants Windows NT user group. Anna, a new accountant, has reported that she has not received the new advertisement, but her colleagues have received it. You realize that Anna is not a member of the Accountants group and then you correct this mistake. What does Anna need to do to receive the advertisement?

○ a. Run the Systems Management Control Panel applet.

○ b. Run the Advertised Programs Control Panel applet.

○ c. Run the Advertised Programs Monitor Control Panel applet.

○ d. Log off and then log back on to the Windows NT domain.

Answer d is correct. The only way Anna can receive the software is by becoming a member of the target collection. Anna needs to log off and then log back on to her computer to become a member of the collection. Answers a, b, and c are all incorrect because the advertisement does not show up on Anna's client computer until she is a member of the target collection.

Question 7

You decided to use SMS Installer to create an Installer executable file to set up a custom application on all of your SMS clients running Windows 95, 98, and NT 4. These machines all have the same configuration settings across their platforms. You've decided to use the SMS Installer Repackage feature. On which machine(s) should you create and compile the Installer's executable?

○ a. Any of the Windows 95, 98, or NT 4 machines

○ b. Any 32-bit Windows machine

○ c. A Windows NT 4 machine and any of the Windows 95 or 98 machines

○ d. A Windows 95, 98, and NT 4 machine

Answer d is correct. To make sure that your software installation is successful, you need to create an Installer executable file for each operating system on a computer that matches the operating system where it is installed. You are going to install the software on three different operating systems, so you need to create a separate Installer executable file for each operating system. Answers a, b, and c do not specify creating the Installer executable file for each operating system separately. Therefore, they are incorrect.

Question 8

> Your central SMS site (with sidecode DUG) has a child site (with sitecode NEA) and a secondary grandchild site (with sitecode UTA). DUG has three distribution points, NEA has four, and UTA has only one. You distributed a software package to all of the distribution points in the hierarchy and configured it to be updated every week on Sunday for the advertised program execution that occurs during each week. On Thursday, you were informed that the drive that stores both the compressed copy and the only package share on the secondary site failed. You also learned that the drive was immediately replaced with a new one. What should you do to repair the missing software distribution files at the secondary site?
>
> ○ a. Wait until Sunday for the files to be regenerated automatically.
>
> ○ b. Use the SMS Administrator console on the central site to refresh the secondary site's distribution point.
>
> ○ c. Use the SMS Administrator console on the central site to update all distribution points.
>
> ○ d. Use the SMS Administrator console on the primary child site to recreate the package from the source files and distribute it to all of the distribution points.

Answer c is correct. You cannot selectively update a compressed copy of a package at child sites, so your only option is to update all of the distribution points. It is Thursday, and users may want to use the package during the work week, so waiting until Sunday is not a good option. Therefore, answer a is incorrect. Answer b is incorrect because it causes SMS to try to re-create the package from the compressed files stored on the secondary site server, but that file is gone. Answer d is incorrect because the source files do not exist on the child site. Although the child site could create this package using the files from one of its distribution points, the management of this package will then be split between two sites, which may cause additional problems.

Need To Know More?

 Microsoft Press. *Microsoft Systems Management Server Administrator's Guide, version 2.0.* Microsoft Press, Redmond, WA, 1999. Chapter 12 discusses the complete software distribution process. Chapter 13 contains detailed information on how to use SMS Installer. Chapter 17 contains more information on using the Y2K feature of SMS.

 Microsoft Press. *Systems Management Server 2.0 Resource Guide, Microsoft BackOffice Resource Kit.* Microsoft Press, Redmond, WA, 1999. Chapter 7 explains how to create PDFs for use with SMS 2.

 www.microsoft.com/smsmgmt/ is the Microsoft Systems Management Server Web page. This Web site contains the latest information about SMS 2, including supported operating systems, upgrade and interoperability information, white papers, and deployment case studies.

Maintenance, Monitoring, And Optimization

9

Terms you'll need to understand:

√ Status messages
√ Status Message Viewer
√ Status filter rules
√ Status summarizers
√ Site system status
√ Component status
√ Advertisement status
√ Package status
√ Windows NT diagnostic tools

√ SMS Service Manager
√ Network Monitor (NetMon) Agent
√ NetMon Experts
√ NetMon Monitors
√ SMS site backup
√ Delete aged objects
√ Update statistics
√ Rebuild indexes

Techniques you'll need to master:

√ Configuring status summarizers
√ Using status summarizer thresholds to determine the health of your site
√ Configuring status filter rules
√ Using NetMon Experts and NetMon Monitors to analyze network traffic
√ Backing up an SMS site

√ Optimizing your SQL Server databases using SMS tools
√ Diagnosing problems on client computers using Windows NT diagnostics and Windows diagnostics tools available through SMS
√ Viewing status summaries in the SMS Administrator console

233

Performance tuning and optimization requires monitoring your site, changing component settings, and upgrading hardware to allow your SMS hierarchy to work flawlessly and deliver the results you expect. This chapter discusses various monitoring methods, including status reporting of SMS processes, SMS client diagnostics, and realtime SMS component tracing. Next, the chapter describes a set of site maintenance procedures that allow for database tuning and recovery. The chapter closes with a few optimization techniques you can use to accommodate more SMS users, decrease SMS processing times, and improve database querying.

Monitoring

Many factors can influence the performance of your SMS site systems: the type of hardware on which you have selected to install SMS, the network that connects your site systems and clients, site configuration, specific help desk activities, or the size of distributed packages. It's not always a straightforward task to determine which of these factors is the source of a performance problem. SMS comes with a set of tools and utilities that you can use to monitor SMS systems, examine rates of SMS activities, and examine computer performance.

Status Reporting

SMS 2 comes with a preconfigured site component and activity status reporting system. The purpose of this system is to allow you to view the health of your SMS site hierarchy at any given point in time. This system reports on the current and past condition and activities of all SMS components, the health of the site servers, the status of package distribution, and the status of advertisements.

Status data is delivered to the SMS Administrator console through status messages that are generated by different server and client components. You can view status messages using standard SMS queries (see Chapter 7 for more information on creating and running SMS queries), built-in status message summary panes (illustrated in Figure 9.1), and Status Message Viewer (also illustrated in Figure 9.1). You can launch Status Message Viewer from any of the status objects in the SMS Administrator console.

The status messages sent to the SMS site server are processed by Status Manager (this thread component of the SMS Executive service is described in Chapter 11), summarized by Status Summarizer (another thread component of the SMS Executive service), and forwarded up the hierarchy (if configured to do so). SMS can also run specific commands, report to the NT Event Log, or send messages to users or user groups based on the number and type of status messages generated by each component.

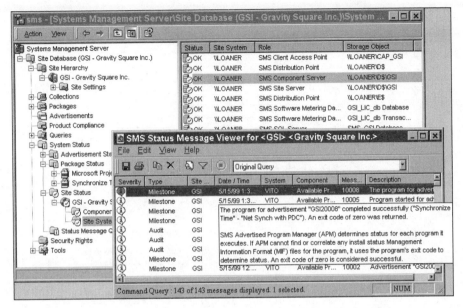

Figure 9.1   Launching Status Message Viewer from the Site System status object.

Several status system configuration settings are located on three nodes in the SMS Administrator console. Status reporting properties are available from the Component Configuration node. Status filter rules and status summarizer configuration are available from their respective nodes under Site Settings. Figure 9.2 shows the location of all three nodes.

Status Reporting Configuration Options

You can use status reporting to control which status messages generated on SMS site systems and SMS clients get reported to the SMS site database and/or logged to the Windows NT Event Log. The options for both server and client components are:

➤ **All milestones with all details** Reports and/or logs all messages

➤ **All milestones** Reports only milestone messages (the default setting)

➤ **Error and warning milestones** Reports only major error and milestone messages

➤ **Error milestones** Reports only event error messages

Milestone messages are reported any time an SMS activity or process completes a major step. You can specify if the details of failures should be reported (not available for all milestones with all details) as well as all of the above settings for Windows NT Event Logging, which is disabled by default.

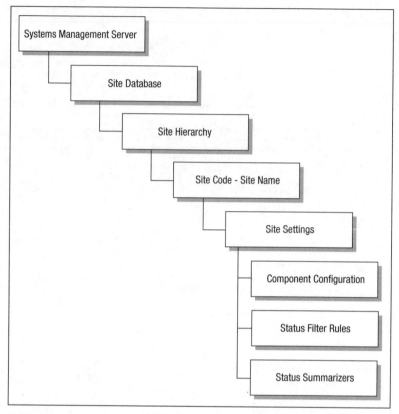

Figure 9.2 Location of the status system configuration objects.

Configuring Status Filter Rules

Several pre-created status filter rules define the action(s) the status system takes when it receives new status messages. You can define an unlimited number of status filter rules. Each status message has to pass through and be evaluated against each rule before it is processed or rejected. You can also specify what the SMS system should do once a specific status message arrives. To specify the type of status message to be filtered, use the General tab of a status filter rule Property dialog box. Each time you create a new status filter rule, SMS will name the dialog box the same as the rule. You can specify the types by:

➤ **Source** Indicates server, client, or SMS Provider

➤ **Sitecode** Indicates the sitecode of the site where the status message originated

➤ **System** Specifies the NetBIOS name of the site system or client

➤ **Component** Allows you to choose the component that generated the status message

➤ **Message Type** Is Milestone, Detail, or Audit

➤ **Severity** Is Informational, Warning, or Error

➤ **Message ID** Indicates the specific message identifier

➤ **Property** Indicates messages with specific properties

➤ **Property Value** Specifies status messages with specific property values

Only status messages that match all of the status filter criteria are designated for processing according to the actions indicated on the status filter rules Actions tab. You can configure and select from the following actions:

➤ Write to the SMS site database and keep messages for a specific number of days (by default, all status messages are written to the database and kept for 30 days)

➤ Report to the Windows NT Event Log (by default, no status messages are reported to the NT Event Log)

➤ Replicate to the parent site at the specified replication priority level (by default, all client-generated messages are replicated to the parent site at low priority)

➤ Run a program specified in the command line (many status filters are configured to display a status message on the site server using the **NET SEND** command)

➤ Do not forward to the status summarizers (see the "Summarizing Status Messages" section later in this chapter for more information on status summarizers)

➤ Do not process lower-priority status filter rules (by default, all status messages are passed through each status filter starting with the one listed at the highest position in the Status Filter Rules node; you can change filter priorities from the Action|All Tasks menu)

 For example, one of the defined status system rules, "Send a message when a site database is low on free space," uses an SMS server as a message source and contains message ID 4707 that is generated by the status summarizer components. The action called by this rule is a **net send** command-line program that displays a message on the site server's screen indicating the problem.

Summarizing Status Messages

With SMS, you can view summaries of status messages, which allow you to more accurately pinpoint where problems are occurring. By quickly looking at the status summaries, you can discover when the site is functioning properly with no warning or error messages being reported. When there is a problem, the summaries report a warning or an error. Then, you can start filtering through the status message system to pinpoint the exact cause of the problem.

You can schedule status messages for summarization based on message type: component status messages, site system status messages, and advertisement status messages. Each of these three groups has different summarization settings.

Component Status Summarizer summarizes the health of the SMS server components. You can enable component status messages for summarization and configure them for replication to the parent site at one of the replication priorities. All component-generated status messages are summarized based on thresholds; the default values are presented in Table 9.1.

These thresholds are configured for each SMS server service and thread (see Chapter 11 for more information on SMS services and threads), and you can adjust them to suit your needs. Every time a number of status messages of a particular type exceeds the specified number, a summary message is created and reported to the local status system for visual indication in the SMS Administrator console. Optionally, the summary message is replicated up to the parent site. For example, refer back to Figure 9.1, which shows the status of all SMS components as OK (and green in color), indicating that no status messages exceeded the warning level or the critical level. Also, the status message count is reset based on the configurable threshold period.

Site System Status Summarizer summarizes the health of all of the site systems in a given site based on their available free disk and database space. The disk and database space messages are summarized (if enabled) on a common SMS schedule similar to the schedule you can configure for the Hardware and Software Inventory Client Agents. You can also enable storage object status messages for replication to the parent site at a specified priority: low, medium, or high.

Table 9.1	Default summarization thresholds for component status messages.	
Type/Threshold	**Warning**	**Critical**
Informational	2000	5000
Warning	10	50
Error	1	5

The thresholds for site system storage objects include settings for Windows NT drives, NT shares, and NetWare volumes—indicated under the default thresholds—and settings for the data and log devices for the SMS site and software metering databases. These settings are shown in Figure 9.3. You can add new specific thresholds for any of the drives, shares, and volumes used by SMS, or you can modify the existing thresholds.

Advertisement Status Summarizer summarizes the state of advertisements in your site, including the total number of clients that have received, started, and run an advertised program. Status messages that indicate the status of advertisement processing and runtime can be enabled for summarization and optionally replicated to the parent site with a configurable replication priority.

Viewing Status Summaries In The SMS Administrator Console

You can view all advertisement-related status summaries in the SMS Administrator console under the Advertisement Status node (refer back to Figure 9.1). These status summaries are grouped by advertisement and by site so that SMS administrators can easily view the status of software distribution, including the number of:

➤ Client machines that have received advertisements

➤ Failure to initiate program execution on client machines

➤ Programs started on client machines

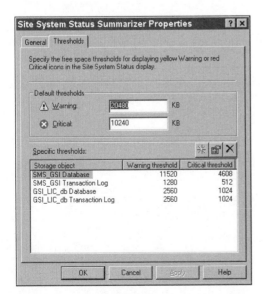

Figure 9.3   Storage object summarization thresholds.

➤ Program errors encountered after successful program launch

➤ Successful execution and completion of an advertised program

Additional information about the names of packages, programs, and targeted collections is also available. You can view the details of software distribution per advertisement or specific site by viewing selected status messages of selected Advertisement Status objects. The available selections for viewable advertisement status messages include received, failures, all messages, and so on. You can also reset the counts for specific messages. This feature is particularly useful if you have advertised a program to run on a recurring basis.

You can also view similar status summaries for packages using the Package Status node (again, refer back to Figure 9.1). In this node, you can view a summary of package distribution to specific sites and specific distribution points. The summary information indicates the source version of the distribution files, the distribution state, and other package information. You can view package distribution details with the scope you specify: per package, per site, or per distribution point. In addition, you can select to view only informational, warning, error, or all messages generated within a specified time period.

You can also view the summary of site systems (based on their available disk space) and site components (based on the summarized service and thread status messages), as shown in Figure 9.1.

Client Diagnostics Utilities

By default, the SMS Administrator console of any SMS site can display the realtime diagnostic information of Windows NT client computers and site systems. You can launch the following diagnostic utilities by right-clicking on the item or from the Action menu of any NT Client object in the SMS Administrator console:

➤ **NT Event Viewer** Use this to list event messages generated on NT machines

➤ **NT Diagnostics** Use this to view OS and hardware information, including environmental variables, network statistics, running services, and so on

➤ **NT Performance Monitor** Use this to monitor utilization of computer resources and the state of processes and threads

Sites with clients configured with the Remote Tools Client Agent can also access the remote diagnostics data of all other Windows clients. These utilities are available from the Remote Tools application, which you launch by right-clicking on any client object within a collection or from the Action menu when the client object is highlighted. The following diagnostic data is available through the Remote Tools application for all machines except Windows NT clients:

➤ Memory

➤ Modules

➤ Tasks

➤ CMOS information

➤ ROM information

➤ DOS Memory Map

In addition, you can perform a ping test (shown in Figure 9.4) to determine the quality of the connectivity between SMS client machines and the SMS Administrator console machine.

SMS Service Manager

You can view the status of SMS components (services and threads) using SMS Service Manager, shown in Figure 9.5. Service Manager allows you to view the state of the SMS services and SMS Executive threads that run on a particular site system. You can also start and stop each service and thread. Finally, using this tool, you can enable tracing (logging) for specific components or multiple components. The SMS Service Manager tool is particularly useful for quickly verifying and modifying the state of SMS components and for enabling tracing.

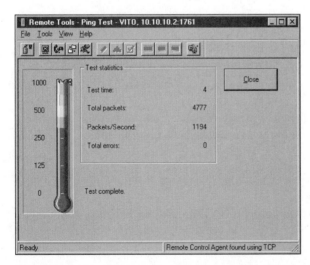

Figure 9.4   Verifying network connectivity with the SMS client using the ping test.

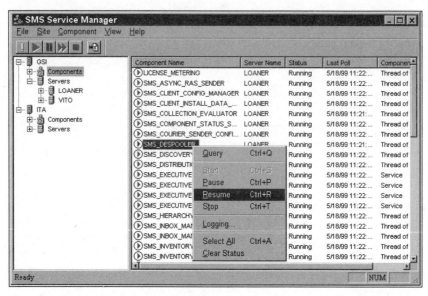

Figure 9.5 Verifying SMS components' status using SMS Service Manager.

You can launch SMS Service Manager from the Tools node of the SMS Administrator console. This tool can provide the status of any site server in any hierarchy provided you have appropriate permissions for it. Figure 9.5 shows SMS Service Manager connected to two SMS site servers that are not part of the same hierarchy.

The pull-down menus of SMS Service Manager allow you to do the following:

➤ Disconnect and connect to SMS site servers

➤ Stop, pause, resume, and start SMS components

➤ Enable tracing (see Chapter 11 for details about tracing)

➤ Query for the updated status of SMS components

Toolbar icons and a right-click menu available from each SMS component allow you to perform some of the actions available from the toolbar pull-down menus (see Figure 9.5).

Each site to which SMS Service Manager connects is represented as an object with two nodes: Components and Servers. The Components node lists all of the services and threads configured on all site systems within a site, whereas the Servers node allows you to view services and threads that are running on a selected site system.

Network Trace

Using Network Trace, you can check the status of SMS site systems within a site, verify connectivity between them, and poll the status of SMS components on each SMS system. Network Trace uses data gathered from Server Discovery and Network Discovery to create a map of SMS site systems and the network routes between them. Using Network Trace, you can also ping a selected site system or router, or all site systems and routers.

 A network connectivity test verifies connectivity between the SMS Administrator console computer and a site system. Just because your console computer can communicate with all site systems does not automatically mean that the systems can communicate with each other—this relationship depends on the Internet Protocol (IP) configuration of your site systems and the SMS Administrator console computer.

To launch Network Trace, use the Action menu of any of the site systems displayed in the SMS Administrator console (Site Systems node). Using Network Trace, SMS administrators can view a graphical representation of the SMS roles each site server is assigned (Trace view) and a representation of all roles on all site systems within a single site, including the network routes connecting them (Site view, shown in Figure 9.6).

 You must enable and run Network Discovery before using Network Trace. Network Trace requires information about routes that connect site systems. If you do not run Network Discovery before using Network Trace, no objects are displayed in either Trace view or Site view.

NetMon

NetMon is an optional SMS tool that captures, filters, and displays packets sent over the network. The captured data can be analyzed right after the network capture session is stopped (see Figure 9.7), or it can be saved for later analysis. You can also modify the captured data and replay it back to the network.

A limited version of NetMon (NetMon agent) is available as a part of the Windows NT 4 operating system. This version allows you to capture data sent to or from the NT machine on which the tool agent runs. NetMon 2, which is bundled with SMS 2, allows you to capture data sent to and from any computer or computers on the network provided that at least one NT machine with

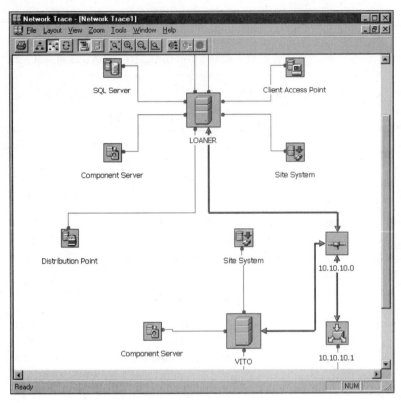

Figure 9.6   Viewing the SMS roles assigned to all site systems within a site.

NetMon agent is present on the segment where you are capturing data. NetMon 2 comes with two new features: NetMon Experts and NetMon Monitors.

In order to capture packets on network segments other than the one where the NetMon station is located, you must config-ure NetMon to use NetMon agents that run on computers lo-cated on other segments. The only requirement for NetMon and NetMon Agents is that the network cards used to capture the data must support promiscuous mode (the ability to cap-ture all packets sent on the network regardless of the destina-tion address). There are versions of NetMon Agents for Windows NT and Windows 9x.

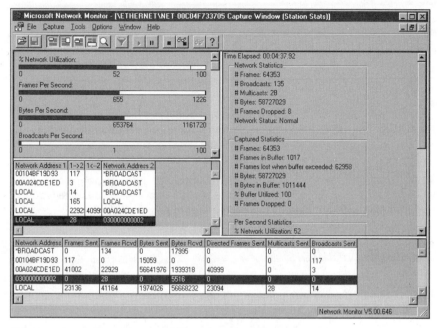

Figure 9.7   Capturing network packets with NetMon.

NetMon Experts

NetMon Experts are post-capture analysis tools that allow you to analyze captured data. SMS 2 comes with a number of pre-created experts, and you can program additional Experts using the documentation included in the NetMon 2 ToolKit—part of the SMS ToolKit. The currently available Experts are listed and described in Table 9.2.

Table 9.2   NetMon 2 Experts.

Expert Name	Description
Average Server Response Time	Determines the average response time of a specified server(s) to network requests
Property Distribution Expert	Calculates statistics for specified protocol properties, for example, Windows Internet Name Service (WINS) resolution requests and responses
Protocol Coalesce Tool	Combines data fragments for a single transmission; creates a new capture file that contains unfragmented sessions

(continued)

Table 9.2 NetMon 2 Experts (continued).	
Expert Name	**Description**
Protocol Distribution	Determines the statistical distribution of protocols based on their data transmission traffic
TCP Retransmit	Determines the level of Transmission Control Protocol (TCP) retransmissions, which indicates network congestion or physical connectivity problems
Top Users	Determines which users were the most active (transmit or receive) on the network during the capture session

NetMon Monitors

NetMon Monitors are pre-capture analysis tools that analyze network traffic for specific events. When these events occur, they generate an administrative warning message. You can configure NetMon Monitors from the Monitor Control Tool, available in the Start|Programs menu under the Systems Management Server program group.

You can configure NetMon Monitors to run locally or on remote computers, which allows you to analyze network data from multiple segments and control it from a single computer. You can also program new NetMon Monitors using the NetMon 2 ToolKit. Table 9.3 shows the Monitors that are available after you install the NetMon optional SMS component.

Table 9.3 NetMon 2 Monitors.	
Monitor Name	**Description**
Internet Control Messaging Protocol (ICMP) Redirect Monitor	Monitors for unauthorized routers and routing table corruption
IP Range Monitor	Monitors for frames originated from devices with specified IP address
IP Router Monitor	Watches specified IP routes and informs about their failures
IPX Router Monitor	Watches specific Internetwork Packet Exchange (IPX) routes and informs about their failures

(continued)

Table 9.3 NetMon 2 Monitors (continued).	
Monitor Name	**Description**
Rogue Monitor	Watches for unauthorized Dynamic Host Configuration Protocol (DHCP) and WINS servers
Security Monitor	Watches for unauthorized instances of NetMon on the network
SYN Attack Monitor	Watches for half-open connections to specified servers (for more information on how to prevent SYN attacks, see the "Need To Know More?" section at the end of this chapter)

When NetMon or NetMon Agent is installed on an NT machine, a new Performance Monitor object is installed—Network Segment. This object allows you to monitor and log network segment characteristics, such as % broadcast frames, % network utilization, and so on.

Performance Monitor

SMS 2 installs a number of performance counters that can help you analyze the processing rates of SMS components, monitor the accumulation of corrupt files, verify the state of SMS components, and examine a variety of other SMS activities. Refer to the "Need To Know More?" section later in this chapter for sources of information on NT Performance Monitor and SMS Performance Monitor objects.

Other Monitoring Tools And Utilities

In addition to the monitoring tools we've covered so far in this chapter, SMS 2 includes other utilities and applications that can help you monitor and verify functionality of the Windows machines and their components on your network. We describe four of these tools—Health Monitor (HealthMon), Web-Based Enterprise Management Test (WBEMTest), SMS Trace, and Tracer—in the following sections.

Health Monitor (HealthMon)

HealthMon allows you to monitor Windows NT 4 Service Pack 4 (SP4) or above computers from a central location. HealthMon is a client/server system that utilizes Windows Management Instrumentation (WMI) on both the client and the server. The server side of HealthMon includes a Microsoft Management Console (MMC) snap-in (shown in Figure 9.8) through which you can add and remove monitored Windows NT computers, configure their monitoring properties, and view the state of the HealthMon clients. A HealthMon client is any machine configured with the HealthMon Client Agent.

You can configure which components of each system (for example, Physical Disk, Processor, or SMS Services) are monitored. You can also configure thresholds for each of the monitored components (for example, percentage of available disk space for logical drives).

 You should be careful when enabling monitoring of system components because only components available on NT machines are reported as being healthy (they can also be reported as being in a warning or critical condition). Components that are not available on NT machines are always reported being in a critical state. For example, the Physical Disk component of a system without disk counters enabled is reported as 100 percent critical.

WBEMTest

Some SMS components don't interact with each other or with the SMS site database directly; they use WMI and store data either permanently or temporarily in the Common Information Model (CIM) repository.

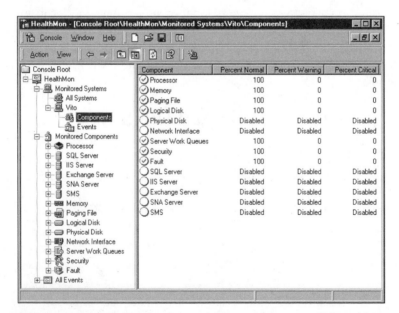

Figure 9.8 Verifying the status of NT systems using the HealthMon console.

WBEMTest allows you to view or populate the contents of the CIM storage space through a Graphical User Interface (GUI). To learn more about WBEMTest, see the references listed in the "Need To Know More?" section of this chapter.

SMS Trace And Tracer

These two tools allow you to view the contents of standard ASCII files. Using any of these tools, you can monitor realtime information written to the SMS log files described in detail in Chapter 11. SMS Trace is a GUI that can open multiple ASCII files, display their entire contents, and display the text that has been appended to them. Tracer is a command-line utility that displays only text appended to ASCII files.

You can view and monitor multiple ASCII files using a single instance of SMS Trace or multiple command consoles that are running Tracer. You should remember that SMS Tracer opens the content of the files, which can consume a large amount of memory if the files are large. Both utilities can consume a large percentage of processor cycles because they continuously process and display the often frequent changes to the files.

Maintenance

Most SMS site systems are pre-configured for self-maintenance. Many site system roles, like logon points, software metering servers, and client access points (CAPs), recover automatically from losing SMS file contents and services. When problems occur with other system roles, like distribution points and sender servers, you need to update or recreate these roles from the SMS Administrator console.

SMS SQL Monitor, an SMS component that maintains database integrity, is configured by default to perform specific SQL database maintenance tasks. It monitors and manages database referential integrity, indexes, keys, and views. SQL Server itself recovers from transactions that stop before they are finished, unexpected service failures due to power shortages, and shortages of disk space.

SQL Maintenance Tasks

SQL maintenance tasks are provided within SMS to assist you in maintaining and optimizing your SMS site database. Depending on your goal and expectations, you might want to modify some of the configurable SMS maintenance tasks. You might also want to periodically back up your SMS site to prepare for the worst possible case—SMS site server or SQL Server database failure. This section discusses common SMS maintenance tasks including database cleanup and SMS site backup. All of the maintenance tasks are available from the Tasks node under the Database Maintenance node in the SMS Administrator console, as shown in the Figure 9.9.

The most important maintenance tasks are SMS site backup (including database backup) and deleting aged database objects.

SMS Site Backup

You can use the SMS Database Maintenance tasks to export the SMS site database and the software metering database. You might also want to export each database's corresponding transaction logs to perform incremental backups. Before exporting transaction logs, you should disable the Truncate Log On Checkpoint option in SQL Server Enterprise Manager for the appropriate database; otherwise, you won't be able to back up (export) the transaction log.

 Truncate Log On Checkpoint is enabled by default after SMS site server installation. When this option is disabled, the transaction log grows until you back it up (export it or dump it). You should expand the transaction log device or allow it to grow to a large size if you plan to disable this option.

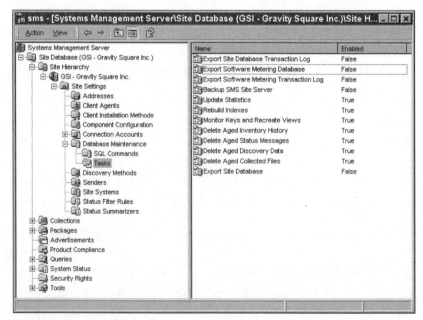

Figure 9.9 Default configurations of Database Maintenance tasks.

All of the export database options require you to pre-create a SQL backup device. The SMS Administrator console also has a predefined task for backing up an SMS site server that includes:

➤ Database backup of both the SMS site and software metering databases

➤ Backup of two main SMS Registry keys:
HKEY_LOCAL_MACHINE\SOFTWARE\Microsoft\NAL and
HKEY_LOCAL_MACHINE\SOFTWARE\Microsoft\SMS

➤ Backup of the main SMS directory shared as SMS_<*sitecode*>

This SMS Site Backup task does not require you to pre-create backup devices, but it does require you to specify a backup destination directory. SMS automatically creates the backup devices, and all backup files are placed in the directory you specify.

All SMS database backup options are called "export tasks" in the SMS Administrator console. Only the SMS site server backup task is called "backup." This terminology can be confusing because in the SQL dialect, backups are called "dumps" rather than "exports."

All SMS export and backup tasks including database, transaction log, and SMS site server backup, have the following default schedule settings:

➤ **Start after** Specifies the time of the day the backup could start (the default setting is 12:00 A.M.)

➤ **Latest start time** Specifies the latest time of the day the backup could start (the default setting is 5:00 A.M.)

➤ **Day of the week** Specifies one or more days of the week the backup should run (by default, Sunday is selected)

Every time a database, transaction log, or site server backup is performed, SQL Monitor stops the SMS services (except for itself) to prevent SMS from accessing the databases during the backup operation. After the backup has finished, SMS restarts the SMS services so all of the systems can function again.

Delete Aged Objects

As computers age and are replaced with newer ones, the data stored in the SMS database becomes old and irrelevant. SMS performs a routine data deletion task that by default deletes the following objects:

➤ Discovery records that have not been updated for more than 90 days

➤ Inventory history 90 days old or older

➤ Status messages (you can configure the age of status messages to be deleted by using status filter rules; you can configure different status messages to be deleted at different ages)

➤ Collected files that are 90 days old or older

All of the delete aged objects tasks are enabled by default to run any time between 12:00 A.M. and 5:00 A.M. each Saturday (aged status messages are deleted daily). You can disable or configure any of these tasks with different schedules and different ages for the objects to be deleted.

Optimization

This section of the chapter describes a number of tuning and optimization techniques that can improve the performance of your SMS system. We do not describe methods for finding performance bottlenecks; we assume in this book that you have discovered performance-related problems yourself, either from the results of system monitoring or feedback from your network administrators, SMS clients, or help desk operators. If so, you might use one or some of the software tuning or hardware tuning optimization methods described here.

Software Tuning Techniques

A number of software tuning settings are pre-configured in SMS and available for modification through the SMS Administrator console. Other settings can be set directly in SQL Server or the Windows NT operating system itself.

SMS Administrator Console Optimization Tasks

All of your SMS configuration settings influence system performance. Enabling hardware inventory and configuring it with a daily schedule place a much bigger load on your server than running an inventory weekly. SMS has a number of settings related only to performance that do not limit the functionality of your site:

➤ **Rebuild Indexes task** This allows for creating, dropping, and recreating SQL data retrieval optimization structures called indexes. The more up-to-date the indexes are, the faster the data can be found. You can configure this setting from the Tasks node of Database Maintenance (refer back to Figure 9.9). By default, this task is scheduled to run anytime between 12:00 A.M. and 5:00 A.M. on Sunday.

➤ **Update Statistics task** This rebuilds statistical data about distribution of data in the SQL indexes. As with the Rebuild Indexes task, this task runs on a schedule (which you configure from the Tasks node of Database Maintenance—refer back to Figure 9.9—and is based on a number of processed objects (which you configure from the Component Configuration node—refer back to Figure 9.9). You can change the number of processed objects by modifying the properties of the Data Processing and Storage object. The default settings update statistics every 1,500 processed discovery records and every 500 processed hardware inventory files.

SQL Optimization Techniques

If you installed your site using Express setup, SQL Server was installed with SMS and configured with the appropriate settings for SMS to perform well under most conditions. If you installed SQL Server yourself, you had to configure it according to recommended settings (listed in Chapter 4). These SQL settings are most likely going to be sufficient for most SMS installations; however, you might want to modify them to fit your specific environment and business model. You can do the following to improve SQL response time:

➤ Add processing power to the SQL Server computer

➤ Increase memory assigned to SQL Server to maximize data caching and minimize paging

➤ Distribute database Input/Output (I/O) operations by placing the database and transaction log devices on multiple drive RAID sets

➤ Separate the data and log devices for the SMS and TEMPDB databases to minimize disk I/O contention

Physical Infrastructure And Performance Optimization

Physical infrastructure usually refers to the hardware components the applications use to operate. These include:

➤ Processor

➤ Disk subsystem

➤ Memory

➤ Network infrastructure

Although different SMS components and SQL Server use different infrastructure elements, discussing their dependencies and optimization techniques is beyond the scope of this book. Generally, it is safe to assume that improving specific hardware components or increasing hardware availability results in improved performance, as described in Table 9.4.

You should remember that "more" of everything is not always the solution. For example, a large number of distribution points might improve the download time of distributed software to client computers, but it takes much longer to set them up and copy the source files to them. You should maintain the right balance of SMS site systems for the number of SMS client machines. One distribution point for 5,000 SMS clients is most likely not enough, yet 500 distribution points for the same number of clients might be too many. You should always monitor your systems and compare current response times and utilization of resources to previous measurements. This technique allows you to more easily notice any signs of performance degradation.

Table 9.4 Basic SMS hardware optimization techniques.

SMS Feature	Optimization Technique
Client installation	Network bandwidth
	Availability of logon points and CAPs
Hardware and software inventory	Availability of CAPs
	Processing power of site server
	Network bandwidth
Help desk activities and reporting	Availability of resources on SMS site database server
	Availability of resources on console machines
Remote control	Network bandwidth
Site to site connectivity	Network bandwidth
	Availability of processing power for sender components (you might need to place sender components on multiple site systems)
Software distribution	Availability of distribution points
	Network bandwidth
	Availability of CAPs
Software metering (Online)	Processing power of software metering servers

Practice Questions

Question 1

> How can you quickly find out how much disk space is free on each of the drives that hosts the SMSLOGON share on your seven domain controllers?
>
> ○ a. Enable disk performance counters on each domain controller and view their % free disk space.
>
> ○ b. View Site System status.
>
> ○ c. View Component status.
>
> ○ d. Run the Server Components Configuration Changes status message query.

Answer b is correct. Site System status allows you to view the status of disk drives on your site systems. Answer a is incorrect because although it provides the data, it is certainly not a quick and easy method. Answer c is incorrect because Component status reports on the state and function of SMS services and threads. Answer d is incorrect because running the Server Components Configuration Changes status message query does not provide information about the available drive space.

Question 2

> Your child SMS site server uses a remote SQL Server 6.5. You are particularly concerned about the SQL Server database running low on disk space. How should you configure the child site to send you both a warning message if the site database free disk space falls below 20MB and a critical status message if it falls below 5MB?
>
> ○ a. Modify the Site System Status Summarizer's thresholds.
>
> ○ b. Modify the Component Status Summarizer's thresholds.
>
> ○ c. Modify the Site database is low on free space status filter rule.
>
> ○ d. Modify the Site database is extremely low on disk space status filter rule.

Answer a is correct. If you want to change the default storage object thresholds for when you receive warning and critical status messages, you modify thresholds using the Site System Status Summarizer Properties dialog box (shown in

Figure 9.3). Answer b is incorrect because doing so would change the thresholds relative to components, but not disk or database space. Answers c and d are incorrect because you set the thresholds for the rules using the thresholds feature rather than by changing status filter rules.

Question 3

You have noticed an unusual number of status messages being sent from your 10 secondary SMS sites. The messages mostly report the event of completing software and hardware inventory collection. You would like to receive only summaries of client advertisements from the secondary sites. What can you do?

○ a. Delete the Replicate all other messages at medium priority filer rule on the parent site.

○ b. Disable replication of all SMS Client messages on the child sites filer rule.

○ c. Disable status summarization of the Advertisement Status Summarizer on the parent site.

○ d. Disable component status summarization on the secondary sites.

Answer b is correct. By default, all client status messages are replicated to the parent at low priority as configured in a status filter rule. Advertisement status message summaries are replicated as well, but you configure these in the status summarizer. To receive only summaries, you need to disable the status filter rule for all client messages. Answers a and c are incorrect because modifying status properties of the primary site does not affect the number of status messages sent from the child sites. Answer d is incorrect because disabling component status summarization at the secondary sites turns off the feature that shows you the status of components at your secondary sites, but it doesn't allow you to receive only summaries of client advertisements from the secondary sites.

Question 4

You want to verify the health of SMS services and their threads on your site system. What could you do? [Choose all correct answers]

❑ a. View component status.

❑ b. Use NetMon.

❑ c. Poll the components on your SMS site server using Network Trace.

❑ d. Use Windows NT Event Viewer.

❑ e. Use Windows NT Diagnostics.

Answers a and c are correct. Component status in the SMS Administrator console reports on the state of each of the SMS services and threads that are installed in your site, and Network Trace allows you to poll components to verify their up or down state. Answer b is incorrect because NetMon allows you to monitor network packets, but it does not allow you to verify the function and state of SMS services and components. Likewise, answers d and e are incorrect because neither Windows NT Event Viewer nor Windows NT Diagnostics reports on the state of SMS services and threads.

Question 5

Your site system is configured with the Simple Network Management Protocol (SNMP) Event To Trap Translator. You want it to send SNMP traps when the storage objects on any site systems in your SMS site cannot be accessed. What can you do?

○ a. Create or modify an existing status filter rule.

○ b. Modify the status summarizer.

○ c. Create and configure a new status summarizer.

○ d. Create an NT Performance Monitor alert.

Answer a is correct. In order to send SNMP traps generated as NT events, you first need to be able to generate NT events. So, you need to configure the status filter rules to generate NT events on specific events—specifically for the Send a message when the site database cannot be accessed rule. Filter rules are the only place where you can configure NT events to be generated. Answers b, c, and d are incorrect because none of them allows you to configure status filter rules, which is a requirement for generating NT events based on SMS status messages.

Question 6

You want to enable tracing of an SMS component on your secondary site server. Which tool should you use?

○ a. Network Trace.

○ b. HealthMon.

○ c. SMS Service Manager.

○ d. You cannot enable trace logs on secondary sites.

Answer c is correct. You can use SMS Service Manager to enable tracing of SMS components on any site server provided you have appropriate privileges. Answers a and b are incorrect because you cannot use Network Trace or HealthMon to enable tracing. Answer d is incorrect because you can enable tracing on secondary sites.

Question 7

You want to run Network Trace to verify network connectivity between your site systems. What should you do before launching the Network Trace tool?

○ a. Enable Windows Networking Logon Discovery.

○ b. Install the SNMP service on the SMS site server.

○ c. Enable and run Network Discovery.

○ d. Install NetMon on the SMS site server and NetMon Agents on all site systems.

Answer c is correct. You must run Network Discovery first or Network Trace does not report any data. Answers a, b, and c are all incorrect because they have nothing to do with a successful Network Trace session.

Question 8

Your SMS site with a local SQL Server 7 was installed two months ago. You configured SQL files to automatically grow without restrictions. You then enabled many attributes in the SMS_DEF.MOF file. The drive that hosts the SMS SQL data file is low on disk space. How can you recover some disk space without sacrificing the system's performance?

○ a. Shrink the SMS site database.

○ b. Modify the Delete Aged Inventory History option to delete data older than 50 days.

○ c. Delete the transaction log file.

○ d. Disable Update Statistics.

Answer b is correct. You can gain some additional disk space by deleting some of the history data stored in the SMS site database. By default, the Delete Aged Inventory History option is configured to delete data older than 90 days; changing it to 50 days frees up disk space. Answer a is incorrect because shrinking the database can only recover unused space, and all the space in your database is used by SMS data. Answer c is incorrect because deleting the transaction log file affects the state of the SMS site, which requires both the data and transaction log devices. Answer d is incorrect because disabling Update Statistics does not free up disk space and may even hurt the performance of your database.

Question 9

You installed your SMS site server using Custom setup. You want to back up your SMS site database, including the transaction log, every day between 11:00 P.M. and 4:00 A.M. What database task or tasks should you enable and configure?

○ a. Enable Truncate Log On Checkpoint.

○ b. Enable Export Site Database and Software Metering Database.

○ c. Enable Export Site Database Transaction Log and Software Metering Transaction Log.

○ d. Enable Backup SMS Site Server.

Answer d is correct. To back up your site database and transaction log, you either need to enable Backup SMS Site Server or both the Export Site Database and Export Site Database Transaction Log tasks. Answer a is incorrect because Truncate Log On Checkpoint prevents you from backing up the transaction log. Answers b and c are incorrect because they provide the wrong combination of tasks required to back up the site database and transaction log.

Question 10

Your primary SMS site server was installed using Custom setup in the server room on an IP segment designated for application servers only. You have installed SMS client software on 1,000 client machines using the Windows NT Remote Client Installation method. Your client machines are located on three IP segments. Each of these IP segments has a Windows NT Server used as a file and print server and one backup domain controller (BDC). What can you do to maximize the performance of distributed software installation?

○ a. Establish SMSLOGON shares on domain controllers located on clients' IP segments.

○ b. Set up all file and print servers as CAPs.

○ c. Set up all file and print servers as distribution points.

○ d. Set up all domain controllers as CAPs.

Answer c is correct. To improve performance of installing distributed software, you need to add more distribution points in your site. Setting up all of the file and print servers as distribution points accomplishes this goal. Answer a is incorrect because establishing logon shares does not provide any performance improvements for software distribution. Answers b and d are incorrect because CAPs do not hold software distribution packages. Creating CAPs closer to the clients would improve the verification of available advertisements, but not the installation of distributed software.

Question 11

Your central site server is connected to 256 secondary sites using an Asynchronous RAS Sender. All 256 modems are connected to the central SMS site server through the port replicator. How can you improve performance of package distribution to the secondary sites?

○ a. Add 256 new modems to the central SMS site server and create 256 additional addresses.

○ b. Create 4 new remote site systems and configure each of them with the Asynchronous RAS Sender and 64 modems.

○ c. Add 256 new modems to the central SMS site server and create 256 additional Asynchronous RAS Senders.

○ d. Install 1 Asynchronous RAS Sender with all 256 modems on a remote site system.

Answer b is correct. It provides the best performance improvement because it moves the load from one machine with 256 modems to 4 machines with 64 modems each. Answers a and c are not possible. You cannot add 256 of the same senders or addresses to a single site from one site server. Answer d could help because it removes some of the load from the site server, but it probably doesn't provide much improvement over the current configuration. Therefore, it is incorrect.

Question 12

You have installed your primary SMS site server and SQL Server 6.5 using Express setup. The site server is configured with two PII 400MHz processors and 256MB of physical memory; it runs only the SMS and SQL Server applications. You configured SQL Server to use 64MB of RAM and 100 user connections. You then noticed occasional high disk activity. You were able to relate this high resource utilization with the activities of the Collection Evaluator thread and the creation of weekly reports. You suspected a memory shortage; you verified that a maximum of 185MB of physical memory is used during the high disk activity time. How can you eliminate the disk thrashing and improve the overall performance of SMS and your site server?

○ a. Add an additional 64MB of physical memory.

○ b. Configure SMS to use 128MB of physical memory.

○ c. Configure SQL Server to use 128MB of physical memory.

○ d. Increase the size of the paging file to at least 350MB.

Answer c is correct. The activities you found responsible for the disk thrashing indicate that you don't have enough SQL cache memory, which causes SQL to access data from the disk instead of from the memory, and you need to increase the cache memory. You can do this by configuring SQL Server to use 128MB of physical memory; your monitoring indicated that you do have available memory that you can assign to SQL. Answer a is incorrect because adding physical memory does not solve the problem if you are not effectively utilizing the memory you have already installed. Answer b is incorrect because the high utilization of Collection Evaluator and weekly reports indicates a problem with SQL Server, not SMS; SMS uses memory dynamically and you cannot configure its memory usage. Answer d is incorrect because the system is not short on virtual memory, which would indicate a lack of page file space.

Question 13

Your SMS site server is servicing 10,000 client machines located on 5 routed IP segments. How can you provide them with the fastest access to the advertisements?

- O a. Configure three CAPs on each segment.
- O b. Configure three distribution points on each IP segment.
- O c. Configure one CAP on each segment.
- O d. Place at least one domain controller on each IP segment.

Answer a is correct. SMS stores advertisements on CAPs. In order to provide clients with faster access to advertisements, you therefore need to increase the number of CAPs on each segment in your site. Answer b is incorrect because distribution points store packages, not advertisements. Answer c is incorrect because having one CAP on each segment does not increase access time as much as having three CAPs on each segment. Answer d is incorrect because adding domain controllers has no effect on advertisements or the software distribution process.

Need To Know More?

 Microsoft Corporation. *Microsoft Systems Management Server Administrator's Guide, version 2.0.* Microsoft Corporation, Redmond, WA, 1999. Chapter 16 provides more detailed information on NetMon and Network Trace. Chapter 18 contains more information about backing up SMS and tuning SQL Server for SMS. Chapter 20 provides a detailed explanation of the status system, how it works, and how to configure it.

 Microsoft Press. *Microsoft BackOffice 4.5 Resource Kit.* Microsoft Press, Redmond, WA, 1999. ISBN 0-7356-0583-1. This resource kit is a great source of information on deploying and maintaining the latest Microsoft BackOffice family members including SQL 7 and SMS 2. A section is dedicated to SMS performance counters (Chapter 27) and performance tuning and optimization techniques (Chapter 11).

 Microsoft Press. *Microsoft Windows NT Workstation Resource Kit.* Microsoft Press, Redmond, WA, 1996. ISBN 1-57231-343-9. This resource kit is the most detailed of all resources on performance and Performance Monitor topics. Part 3 describes different monitoring tools and utilities with a special emphasis on Performance Monitor. Chapters 12 through 16, which describe methods used to detect system bottlenecks, are must-reads for all NT and SMS administrators concerned about the performance of their systems.

 www.microsoft.com/smsmgmt/ is the Microsoft Systems Management Server Web page. This Web site contains the latest information about SMS 2, including supported operating systems, upgrade and interoperability information, white papers, and deployment case studies.

  www.microsoft.com/technet/ is a great source for detailed information related to Microsoft products. Searching for "SYN Attack" will point you to articles on this security issue. Note that the CD version of Technet has many more articles than the Web version.

http://msdn.microsoft.com is an additional source of information related to Microsoft products intended mostly for programmers. Searching for "WBEMTest" will point you to articles (including many SMS-related articles) that describe how to use this tool. Searching for "NetMon" results in a number of pointers to techniques used to build NetMon Experts and NetMon Monitors. Microsoft Developer Network subscription CD-ROMs are also available.

Troubleshooting SMS

10

. . . .

Terms you'll need to understand:

√ Discovery Data Manager (DDM)

√ Client installation log files

√ Copy Queue Manager

√ Inventory Processor

√ Inventory Data Loader

√ Inbox Manager Assistant

√ Inbox Manager

√ Offer Manager

√ Remote Control Hardware Manager

√ SMS Registry keys

√ SQL database consistency checker (**dbcc**) commands

√ Site reset

Techniques you'll need to master:

√ Troubleshooting primary and secondary site server installation

√ Troubleshooting client discovery and installation

√ Troubleshooting inventory collection and processing

√ Understanding the software distribution process

√ Recognizing remote control problems and learning ways to solve them

√ Troubleshooting software metering configurations

√ Becoming familiar with requirements for Simple Network Management Protocol (SNMP) integration

√ Preparing a site for SMS component restore

√ Restoring the SMS site server and databases

Generally, system failures or incorrect SMS configurations cause SMS-related problems. This book doesn't aim to teach you methods for maintaining your systems with 99.99 percent uptime; however, we do intend to make you aware of the most common SMS configuration problems and the techniques that will help you find the source of those problems. Then, you will be prepared to answer test questions related to troubleshooting.

Troubleshooting a complex system like SMS 2 requires extensive knowledge of SMS architecture and processes as well as an ability to track system status and activities. Earlier chapters in this book provide information that will help you learn to troubleshoot in the SMS environment. They also describe SMS architecture and features as well as monitoring tools. This chapter concentrates on SMS process flows and common problems that you may encounter when using specific SMS features. We conclude with a short discussion on SMS site systems recovery.

Tracking And Troubleshooting SMS Processes

Before you can troubleshoot problems that appear in your SMS hierarchy, you first need to understand the SMS processes that are related to specific features. You also need to understand how SMS performs activities before you attempt to troubleshoot them. The following sections describe the most common problems related to specific SMS features and the process flows you need to know to solve them.

Primary Site Server Installation

It's fairly simple to install the primary site server. If any problems are detected, the installation wizard stops and reports them. These problems are usually related to incorrect security permissions, low disk space, incorrect or missing SQL devices, or a lack of the software required for installation.

 You should remember the differences between the Express and Custom setup methods. It is important to know which method is available when and what features are being installed and enabled by default by each of them. For details, refer to Chapter 4.

Secondary Site Server Installation

Installation of secondary sites is much more susceptible to failure because it requires more parameters than primary site installation. When you install a secondary site from a local Windows NT machine, make sure that you specify the correct:

➤ Sitecode of the primary parent site

➤ NetBIOS name of the primary parent site

➤ Secondary site SMS Service account

➤ NT account that has access to the SMS_*SITE* share on the primary parent site

You need this information so that the secondary site can communicate with the primary site. The actual connectivity between the sites does not have to be present during secondary site installation. However, the secondary site is not configurable or functional before it attaches to its parent site. You should also remember to create an address from the parent site to the secondary site or you will not be able to manage the secondary site.

When you install a secondary site using the Secondary Site Creation Wizard from the parent site, you need to correctly specify the following information:

➤ Parameters of an address from the primary site to the secondary site (without them, the secondary site is not installed)

➤ Parameters of an address from the secondary site to the primary site (without them, the primary site never learns that you have successfully installed the secondary site)

➤ The security account that SMS will use to run SMS services on the secondary site

It is also essential for the primary site to have access to the secondary site server under an account that has Administrative privileges. Either the SMS Service account or the primary-to-secondary address account requires these privileges; they are used to connect to the administrative share of the secondary site server as well as to install and start the installation service.

Common secondary site installation mistakes include:

➤ The lack of platform support files if the source files are being copied from the primary site to the secondary site server, and if the servers are running on different platforms (x86 and Alpha)

➤ Not enough drive space (100MB on a system drive and an additional 500MB on any NTFS drive)

➤ A missing SMS 2 installation CD-ROM on the secondary site if the Secondary Site Creation Wizard is instructed to use it

➤ An incorrect drive letter specified to install the main SMS directory on the secondary site server

To troubleshoot the installation, you can check HMAN.LOG for events that refer to the compression of source files to be sent to the secondary site server and SENDER.LOG for information regarding the transfer of files to the secondary site server, installation of the setup service, and the startup of that service.

Client Discovery

Once you understand the discovery process flow, troubleshooting discovery can be very easy. SMS components produce Discovery Data Records (DDRs) and pass them to DDM for processing. DDRs can originate at any of the sources listed in Table 10.1.

Each of the discovery sources passes DDRs to different site components and directories. For example, logon DDRs are passed to logon points, Heartbeat Discovery records are passed to client access points (CAPs), and user and user group DDRs are produced directly on the site server, where they are then processed. All DDRs eventually end up in the DDM inbox of primary sites, where they are parsed and processed. Then, they all go to the parent site (if present).

Most discovery problems are related to incorrect configuration of Network Discovery (see Chapter 5 for details about configuring this method) and excessive site system utilization caused by unnecessarily frequent generation of

Table 10.1   Sources of DDRs.

Discovery Method	DDR Source
Heartbeat Discovery	SMS client machines produce DDRs based on a predefined schedule
Logon Discovery	SMS server or client machines processing logon scripts with a call to SMSLS.BAT or running the SMSMAN.EXE or SMSMAN16.EXE file
Network Discovery	SMS site server produces DDRs for all resources found within the scopes defined in the Network Discovery Properties dialog box
Server Discovery	SMS site server produces DDRs for all site systems
User Discovery	SMS site server produces DDRs for each user found in the NT domain security database
User Group Discovery	SMS site server produces DDRs for each global user group found in the NT domain security database

DDRs; for instance, User Discovery and User Group Discovery can cause a large number of DDRS to be generated frequently. You can monitor discovery processing using SMS performance counters or by tracing the DDM log file—DDM.LOG.

Client Installation

You can install clients using three methods: logon scripts, manual installation, and remote installation on NT client machines. Each of these installation methods reports its activities in a separate log file on the client machine. In addition, remote installation on NT client machines is performed from the site server and is logged there. The log files listed in Table 10.2 will help you troubleshoot most client installation problems.

Clients log their activities to other log files as well. Depending on the client operating system, as well as the type and the number of enabled client agents, you will need to examine several log files to verify the origin of a problem.

Generally, client installation problems are related to any the following:

➤ Site boundaries are incorrectly configured; clients are not installed because they are not assigned

➤ There is not 30MB of free disk space on the client system drives

➤ The Windows NT Remote Client Installation method does not have Administrative privileges to the NT machines

➤ The incorrect installation method or no installation method is enabled

Hardware Inventory

An optional Hardware Inventory Client Agent produces hardware inventory. You can enable this client agent before or after client installation. Make sure you give your SMS clients enough time (up to 23 hours) to synchronize their configuration with the CAP before you start troubleshooting problems related to newly configured client agents.

Table 10.2 Log files for client installation.	
Installation Method	**Log File**
Logon script installation	WN_LOGON.LOG
Manual installation	WNMANUAL.LOG
Windows NT Remote Client Installation	CCM.LOG (on the site server) WNREMOTE.LOG (on the client)

Any changes made to the client configuration are made available to the clients through the CAP(s). Client Configuration Installation Manager (CCIM) connects to a CAP every 23 hours, when users logon to the network, or when users restart Windows NT client computers. The configuration changes are immediately applied to the client (with the exception of some Remote Tools Client Agent settings, which are described in the "Remote Control" section later in this chapter).

Hardware inventory data is created on client machines based on the principal site's schedule (see Chapter 6 for details on the principal site and client configuration) or on agent startup if the last schedule was missed. This inventory data is stored in the Common Information Model (CIM) repository on 32-bit clients and passed in a Management Information Format (MIF) file from any SMS client to the CAP. Copy Queue Manager carries out all client communication with the CAP.

The inventory file is then moved to the site server, where it is processed by Inventory Processor (which runs on both primary and secondary sites) and Inventory Data Loader (which runs on primary sites only). Inventory Processor calculates the history of hardware inventory files generated on 16-bit SMS clients and adds a binary header to all inventory files, which are then passed to Inventory Data Loader. Inventory Data Loader finds the owner of the inventory file based on the binary header, parses the inventory file, and updates the SMS site database. If any inconsistencies are found in an inventory file, Inventory Data Loader rejects it and requests a hardware inventory resynchronization.

As you see from the above hardware inventory process flow, several components participate in hardware inventory collection and processing. Each of these components generates status messages and can log its activities to ASCII log files, which you can view for signs of possible problems.

In addition, NOIDMIF and IDMIF files are a part of the hardware inventory collection process. When these files are present in the appropriate clients' directories, the inventory agent picks them up and checks them for accuracy. If correct, the data stored in the NOIDMIF and/or IDMIF files is included in the hardware inventory file that is passed to the CAP. If the data is incorrect, an error is written to the hardware inventory log file (HINV32.LOG or HINV.LOG), and the malfunctioning file is moved to the client's BADMIFs directory.

Software Inventory

As with hardware inventory, an optional client agent (Software Inventory Client Agent) produces software inventory. If enabled, this agent is updated with a new configuration on a 23-hour schedule and runs on a schedule configured at the principal site.

The Software Inventory Client Agent produces the software inventory data file on a schedule or when the agent starts up (if the last scheduled cycle was missed). As with hardware inventory, only 32-bit client computers produce incremental software inventory files. As soon as client components can connect with the CAP, Copy Queue Manager passes the software inventory file to the CAP. The inventory file is then moved to the site server, where Software Inventory Processor processes it. All corrupt software inventory files, as well as inventory files that contain data inconsistent with that stored in the SMS site database, are discarded, and the computers are requested to produce a resynchronization file—a full software inventory. All software inventory files are then passed up the hierarchy all the way up to the central site.

All components that produce, move, and process software inventory files can log their activities to log files as well as create status messages. Remember that Inbox Manager Assistant—an SMS component that runs on the NT CAP(s)—moves all client files from the NT CAP(s) to the site server almost immediately. Inbox Manager—an SMS component that runs on the site server on an hourly cycle—picks up client files moved to NetWare CAP(s). You need to know which log files to examine for potential problems based on the location of the CAP(s).

The most common software inventory problems are related to the following:

➤ Delays being associated with moving inventory files from NetWare CAP(s) to the site server

➤ The inventory exceeding the maximum allowed size (if this happens, the inventory is not sent from the client)

Software Distribution

As with the optional Hardware and Software Inventory Client Agents, the Advertised Programs Client Agent's configuration is updated on a 23-hour cycle. However, the agent itself verifies the availability of new or modified advertisements on a schedule that you can configure (60 minutes is the default).

Offer Manager (a thread of the SMS Executive service) produces the advertisements based on a collection refresh interval. As the collection is refreshed and its member list is updated, Offer Manager updates the advertisements for both primary and secondary sites. The advertisements are in the form of instruction files stored in the OFFERINF.BOX directory on each CAP in sites where the targeted clients are assigned.

 If the site did not receive a distribution package, the instruction files are not created for any of its clients. If the clients you are targeting for collection reside in multiple sites, you must distribute the software package to at least one distribution point for each of these sites; otherwise, not all targeted clients will receive the advertised software. You must distribute packages even if they contain no source files. For a detailed discussion on software distribution, see Chapter 8.

You must properly configure advertisements that are distributed to sites located in different time zones. By default, all advertisement time properties are configured in local time, which means that an advertisement scheduled in London with mandatory assignment for 11:00 A.M. is also scheduled for 11:00 A.M. in New York and Portland according to their local times. If you want to advertise the software to run exactly at the same time across the time zones, you should schedule it using Greenwich Mean Time (GMT). The advertisements are made available to clients according to the site server's time, and they run according to the client time; it is crucial to keep the time of all of your systems synchronized.

The most common software distribution problems are related to:

➤ Packages not being distributed to distribution points in sites with targeted clients

➤ The Advertised Programs Client Agent being configured to check for the availability of advertisements infrequently

➤ Advertisements being configured with the Offer After Time setting being configured to a future time.

➤ Collections not being set for automatic updates or being set for infrequent updates

➤ Users being added to new user groups and not receiving advertisements without logging off and on to the network (this action is necessary to update their user group membership)

➤ Program and batch files being incorrectly configured

You can use several files located on the site server and CAP(s) to examine the consistency of advertised programs, instruction files, and pointers to the distribution points. Table 10.3 lists these files and includes their locations and descriptions.

Remote Control

The Remote Tools Client Agent requires a little more maintenance than the other client agents. This is due to the advanced acceleration and compression features available for NT systems as well as granular security requirements.

Table 10.3 Files associated with software distribution.

File Name	File Location	File Description
*<sitecode>*000N.INS[1]	SMS\INBOXES\ OFFERINF.BOX CAP\OFFERINF.BOX	Instruction file that lists sets of advertisement IDs with the targeted collection IDs
*<sitecode>*000N.OFR	SMS\INBOXES\ OFFERINF.BOX CAP\OFFERINF.BOX	Offer file that includes information about the package ID, program, and collection
*<sitecode>*SYSTM.LKP	SMS\INBOXES\ OFFERINF.BOX CAP\OFFERINF.BOX	System lookup file that lists systems by globally unique identifier (GUID) and names of their instruction files
*<sitecode>*USER.LKP	SMS\INBOXES\ OFFERINF.BOX CAP\OFFERINF.BOX	User lookup file that lists NT users and the names of their instruction files
*<sitecode>*USRGRP.LKP	SMS\INBOXES\ OFFERINF.BOX CAP\OFFERINF.BOX	User group lookup file that lists NT user groups and names of their instruction files
*<sitecode>*000N.NAL	SMS\INBOXES\ PKGINFO.BOX CAP\PKGINFO.BOX	Network abstraction layer package file that lists all Universal Naming Convention (UNC) paths to pack ages stored on distribution points
*<sitecode>*000N.PKG	SMS\INBOXES\ PKGINFO.BOX CAP\PKGINFO.BOX	Package file that shows package and program properties
*<sitecode>*000N.ICO	SMS\INBOXES\ PKGINFO.BOX CAP\PKGINFO.BOX	Icon file that is associated with the package

[1]N stands for the consecutive hexadecimal integer.

Basic configuration of the Remote Tools Client Agent is updated on a 23-hour cycle and when users logon to the network. Two settings of the Remote Tools Client Agent are not always updated automatically: screen capture acceleration and remote capture data compression. These settings are correctly applied only during agent installation. If either of them is changed later on, the agent requires that you do one of the following:

➤ Uninstall and reinstall of the Remote Tools Client Agent

➤ Repair the installation

➤ Run Remote Control Hardware Munger (see Chapter 6 for details)

  The high compression level of remote capture data is available only if screen capture acceleration is enabled. For details on these two advanced remote control features, refer to the "Need To Know More?" section at the end of this chapter.

Help desk personnel and SMS administrators require a specific security configuration in order to remotely control client machines. These rights include:

➤ Presence in the Permitted Viewers list in the client agent's Properties dialog box (CCIM downloads this list, if modified, to each client)

➤ Rights to view and remote control the resource from the SMS Administrator console (see Chapter 3 for details)

➤ Administrative rights to the NT client machine

It is also important to make sure that both the controlling and the controlled machines run the same protocol and that the Remote Tools Client Agent listens to the requests using this protocol.

  The Remote Tools Client Agent can listen to the remote requests on only one network interface card (NIC). If a client has multiple NICs, you might want to configure the Remote Tools Client Agent to listen on the other NIC than the one initially set up. Refer to the "Need To Know More?" section later in this chapter for references regarding this setting.

The most common remote control problems are caused by:

➤ The lack of a common protocol between the controlling and the controlled machine

➤ The incorrect protocol being selected in the Remote Tools Client Agent Properties dialog box

➤ The lack of security rights

➤ The Remote Tools Client Agent listening on the wrong NIC (if multiple NICs are present)

➤ Multisite agent settings (the most restrictive are always used)

Software Metering

The SMS Software Metering feature is relatively complex due to a number of components and their large number of SMS Administrator console settings. By far, the most common problem you can encounter with software metering is incorrect configuration. Before attempting to troubleshoot software metering problems, make sure that:

➤ The software metering database is operational

➤ The software metering server or servers are set up and operational

➤ The Software Metering Client Agent is enabled, configured for either online or offline mode, and installed on the client computers

➤ SMS clients can connect to at least one software metering server

You should also make sure that your products and product suites are configured properly for metering and/or licensing. Verify that:

➤ The correct programs are in the Exclude list

➤ Programs that are to be monitored but not licensed are not configured for license enforcement

➤ Programs that are to be licensed are set with the correct number of licenses (make sure you understand the implications of disabling trend analysis, as described in Chapter 7)

➤ Programs that are licensed as standalone and as parts of application suites are licensed appropriately

Be aware of the time settings of the client agent and software metering components; these time settings allow you to control system resource utilization, but might introduce delays in functionality. For example, callback settings might delay application availability on a client, although the license has already been released.

SNMP Integration

When configuring the SNMP agent on your SMS NT clients (this agent is available only for NT clients), you need to remember a few things:

➤ SNMP and SNMP Trap NT services must be configured and started on client computers (if these networking services are installed after the NT service pack was applied, you have to reinstall the service pack)

➤ The Event To Trap Translator Client Agent must be enabled and started on client machines (it might take up to 23 hours for SMS to install this client)

➤ Each client must be configured with specific NT events to be translated to SNMP traps (see Chapter 6 for details)

SMS Site System Recovery

An SMS site consists of many components located on multiple servers and client machines. Some of the server components are self-restorable and can recover themselves from most failures. SMS can automatically restore CAPs, metering servers, and logon points. If distribution points fail, you need to reinitiate them from the SMS Administrator console; if the SMS SQL databases fail, you should restore them from backup.

SMS comes with its own backup tasks (described in Chapter 9). SMS does not have its own restore procedures; therefore, you need to understand how they should be performed and in what order. This section describes elements of an SMS site that require a complete restore procedure as well as explains the steps required for the site restore.

Restoring The SMS Site Server And SQL Databases

Once you have a functional SMS site, it is important to develop a plan for backing up and restoring your site servers and databases in case of a failure. The crucial elements of SMS sites and databases that are backed up and might need to be restored are listed in Table 10.4.

All of the SMS elements listed in Table 10.4 are automatically backed up by the Backup SMS Site Server task (discussed in Chapter 9). You should restore all of these SMS elements when performing SMS site recovery.

Table 10.4	Main SMS site components that require backup and restore.[1]
Site Element	**Description**
SMS directory	Is called SMS by default, but you can rename it during SMS setup; it's shared as SMS_<sitecode> and contains the main SMS files
SMS SQL database (also known as the SMS site database)	Stores SMS configuration information and client data
SMS SQL transaction log	Is used to support the SMS SQL database
Software metering SQL database	Stores metering data
Software metering SQL transaction log	Is used to support the metering SQL database
NAL Registry key	Is located under HKEY_LOCAL_MACHINE\ SOFTWARE\Microsoft\NAL; stores network abstraction layer information
SMS Registry key	Is located under HKEY_LOCAL_MACHINE\ SOFTWARE\Microsoft\SMS; stores some of the SMS component configuration data

[1]*Some components are not included (Crystal Info services, Network Monitor Control service, Web Based Enterprise Management (WBEM) or Windows Management Instrumentation (WMI), and so on).*

Preparing For A Restore

Before restoring the SMS site and/or databases, you should prepare the NT Server for the SMS site and optionally for the site and software metering databases if they are installed on remote NT machines.

You can restore the SMS site and site database servers on NT Servers with the following properties identical to those on the original site server:

➤ The platform (x86 or Alpha)

➤ The domain membership and domain role

➤ The NetBIOS name

Once the NT Server or Servers are ready for an SMS restore, you need to install a new SMS site with the same settings as those of the original one. These settings include:

➤ The service account names and permissions

➤ The sitecode

➤ Optional components

➤ The location of the SMS site database

➤ The location of the software metering database

➤ SQL 6.5 device names or the SQL 7 database name

➤ The location of SMS Provider

➤ The drive letter of the main SMS directory

Restoring The Site Server And SQL Databases

After a new site is installed, you should close all SMS applications and tools, stop all SMS services and the Windows Management service, and restore all backed up SMS elements. After the restore operation, but prior to restarting the site, you could run one or more of the following SQL commands to verify database integrity:

➤ **dbcc checkalloc** To check the allocation and use of all pages within a specified database (on SQL 6.5, you should use **dbcc newalloc**)

➤ **dbcc checkcatalog** To check the consistency among (and within) the system tables in the specified database

➤ **dbcc checkdb** To check the allocation and structural integrity of all objects in the specified database

➤ **dbcc checktable** To check the structural integrity of some objects in the specified database; not required if you use **dbcc checkdb**

You should also run the above **dbcc** commands prior to each backup.

After the restore procedure is completed, you should restart all involved systems and then verify their functionality. You might also need to run a site reset—one of the SMS setup options—to re-create accounts and connectivity among all site systems in your site. As a last step, you should verify the configuration of the site to make sure that there are no major differences between the site's state from before the failure and after the restore; these differences can be present if anything changed in the site configuration between the time of the last backup and the moment of site failure.

If you are to restore the SQL database(s) only, you should follow the same steps listed above, except for the ones related to the site restore. You need to close all SMS applications and tools, stop the SMS services and the Windows Management service, restore the site and/or software metering database, check the integrity of the restored database(s), and restart the site. You might also need to run a site reset to resynchronize the site with the restored database(s).

Practice Questions

Question 1

> You used Express setup to install a primary SMS site server on a backup
> domain controller (BDC) of a master domain that hosts 10,000 user accounts.
> Your domain spans 28 fast Internet Protocol (IP) segments, includes 2 other
> domain controllers, and authenticates over 8,000 users a day. Not long after
> SMS site installation, you noticed unusually high site server CPU utilization
> and excessive disk activity. What is the most likely cause of this behavior?
>
> ○ a. User Account Discovery
>
> ○ b. Windows Networking Logon Discovery
>
> ○ c. Network Discovery
>
> ○ d. Heartbeat Discovery

Answer a is correct. User Account Discovery and User Group Discovery are
the two types of discovery that might overwork the system. Answer b is incorrect because it uses logon scripts to gather data, and logon script modification
is not enabled by Express setup. Answer c is incorrect because Network Discovery is not enabled by default during Express setup. Answer d is incorrect
because Heartbeat Discovery works only after you have installed clients, and
you haven't installed clients yet.

Question 2

> You have initiated the installation of a secondary SMS site server using the
> Secondary Site Creation Wizard. Both Windows NT Servers (primary and second-
> ary) are member servers of the same domain and are on the same LAN. You
> used the same SMS Service account for the SMS services. After a day, you
> notice that the secondary site is not set up yet, although the primary site and all
> remote CAPs are running. What is the most likely cause of the problem?
>
> ○ a. The SMS Service account is not a member of the Domain Admins
>   global group.
>
> ○ b. The SMS Service account does not have Logon as a service
>   advanced user rights on the primary domain controller (PDC).
>
> ○ c. The SMS Service account does not have Logon as a service
>   advanced user rights on the secondary site server.
>
> ○ d. The Site System Connection account has an invalid password.

Answer c is correct. The question states that you use the same SMS Service domain account for the primary site server and the secondary site server; however, the account must have Logon on as a service advanced user rights on both computers. Another required step before secondary site installation is to grant those rights on the secondary site server (answer c). Answer a is incorrect because the primary site and its remote systems are operational on the domain. Answer b is incorrect because SMS does not require those rights on a PDC to function correctly. Answer d is incorrect because the Site System Connection account is not relevant for installation.

Question 3

On Monday morning, you enabled Network Discovery on your primary SMS site server and discovered over 500 Windows NT 4 Workstation machines that you purchased and configured last week. At the end of the day, you enabled the Windows NT Remote Client Installation method. The next day, you came early to work to check on the status of the SMS client installation. You noticed that almost 450 Client Configuration Requests (CCR files) were queued up in the \INBOXES\CCRRETRY.BOX directory. What is the most likely cause of the problem?

○ a. Most of the Windows NT 4 Workstations machines don't have Service Pack 4 (SP4) installed.

○ b. Most of the Windows NT 4 Workstations machines don't have large enough C: drives.

○ c. Most of the Windows NT 4 Workstations machines were off since the last evening.

○ d. Most of the Windows NT 4 Workstations machines were locked with users with no local Administrative privileges logged on.

Answer c is correct. You enabled Windows NT Remote Client Installation after business hours. When you came to work early the next morning, most NT machines were still turned off, so Client Configuration Manager (CCM) could not access them. Answers a and d are incorrect because they are not relevant and do not cause this problem. Answer b is possible if the client machines have fewer than 30MB of free disk space on the system drive; however, because all of the machines are new, this is unlikely (and the question does not state that C: drive is their system drive). Therefore, answer b is incorrect.

Question 4

> You have installed SMS 2 client software on all computers in your site. On Monday morning, you decided to enable hardware and software inventory. At the end of the day, you noticed that only 15 percent of all the computers reported inventory to the SMS site database. What is the most likely cause of the problem?
>
> ○ a. The Advertised Programs Client Agent is configured to check for available programs every 23 hours.
>
> ○ b. CCIM has not refreshed the SMS client configuration on all of the client machines.
>
> ○ c. The advertisement that includes hardware and software inventory did not yet arrive at all of the distribution points.
>
> ○ d. Inbox Manager has not yet refreshed all of the CAPs.

Answer b is correct. You should wait 23 hours before being concerned about hardware and software inventory not being reported to the SMS site database because CCIM has a 23-hour refresh cycle. Answer a is incorrect because checking for available programs is not related to hardware and software inventory. Answer c is incorrect because advertisements at distribution points do not have anything to do with inventory. Answer d is incorrect because some of the clients have reported inventory.

Question 5

> You have written a custom application that queries clients for a hardware component not reported by the inventory agent and that creates a NOIDMIF. You distributed the application to all clients and modified logon scripts to initiate it every time clients log on to the Windows NT domain. You notice that there is no NOIDMIF data in the SMS site database, but Inventory Data Loader is reporting successful MIF processing. You verified that your application runs, creates NOIDMIFs, and places them in the proper directory. What could be the cause of the problem?
>
> ○ a. Inventory Processor has stopped.
>
> ○ b. The Copy Queue thread on the clients is not operational.
>
> ○ c. NOIDMIF has an incorrect syntax.
>
> ○ d. Custom computer hardware should be reported in the form of an IDMIF.

Answer c is correct. Once you have verified that Inventory Data Loader is working properly and the NOIDMIFs are being created, the only remaining possibility is incorrect syntax in the NOIDMIF. Answer a is incorrect because it contradicts information you have in the question, which states that Inventory Data Loader is working properly. Answer b is incorrect because inventory data is passed to the site systems for processing, and therefore, the Copy Queue Manager components must be operational on client machines. Answer d is incorrect because a NOIDMIF (not an IDMIF) does allow you to report custom hardware component information for system architecture.

Question 6

You are in the process of rolling out SMS client software to machines in your site. You created a program and advertised it to the All Windows 98 Systems collection. Eve has noticed SMS client software being installed on her new Windows 98 computer and has asked you about the availability of an advertised program; it was not available in her Advertised Program Monitor even after she refreshed. What is the most likely reason why the program is not available on Eve's machine?

- O a. The hardware inventory collected on Eve's machines has not been processed yet.

- O b. CCIM running on Eve's machine has not refreshed the SMS client software configuration.

- O c. The All Windows 98 Systems collection has not been updated since Eve's machine was configured with the SMS client software.

- O d. The Advertised Software Client Agent is configured to check for available programs every 12 hours.

Answer c is correct. The most likely cause of the problem is that the Windows 98 Systems collection has not been updated since Eve's computer was installed. Answer a is incorrect because hardware inventory collection is not relevant to software distribution based on discovery data (the All Windows 98 Systems collection is based on discovery data). Answer b is incorrect because it is not relevant to software distribution. Answer d is incorrect because it is irrelevant; the question states that she already refreshed the Advertised Software Client Agent.

Question 7

> You just added Jeremy to the list of Permitted Viewers of the Remote Tools
> Client Agent. Jeremy reported that he cannot connect to four Windows NT
> client computers that he tried to control remotely; he is being denied access
> to these computers. What are the most likely causes of this behavior? [Choose
> all correct answers]
>
> ❑ a. Jeremy is not a member of the Domain Admins domain global
>   group.
>
> ❑ b. CCIM on the four Windows NT machines has not refreshed the client
>   configuration.
>
> ❑ c. Jeremy is not a member of the Administrators domain local group.
>
> ❑ d. Jeremy is not a member of the Administrators local group on any of
>   the four Windows NT machines.

Answers b and d are correct. Jeremy has to be a local workstation administrator
(answer d) and the machines must have information about him before he can
control them remotely. CCIM must refresh the client configuration for the
machines to have this information (answer b). Answer a is incorrect because
Jeremy does not have to be either a domain admin or a domain administrator
to be able to remote control these machines.

Question 8

> You have installed a primary SMS site server, created a software metering
> site server, enabled the Software Metering Client Agent, and configured some
> applications for licensing. A number of users reported that they have been
> denied the runtime of a specific application for over an hour and requested a
> callback, but nothing has happened since then. This application has 30 li-
> censes defined and only 20 are in use. What can you do?
>
> ○ a. Increase the callback-polling duration.
>
> ○ b. Increase the number of retries.
>
> ○ c. Decrease the delay before retrying.
>
> ○ d. Disable Enforce license limit for this product.

Answer a is correct. The problem is that the released licenses are not being
given to the users because their callback requests are not present on the metering server(s). If you increase the callback-polling duration, the request for the
application license remains in the wait queue longer; therefore, the request has

a better chance of receiving a released license. Answer b is incorrect because increasing the number of retries has no effect on licenses requested via callback. Answer c is incorrect because the delay before retrying also has no effect on licenses requested via callback. (Both settings—the number of retries and the delay before retrying—specify how many times and how often the metering agent should try to reconnect to the metering server before switching to offline mode.) Answer d is incorrect because if you disable license enforcement, you might violate your licensing agreements.

Question 9

> You want to monitor the creation of the advertisements and the process of placing them on all CAPs. What are the best tools to use to monitor both processes? [Choose all correct answers]
>
> ❑ a. Tracer
>
> ❑ b. SMS Trace
>
> ❑ c. Network Monitor
>
> ❑ d. Health Monitor

Answers a and b are correct. Only tracing tools can monitor both processes. Answer c is incorrect because Network Monitor could monitor the process of transferring advertisement instruction files to CAPs (if they are on the remote servers); however, it does not monitor the process of creating them. Answer d is incorrect because HealthMon does not monitor any SMS component processes.

Question 10

> You wanted to configure your Windows NT 4 Workstation (SP4) computers with an Event To Trap Translator Client Agent. You installed and configured the SNMP service, and then you enabled the Event To Trap Translator Client Agent. After two days, the agents are still reported as not running. What could be the cause of the problem?
>
> ○ a. CCIM on the clients has not refreshed their configuration.
>
> ○ b. You have not reinstalled SP4.
>
> ○ c. Clients have not configured their translator with the event filters.
>
> ○ d. You have not configured the client with the event filters.

Answer b is correct. You are required to reapply the service pack after SNMP is installed. Answer a is incorrect because it's been over two days since you enabled the agent, and the agent should be functional within 23 hours. Answers c and d are incorrect because the event filters are not required for the Event To Trap Translator Client Agent to run.

Question 11

A disk drive on a Windows NT component site server that hosts a CAP has crashed. What do you have to do after replacing the drive?

○ a. Re-create the Windows NT site system in the SMS Administrator console.

○ b. Create the CAP share manually and copy its content from a different CAP of the same site.

○ c. Create the CAP share manually and copy its content from the SMS installation CD-ROM.

○ d. Nothing.

Answer d is correct. Inbox Manager updates CAPs on an hourly schedule. It re-creates the share and copies all necessary files. Answer a is incorrect because you do not need to create the site system in the SMS Administrator console to restore a CAP. Answer b is incorrect because SMS performs these functions automatically. Answer c is incorrect because this solution is not even possible.

Question 12

Your firm has merged with another large company. At the meeting of IT personnel, it was decided that your primary SMS site will be attached to the central SMS site (sitecode IRL) located in New York. The sites will be communicating over the new Asynchronous Transfer Mode (ATM) switched network. You created the Standard Sender address and configured it with the central site's sitecode (IRL), server name, and authentication data. You then set IRL as your parent site. Two days later, you received an email from the administrator of IRL asking whether you had attached your site to his; your site is still not visible in IRL's SMS Administrator console. Both servers can ping each other using IP addresses and names registered in the Doman Name Service (DNS) database. What are the possible causes of the problem? [Choose all correct answers]

❑ a. The central SMS site does not have an address to your site.

❑ b. The NetBIOS to IP resolution is not available between the two sites.

❑ c. A firewall has to be configured specifically for SMS site-to-site communication.

❑ d. You have incorrectly entered the name of the IRL site server in the Standard Sender Address Properties dialog box.

Answers b and d are correct. The servers can ping using IP and DNS, but they might not be able to resolve NetBIOS names—pinging using NetBIOS names was not tried. You created the address with the right sitecode, but the server name and the authentication information could be incorrect. Answer a is incorrect because the address from the central site to the child site is not required to transfer site information up the hierarchy. Answer c is incorrect because a firewall does not have to be configured specifically for SMS to function.

Need To Know More?

 Microsoft Corporation. *Microsoft Systems Management Server Administrator's Guide, version 2.0.* Microsoft Corporation, Redmond, WA, 1999. The entire guide is an excellent resource for troubleshooting SMS site systems and clients. Chapter 18 describes the steps required to perform a backup and restore of an SMS site server and its databases. In addition, Appendix D illustrates most of the SMS system processes.

 Microsoft Press. *Microsoft Systems Management Server Resource Guide.* Microsoft Press, Redmond, WA, 1999. ISBN 0-7356-0583-1. This is one volume of the *Microsoft BackOffice 4.5 Resource Kit.* Chapter 9 discusses the various Remote Tools Client Agent settings, including the advanced ones.

 Microsoft Press. *Microsoft Windows NT Workstation Resource Kit.* Microsoft Press, Redmond, WA, 1996. ISBN 1-57231-343-9. The entire book is a great source of information about Windows NT, its architecture, security, and networking. Chapters 23 and 24 are excellent references to learn about Registry backup, restore, and manual editing.

 Microsoft Press. *Microsoft SQL Server 7.0 System Administration Training Kit.* Microsoft Press, Redmond, WA, 1999. ISBN 1-57231-827-9. This hands-on training manual is a great source of information about SQL 7. Chapters 8, 9, and 10 have valuable information about the backup and restore techniques of SQL 7 databases, including new differential backup. In addition, Chapter 14 walks you through the SQL monitoring procedures, including the **dbcc** statements.

 Solomon, David W., Ray Rankins, and David S. Solomon. *Microsoft SQL Server 6.5 Unleashed, Second Edition.* Sams Publishing, Indianapolis, IN, 1996. ISBN 0-672-30956-4. Chapter 30 has some valuable information about backing up and restoring SQL databases. Chapter 29 explains SQL 6.5 **dbcc** statements.

 www.microsoft.com/smsmgmt/ is the Microsoft Systems Management Server Web page. This Web site contains the latest information about SMS 2, including supported operating systems, upgrade and interoperability information, white papers, and deployment case studies.

Infrastructure
And Tracing

. . . .

Terms you'll need to understand:

√ SMS services

√ SMS Executive threads

√ SMS client processes

√ SMS client threads

√ Logging

√ Tracing

Techniques you'll need to master:

√ Identifying SMS services and SMS Executive threads

√ Delineating SMS support tools from core services and threads

√ Recognizing SMS client processes and threads

√ Enabling tracing of SMS server activities

√ Knowing which SMS server components report their events to which log files

√ Knowing which activities are reported to each client log file

SMS is a complex client/server system that is composed of many components: services, processes, and threads that run on SMS site systems and SMS client computers. Each SMS feature uses specific services, processes, and threads to accomplish tasks. SMS also includes a tracing (or logging) feature that allows you to trace specific activities for troubleshooting purposes. This chapter summarizes the functions of the SMS components and lists all of the log files that report SMS activities. A Windows Management Instrumentation (WMI) component description is not included in this chapter. WMI, which is Microsoft's implementation of Web-Based Enterprise Management (WBEM), is an important part of the SMS infrastructure, but its processes and logging capabilities are beyond the scope of this book. This chapter discusses the 32-bit components and log files, but does not discuss 16-bit SMS client components and log files.

SMS Infrastructure

To fully understand SMS functionality and to prepare yourself for the SMS 2 exam, you need to be familiar with SMS server and client components and the functions they perform. Many of these components are created during SMS server or client installation and are continuously active. Some work based on a fixed or configurable schedule; others are installed only if you select optional SMS components during installation or after you enable specific client agents. The next two sections list the server and client components, describe their location and functionality, and specify if they run on a schedule or non-stop.

Server Services And Threads

Most of the SMS processes run as Windows NT services on SMS primary and secondary site servers and other site systems. The SMS Executive service is the main SMS worker process that runs as an NT Service. This process has many threads, each responsible for different SMS functionality. Other SMS services are necessary for SMS to function, but they perform supporting roles to the SMS Executive service. Table 11.1 lists all of the Windows NT SMS Services.

A process is an address space and a set of control information required for the execution of a set of threads. We usually refer to a program or an application as a process, but a program or an application is usually composed of multiple processes that are composed of one or multiple threads. Some SMS processes are configured to run as Windows NT services.

The SMS Administrator console is installed on each primary site server by default, so services, threads, and processes specified as running on the SMS Administrator console machine can also run on primary SMS servers.

Table 11.1   SMS Services.

Service Name	Location	Description
Info Agent	SMS site server[1]	Retrieves data to create reports
Info Aps	SMS site server[1]	Manages all Crystal components and scheduling
Info Sentinel	SMS Administrator console computer[1]	Manages communication between the SMS Administrator console with the Crystal snap-in and Crystal services running on the SMS site server
Monitor Control Service	SMS Administrator console computer	Runs real-time Network Monitor monitors
NT Logon Discovery Agent	Logon point	Moves logon discovery DDRs to all sites with logon discovery enumerating each logon point's NT domain
SMS Executive	SMS site server, CAP, SMS Sender Server	Main SMS component; performs most of the SMS operations distributed into multiple functionality threads
SMS License Server	Software metering server	Services SMS client registrations of metered and licensed applications; this service manages application usage (grants and denies use) and stores usage data in the local cache
SMS Site Component Manager	SMS site server	Monitors and manages functionality of all other SMS services, including the SMS Executive threads
SMS SQL Monitor	SMS SQL Server	Monitors and maintains SMS-related SQL operations; notifies SMS components about configuration changes and scheduled actions

[1]*Primary SMS site server only.*

SMS Executive threads are components that run underneath the SMS Executive service. If the SMS Executive service isn't running, none of these threads is running. Table 11.2 lists all threads of the SMS Executive NT service.

Some additional supporting SMS processes run only on site systems or the SMS Administrator console computer. When the site server performs any or all of the site system roles, they run on the site server. When a role is assigned to another computer in the site, these processes run on the assigned site system, as described in Table 11.3. These SMS processes run only when started by the user or an SMS Service (Crystal agent only).

Table 11.2 SMS Executive threads.

Thread Name	Location	Startup Type	Description
Asynchronous RAS	SMS sender server	Automatic	Manages communication between sites using asynchronous Remote Access Server (RAS) connectivity
Client Configuration Manager	SMS site server	Automatic	Initiates SMS client software installation on receiving a Client Configuration Request (CCR file) from Discovery Data Manager (DDM) or an NT client without Administrative privileges
Client Installation Data Manager	SMS site server	Automatic	Manages all client installation files on the SMS site server
Collection Evaluator	SMS site server	Automatic	Reevaluates collections on a predefined schedule
SMS Component Status Summarizer	SMS site server	Automatic	Summarizes the status of each component within an SMS site
Courier Sender Confirmation	SMS site server	Automatic	Monitors confirmation messages sent from the subsite(s) when courier packages arrive
Despooler	SMS site server	Automatic	Decompresses files received from parent and child sites and passes them to the appropriate component's inboxes
Discovery Data Manager	SMS site server	Automatic	Processes DDR files, manages site boundaries, creates CCR files, and passes them to the Client Configuration Manager's inbox; generates a discovery dump when attached to a new parent site

(continued)

Table 11.2   SMS Executive threads (continued).

Thread Name	Location	Startup Type	Description
Distribution Manager	SMS site server	Automatic	Manages package distribution within the site and compresses packages to be sent to subsites
Hierarchy Manager	SMS site server	Automatic	Retrieves changes to the site control file from the SMS site database and passes them to Site Control Manager for processing; updates the database image of the site control file; pre-epares compressed SMS installation source files for the secondary site
Inbox Manager	SMS site server	Automatic	Synchronizes all CAPs within a site; downloads client files from CAPs located on NetWare servers; installs some remote site systems
Inbox Manager Assistant	CAP	Automatic	Moves files from CAP inboxes to the appropri-ate component inboxes on the SMS site server
Inventory Data Loader	SMS site server[1]	Automatic	Parses hardware inventory files and uploads their data to the SMS site database; generates an inventory dump when attached to a new parent site
Inventory Processor	SMS site server	Automatic	Calculates delta information of hard-ware inventory collected on 16-bit client ma-chines; adds a binary header to 32-bit client hardware inventory

(continued)

Table 11.2   SMS Executive threads (continued).

Thread Name	Location	Startup Type	Description
ISDN RAS Sender	SMS sender server	Automatic	Manages communication between sites using the existing ISDN RAS connectivity
LAN Sender	SMS sender server	Automatic	Manages communication between sites using the existing local area network (LAN) or wide area network (WAN) circuits
License Metering	SMS site server	Automatic	Manages application licenses at a site and replicates them between the sites
License Server Manager	SMS site server	Automatic	Installs, deinstalls, and monitors the status of metering server(s)
NDS Logon Discovery Manager	SMS site server	Automatic	Manages NetWare Novell Directory Services (NDS) Logon Discovery settings
NDS Logon Installation Manager	SMS site server	Automatic	Manages NetWare NDS Client Logon Installation settings
NDS Logon Server Manager	SMS site server	Automatic	Synchronizes all NetWare NDS servers with NDS Logon Client Installation and Discovery files; modifies NDS container logon scripts
NetWare Bindery Logon Discovery Manager	SMS site server	Automatic	Manages NetWar Bindery Logon Discovery settings
NetWare Bindery Logon Installation Manager	SMS site server	Automatic	Manages NetWare Bindery Logon Client Installation settings

(continued)

Table 11.2   SMS Executive threads (continued).

Thread Name	Location	Startup Type	Description
NetWare Bindery Logon Server Manager	SMS site server	Automatic	Synchronizes all Net-Ware Bindery servers with NetWare Bindery logon installation and discovery files; modifies bindery logon scripts
NetWare Bindery Server Discovery Agent	SMS site server	Scheduled	Creates DDR files for NetWare Bindery site systems
Network Discovery	SMS site server	Scheduled	Creates DDR files based on the collected information from the network scan
NT Logon Discovery Manager	SMS site server	Automatic	Manages the Windows Logon Discovery method settings
NT Logon Installation Manager	SMS site server	Automatic	Manages Windows Logon Client Installation method settings
NT Logon Server Manager	SMS site server	Automatic	Synchronizes all domain controllers in domains enumerated by the Windows logon discovery and logon installation methods; modifies NT domain logon scripts and user profiles
NT User Discovery Agent	SMS site server	Scheduled	Creates user DDR files by querying the Security Accounts Manager (SAM) database of primary domain controllers (PDCs)
NT User Group Discovery Agent	SMS site server	Scheduled	Creates user group discovery records (DDR files) by querying the SAM database of PDCs

(continued)

Table 11.2 SMS Executive threads (continued).

Thread Name	Location	Startup Type	Description
Offer Manager (Advertisement Manager)	SMS site server	Automatic	Creates software distribution instruction files based on advertised software and result sets of targeted collections
Offer Status Summarizer (Advertisement Status Summarizer)	SMS site server	Automatic	Summarizes the status of software distribution
Replication Manager	SMS site server	Automatic	Collects and manages files queued for sending to and from parent and child sites
Scheduler	SMS site server	Automatic	Compresses files stored in Replication Manager inboxes and schedules them to be sent to their destinations; routes inter-site packages between sites
Site Control Manager	SMS site server	Automatic	Processes changes to the site control file; creates heartbeat site control files and passes them to the Replication Manager for transfer to the parent site
Site System Status Summarizer	SMS site server	Automatic	Summarizes the status of the site systems in the SMS site
SNA RAS Sender	SMS sender server	Automatic	Manages communication between sites using RAS over Systems Network Architecture (SNA) connectivity
Software Inventory Processor	SMS site server[1]	Automatic	Processes software inventory files
Status Manager	SMS site server	Automatic	Processes status messages

(continued)

Table 11.2   SMS Executive threads (continued).

Thread Name	Location	Startup Type	Description
Windows NT Server Discovery Agent	SMS site server	Scheduled	Creates DDRs for Windows NT SMS site systems
X.25 RAS Sender	SMS sender server	Automatic	Manages communication between sites using X.25 RAS connectivity

[1]Primary SMS site server only.

Table 11.3   Additional SMS processes.

Process Name	Location	Description
Reports Agent	SMS site server[1]	Used to create reports when scheduled from the SMS Administrator console
Info Report Designer	SMS Administrator console machine	Used to design new reports and modify existing ones; launched from the SMS Administrator console
Courier Sender Manager	SMS Administrator console machine	Used to create and receive Courier Sender packages when a package is scheduled for distribution
Remote Tools console	SMS Administrator console machine	Used for remote control of client machines; launched from the SMS Administrator console
Software Metering console	SMS Administrator console machine	Used to manage metered and licensed applications; launched from the SMS Administrator console
SMS Service Manager	SMS Administrator console machine	Used to view SMS services and threads; launched from the SMS Administrator console
Network Monitor	SMS Administrator console machine	Used to monitor and analyze network traffic; launched from the SMS Administrator console or from the Start|Programs menu

(continued)

Table 11.3	Additional SMS processes (continued).	
Process Name	**Location**	**Description**
Network Monitor Control Tool	SMS Administrator console machine	Used to configure and start real-time time monitors; launched from the SMS Administrator console or from the Start|Programs menu
SMS Setup	SMS Administrator console machine	Used to modify SMS installation; launched from the Start|Programs menu
Event To Trap Translator	SMS Administrator console machine	Used to configure NT events to be translated to Simple Network Management Protocol (SNMP) traps; launched from the Action menu of any Windows NT client object in the SMS Administrator console

[1]Primary SMS site server only.

Client Processes

SMS client components run in different forms on different operating system machines. On all 32-bit operating system machines, the client software runs as:

➤ NT services (NT clients only)

➤ Processes

➤ Control Panel applets

All SMS client components run on client machines and are not launched over the network. Table 11.4 lists all of the processes and threads that run on 32-bit SMS client machines and summarizes their functionality and usage.

Table 11.4	SMS client components that run on 32-bit operating system machines.	
SMS Client Component Name	**Startup Type**	**Description**
Client Configuration Installation Manager	Scheduled	Synchronizes SMS client files and configuration by connecting to a CAP every 23 hours or on restart/ logon; a thread of SMS Client Service

(continued)

Table 11.4   SMS client components that run on 32-bit operating system machines (continued).

SMS Client Component Name	Startup Type	Description
Available Programs Manager	Automatic	Manages advertisements and agent installation; schedules them, starts them, and reports their success or failure
Advertised Programs Monitor	Automatic	Used to view advertised programs; is started by SMS Application Launcher
Advertised Programs Wizard	Manual	Is a separate application used to run advertised software
Copy Queue	Automatic	Copies client data to CAP(s); is a thread of SMS Client Service
Hardware Inventory Agent	Scheduled	Is used to collect hardware inventory by querying the Common Information Model (CIM) database
License Metering Client	Automatic	Is a separate process that watches started processes, passes captured information to the metering server, and grants or denies application runtime
NT Event To SNMP Trap	Automatic	Converts Windows NT Translator Agent events, based on the file rules, to SNMP traps
SMS Application Launcher	Automatic	Is used to start the user context and scheduled SMS client components; starts them on a schedule, restarts them if they fail, and so on
SMS Client Service	Automatic	Is the main SMS multithreaded client process; runs as a service on Windows NT computers
SMS Remote Control Agent	Automatic	Listens for the remote control session signals and manages the client side of the session; runs as a service on Windows NT and as a pseudo-service on Windows 9X computers

(continued)

Table 11.4 SMS client components that run on 32-bit operating system machines (continued).

SMS Client Component Name	Startup Type	Description
Software Inventory Agent	Scheduled	Used to collect software inventory
Systems Offer Data Provider	Scheduled	Used to retrieve software distribution information targeted for SMS systems
User Groups Offer Data Provider	Scheduled	Used to retrieve software distribution information targeting NT user groups
Users Offer Data Provider	Scheduled	Used to retrieve software distribution information targeting NT users

SMS Tracing

Almost every component that runs on an SMS site system or an SMS client can report its activities to ASCII files called *logs* or *traces*. The following section describes SMS server and client tracing defaults and the information reported to each log.

Server Log Files

By default, most of the SMS server logs are disabled. You can enable and disable SMS tracing—reporting to the log files—from SMS Service Manager, shown in Figure 11.1. You can enable tracing by component, or you can have multiple components report their activities to a single log file. To report their activities to one log file, enable the Use Same File For All Selected Components option in the SMS Service Manager (shown in Figure 11.1).

You can control multiple SMS sites and modify all of their tracing activities from a single SMS Service Manager. The log files that are generated by different SMS site system components are listed in Table 11.5.

Client Log Files

Client log files report SMS processing that occurs on each SMS client computer. All SMS client logs are enabled by default and they are stored in the %*WINDIR*%\MS\SMS\LOGS directory on each SMS client machine. Table 11.6 lists most of the 32-bit SMS client log files.

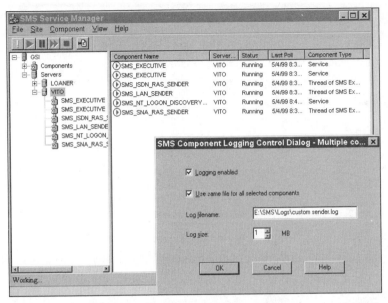

Figure 11.1 Enabling tracing of multiple components to a single log file.

Table 11.5	SMS site systems logs.
Log File Name	**Component That Logs To The File**
CCM.LOG	Client Configuration Manager
CIDM.LOG	Client Installation Data Manager
COLLEVAL.LOG	Collection Evaluator
COMPSUMM.LOG	Component Status Summarizer
COURSEND.LOG	Courier Sender Manager
CSCNFSVC.LOG	Courier Sender Confirmation
DATALDR.LOG	Inventory Data Loader
DDM.LOG	Discovery Data Manager (DDM)
DESPOOL.LOG	Despooler
DISTMGR.LOG	Distribution Manager
HMAN.LOG	Hierarchy Manager
INBOXAST.LOG	Inbox Manager Assistant
INBOXMGR.LOG	Inbox Manager
INVPROC.LOG	Inventory Processor
LICSRVC.LOG	License Metering
CONLICSVCFG.LOG	License Server Manager

(continued)

Table 11.5 SMS site systems logs (continued).

Log File Name	Component That Logs To The File
ND_LOGON.LOG	NDS Logon Server Manager
NDLGDSCM.LOG	NDS Logon Discovery Manager
NDLGINST.LOG	NDS Logon Installation Manager
NETDISC.LOG	Network Discovery
NT_LOGON.LOG	NT Logon Server Manager
NTLGDSCA.LOG	NT Logon Discovery Agent
NTLGDSCM.LOG	NT Logon Discovery Manager
NTLGINST.LOG	NT Logon Installation Manager
NTSVRDIS.LOG	Windows NT Server Discovery Agent
NTUG_DIS.LOG	NT User Discovery Agent
NTUSRDIS.LOG	NT User Group Discovery Agent
NW_LOGON.LOG	NetWare Bindery Logon Server Manager
NWLGDSCM.LOG	NetWare Bindery Logon Discovery Manager
NWLGINST.LOG	NetWare Bindery Logon Installation Manager
NWSVRDIS.LOG	NetWare Bindery Server Discovery Agent
OFFERMGR.LOG	Offer Manager (Advertisement Manager)
OFFERSUM.LOG	Offer Status Summarizer (Advertisement Status Summarizer)
REPLMGR.LOG	Replication Manager
SCHED.LOG	Scheduler
SENDER.LOG	LAN Sender, Asynchronous RAS Sender, ISDN RAS Sender, SNA RAS Sender, X.25 RAS Sender
SINVPROC.LOG	Software Inventory Processor
SITECOMP.LOG	SMS Site Component Manager
SITECTRL.LOG	Site Control Manager
SITESTAT.LOG	Site System Status Summarizer
SMSDBMON.LOG	SMS SQL Monitor
SMSEXEC.LOG	SMS Executive
SMSPROV.LOG	SMS Provider
SRVACCT.LOG	Setup or any component that modifies the NT account database
STATMGR.LOG	Status Manager

Table 11.6   SMS client logs.

Log File Name	Description
APASETUP.LOG	Reports on Available Programs Manager installation
CCIM32.LOG	Reports the activities associated with client configuration synchronization
CLICORE.LOG	Reports on the installation of core SMS client components
CLINST.LOG	Reports on the installation of the License Metering Client Agent
CLISVC.LOG (CLISVC95.LOG)	Reports on the state of all SMS components
CQMGR32.LOG	Logs communication with CAP events
HINV32.LOG	Reports the Hardware Inventory Agent's activities
INHINV32.LOG	Reports the progress of Hardware Inventory Agent installation
LAUNCH32.LOG[1]	Reports on the state of schedules and the user context SMS components
LICCLI.LOG (LICCLI95.LOG)	Reports the license metering agent's activities
ODPSYS32.LOG	Reports the activities of the Systems Offer Data Provider
ODPUSR32.LOG (ODPUSR9X.LOG)	Reports the activities of the Users Offer Data Provider
ODPWNT32.LOG (ODPWNT9X.LOG)	Reports the activities of the User Groups Offer Data Provider
PEA32.LOG[1]	Reports advertised programs execution in the user context
REMCTRL.LOG	Reports Remote Tools Client Agent installation
SINV32.LOG	Reports the Software Inventory Agent's activities
SMSAPM32.Log	Reports the activities associated with scheduling and running of distributed software; reports advertised software execution in the administrative context
SMSCLI.LOG	Reports the activities of Advertised Programs Control Panel applet

(continued)

Table 11.6   SMS client logs (continued).

Log File Name	Description
SMSCLREG.LOG	Reports Registry cleanup during the component uninstall process
SMSMON32.LOG	Reports the activities of the Advertised Programs Monitor
SMSWIZ32.LOG	Reports the activities associated with advertised software runtime initiated by a user
STSINSTL.LOG	Reports on the installation of the NT Event To SNMP Trap Translator Agent
SWDIST.LOG	Reports on the installation of the Available Programs Manager, Available Programs Monitor, and all Offer Data Providers
WN_LOGON.LOG	Reports the progress of logon client installation
WNMANUAL.LOG	Reports the progress of manual client installation
WNREMOTE.LOG[1]	Reports the progress of remote client installation

[1]Windows NT only.

Practice Questions

Question 1

You have enabled Network Discovery and scheduled it to run between 1:00
A.M. and 5:00 A.M. on Saturday. When you arrived at work on Monday, you
noticed that almost no clients were discovered on your 5,000-user Internet
Protocol (IP) network. Which logs should you view to find out what went wrong?
[Choose all correct answers]

❏ a. DESPOOL.LOG

❏ b. DDM.LOG

❏ c. NT_LOGON.LOG

❏ d. NETDISC.LOG

Answers b and d are correct. DDM and Network Discovery are the only two
SMS Executive threads that are involved in Network Discovery; therefore, you
should check their log files. DDM.LOG contains information that lets you
determine whether DDM failed to process the DDRs that Network Discovery created. NETDISC.LOG contains information about the operation of
Network Discovery. Answer a is incorrect because DESPOOL.LOG contains
information about the operation of DESPOOLER, which is not involved in
Network Discovery. Answer c is incorrect because NT_LOGON.LOG contains information about NT Logon Server Manager, which also is not used in
Network Discovery.

Question 2

You have created a new SMS site system and configured it to be a software
metering server. Which log file can you check to verify proper installation
of the metering services on that server?

○ a. LICSRVC.LOG

○ b. REMODBC.LOG

○ c. LICCLI.LOG

○ d. LICSVCFG.LOG

Answer d is correct. LICSVCFG.LOG reports activities of the License Server
Manager, the thread that reports events related to metering server installation.

Answer a is incorrect because LICSRVC.LOG reports the actions related to license management. Answer b is incorrect because REMODBC.LOG can be enabled on the metering server itself to monitor metering server operations. Answer c is incorrect because it records the activities of the License Metering Client Agent on the client computer.

Question 3

> Which client log will you view to verify that a client has connectivity with the CAP?
>
> ○ a. CLISVC.LOG
>
> ○ b. CQMGR32.LOG
>
> ○ c. SMSAPM32.LOG
>
> ○ d. SMSCLI.LOG

Answer b is correct. Copy Queue (a thread of the SMS Executive service) connects to the CAP and uploads and downloads the files. CQMGR32.LOG reports the activities of Copy Queue. Answer a is incorrect because CLISVC.LOG reports on the state (on or off) of SMS components running on client computers. Answer c is incorrect because SMSAPM32.LOG reports software distribution activities on clients. Answer d is incorrect because SMSCLI.LOG reports activities of the Advertised Programs Control Panel applet on clients.

Question 4

> You want to monitor processor utilization of the Hardware Inventory Client Agent on your Windows NT 4 Workstation machine. Which object should you add to the Performance Monitor log? [Choose all correct answers]
>
> ❏ a. Process
>
> ❏ b. Processor
>
> ❏ c. Thread
>
> ❏ d. System

Answers a and c are correct. Because the Hardware Inventory Client Agent is a separate process that performs only hardware inventory activities, you can log either process or thread CPU utilization. If the Hardware Inventory Client

Agent was a thread of a multithreaded process performing other functions, you would not obtain the required results from the process object. Answers b and d are incorrect because they allow only for monitoring of processor utilization due to all processes running on the client machine.

Question 5

You want to monitor memory and processor utilization caused by the creation of advertisement instruction files. Which Performance Monitor objects should you log to file? [Choose all correct answers]

❏ a. Thread

❏ b. Process

❏ c. System

❏ d. Cache

Answers a and b are correct. Offer Manager creates instruction files, and it is a thread of SMS Executive service. Therefore, you need to log both thread and process. You need to log the thread object for %CPU utilization. The thread object does not show memory utilization, so you also need to log the process object to see how much memory the SMS Executive service used at the same time the Offer Manager thread was active. Answer c is incorrect because it doesn't allow for the measurement of memory utilization. It does allow you to measure CPU utilization caused by all processes on the system. Answer d is incorrect because it does not provide figures for either memory or processor utilization, and it cannot monitor processes and threads..

Need To Know More?

 Microsoft Corporation. *Microsoft Systems Management Server Administrator's Guide, version 2.0.* Microsoft Corporation, Redmond, WA, 1999. Appendix C provides more information on the various SMS components that run on both servers and clients. Appendix D will help you match the processes, threads, and log files.

 Microsoft Corporation. *Systems Management Server 2.0 Resource Guide, Microsoft BackOffice Resource Kit.* Microsoft Corporation, Redmond, WA, 1999. Microsoft Corporation. ISBN 0-7356-0583-1. Part 8 contains many references to SMS processes, services, threads, and log files.

 Solomon, David A. *Inside Windows NT (Microsoft Programming Series), Second Edition.* Microsoft Press, Redmond, WA, 1998. ISBN 1-57231-677-2. Chapter 4 has a detailed explanation of NT processes and threads, including a discussion about performance counters and monitoring tools. This is probably the best book that explains Windows NT architecture, performance, and advanced debugging and troubleshooting techniques. It's a must-have book for anyone who works with Windows NT at a low programming and system architecture level.

 www.microsoft.com/smsmgmt/ is the Microsoft Systems Management Server Web page. This Web site contains the latest information about SMS 2, including supported operating systems, upgrade and interoperability information, white papers, and deployment case studies.

Sample Test

In this chapter, we provide pointers to help you develop a successful test-taking strategy, including how to choose proper answers,
how to decode ambiguity, how to work within the Microsoft testing
framework, how to decide what you need to memorize, and how to
prepare for the test. At the end of the chapter, we include 52
questions on subject matter pertinent to Microsoft Exam 70-086,
"Implementing and Supporting Microsoft Systems Management
Server 2.0" Good luck!

Questions, Questions, Questions

There should be no doubt in your mind that you are facing a test full of specific and pointed questions. If the version of the SMS 2 exam that you take is fixed-length, it will include 52 questions, and you will be allotted 90 minutes to complete the exam. You will receive a passing score if you answer at least 66 percent of the answers correctly. If it's an adaptive test (the software should tell you this as you begin the exam), it will consist of somewhere between 25 and 35 questions (on average) and take somewhere between 30 and 60 minutes.

Whichever type of test you take, for this exam, questions belong to one of five basic types:

➤ Multiple choice with a single answer

➤ Multiple choice with multiple answers

➤ Multipart with a single answer

➤ Multipart with multiple answers

➤ Questions that require you to analyze the SMS configuration shown in a figure

Always take the time to read a question at least twice before selecting an answer and look for an Exhibit button. Exhibits include graphics information related to a question. An *exhibit* is usually an SMS hierarchy or network diagram that you must examine to analyze the question's contents and formulate an answer. The Exhibit button brings up graphics and charts used to help explain a question, provide additional data, or illustrate hierarchy layout or program behavior. Always carefully examine the exhibit as you study each question.

Not every question has only one answer; many questions require multiple answers. Therefore, you should read each question carefully, determine how many answers are necessary or possible, and look for additional hints or instructions when selecting answers. Such instructions often occur in brackets, immediately following the question itself (multiple-answer questions).

Picking Proper Answers

Obviously, the only way to pass any exam is to select enough of the right answers to obtain a passing score. However, Microsoft's exams are not standardized like the SAT and GRE exams; they are far more sophisticated and ambiguous. In some cases, questions are strangely worded, and deciphering them can be a real challenge. In those cases, you may need to rely on answer-elimination skills. Almost always, at least one answer out of the possible choices for a question can be eliminated immediately because it matches one of these conditions:

➤ The answer does not apply to the situation.

➤ The answer may be eliminated because of information in the question itself.

After you eliminate all answers that are obviously wrong, you can apply your retained knowledge to eliminate further answers. Look for items that sound correct but refer to actions, commands, or features that are not present or not required in the situation that the question describes.

If you're still faced with a blind guess among two or more potentially correct answers, reread the question. Try to picture how each of the possible remaining answers would alter the situation. Be especially sensitive to terminology; sometimes the choice of words ("remove" instead of "disable") can make the difference between a right answer and a wrong one.

Only when you've exhausted your ability to eliminate answers but remain unclear about which of the remaining possibilities is correct should you guess at an answer. An unanswered question offers you no points, but guessing gives you at least some chance of getting a question right; just don't be too hasty when making a blind guess.

 If you're taking a fixed-length exam, you can wait until the last round of reviewing marked questions (just as you're about to run out of time or out of unanswered questions) before you start making guesses. If you're taking an adaptive test, you can't mark the questions to return to them later. That means you'll have to guess before moving on, if you don't know the answer. Either way, guessing should be a last resort.

Decoding Ambiguity

Microsoft exams have a reputation for including questions that can be difficult to interpret, confusing, or ambiguous. In our experience with numerous exams, we consider this reputation to be completely justified. The Microsoft exams are tough, and they're deliberately made that way.

The only way to beat Microsoft at its own game is to be prepared. You'll discover that many exam questions test your knowledge of things that are not directly related to the issue raised by a question. This means that the answers you must choose from, even incorrect ones, are just as much a part of the skill assessment as the question itself. If you don't know something about many aspects of SMS 2, you may not be able to eliminate obviously wrong answers because they relate to a different area of SMS 2 than the one that's addressed by the question at hand. In other words, the more you know about the software, the easier it will be for you to tell right from wrong.

Questions often give away their answers, but you have to be Sherlock Holmes to see the clues. Often, subtle hints appear in the question text in such a way that they seem almost irrelevant to the situation. You must realize that each question is a test unto itself and that you need to inspect and successfully navigate each question to pass the exam. Look for small clues, such as the mention of sitecodes, site types, security permissions and names, and configuration settings. Little things such as these can point to the right answer if properly understood; if missed, they can leave you facing a blind guess.

Another common difficulty with certification exams is vocabulary. Microsoft has an uncanny knack for naming some utilities and features entirely obviously in some cases and completely inanely in other instances. Be sure to brush up on the key terms presented at the beginning of each chapter. You may also want to read through the glossary at the end of this book the day before you take the test.

Working Within The Framework

The test questions appear in random order, and many elements or issues that receive mention in one question may also crop up in other questions. It's not uncommon to find that an incorrect answer to one question is the correct answer to another question, or vice versa. Take the time to read every answer to each question, even if you recognize the correct answer to a question immediately. That extra reading may spark a memory—or remind you about an SMS feature or function—that helps you on another question elsewhere in the exam.

If you're taking a fixed-length test, you can revisit any question as many times as you like. If you're uncertain of the answer to a question, check the box that's provided to mark it for easy return later on. You should also mark questions you think may offer information that you can use to answer other questions. On the fixed-length tests we've taken, we usually mark somewhere between 25 and 50 percent of the questions. The testing software is designed to let you mark every question if you choose; use this framework to your advantage. Everything you'll want to see again should be marked; the testing software can then help you return to marked questions quickly and easily.

For fixed-length tests, we strongly recommend that you first read through the entire test quickly, before getting caught up in answering individual questions. This will help to jog your memory as you review the potential answers and can help identify questions that you want to mark for easy access to their contents. It will also let you identify and mark the tricky questions for easy return. The key is to make a quick pass over the territory to begin with—so that you know what you're up against—and then to survey that territory more thoroughly on a second pass, when you can begin to answer all questions systematically and consistently.

If you're taking an adaptive test, and you see something in a question or one of the answers that jogs your memory on a topic, or that you feel you should record if the topic appears in another question, write it down on your piece of paper. Just because you can't go back to a question in an adaptive test doesn't mean you can't take notes on what you see early in the test, in hopes that it might help you later in the test.

For adaptive tests, don't be afraid to take notes on what you see in various questions. Sometimes, what you record from one question, especially if it's not as familiar as it should be or reminds you of the name or use of some utility or interface details, can help you on other questions later on.

Deciding What To Memorize

The amount of memorization you must undertake for an exam depends on how well you remember what you've read, and how well you know the software by heart. If you're a visual thinker and can see the drop-down menus and dialog boxes in your head, you won't need to memorize as much as someone who's less visually oriented. However, the exam will stretch your abilities to memorize hierarchy design principles, server and client installation and configuration, product features and functions, and troubleshooting and maintenance details.

At a minimum, you'll want to memorize the following kinds of information:

➤ Important SMS hierarchy design terms and principles

➤ The features and functions associated with discovering resources and installing clients

➤ Default installation configurations using Express setup and Custom setup

➤ The main features of SMS, their configuration, and the circumstances under which you would use each of them

➤ How to use various tools to assist you in troubleshooting and maintaining SMS

➤ How to design and optimize the SMS system for operation in different computing environments

If you work your way through this book while sitting at a machine with SMS 2 installed and try to manipulate this environment's features and functions as they're discussed throughout, you should have little or no difficulties mastering this material. Also, don't forget that The Cram Sheet at the front of the book is designed to capture the material that's most important to memorize; use this to guide your studies as well.

Preparing For The Test

The best way to prepare for the test—after you've studied—is to take at least one practice exam. We've included one here in this chapter for that reason; the test questions are located in the pages that follow (and unlike in the preceding chapters in this book, the answers don't follow the questions immediately; you'll have to flip to Chapter 13 to review the answers separately).

Give yourself 90 minutes to take the exam, and keep yourself on the honor system—don't look at earlier text in the book or jump ahead to the answer key. When your time is up or you've finished the questions, you can check your work with the answers presented in Chapter 13. Pay special attention to the explanations for the incorrect answers; these can also help to reinforce your knowledge of the material. Knowing how to recognize correct answers is good, but understanding why incorrect answers are wrong can be equally valuable.

Taking The Test

Relax. Once you're sitting in front of the testing computer, there's nothing more you can do to increase your knowledge or preparation. Take a deep breath, stretch, and start reading that first question.

You don't need to rush, either. You have plenty of time to complete each question and to return to those questions that you skip or mark for return (if you're taking a fixed-length test). If you read a question twice and remain clueless, you can mark it if you're taking a fixed-length test; if you're taking an adaptive test, you'll have to guess and move on. Both easy and difficult questions are intermixed throughout the test in random order. If you're taking a fixed-length test, don't cheat yourself by spending too much time on a hard question early on in the test, thereby depriving yourself of the time you need to answer the questions at the end of the test. If you're taking an adaptive test, don't spend more than five minutes on any single question—if it takes you that long to get nowhere, it's time to guess and move on.

On a fixed-length test, you can read through the entire test, and before returning to marked questions for a second visit, you can figure out how much time you've got per question. As you answer each question, remove its mark. Continue to review the remaining marked questions until you run out of time or complete the test.

On an adaptive test, set a maximum time limit for questions and watch your time on long or complex questions. If you hit your limit, it's time to guess and move on. Don't deprive yourself of the opportunity to see more questions by taking too long to puzzle over questions, unless you think you can figure out the answer. Otherwise, you're limiting your opportunities to pass.

That's it for pointers. Here are some questions for you to practice on.

Sample Test

Question 1

Which of the following Windows NT 4 servers can be installed as a central SMS site server? [Choose all correct answers]

❑ a. Pentium 200 PDC with 650MB of free disk space on an NTFS system drive

❑ b. Pentium II 450 Windows NT member server with 1GB of free disk space on drive F: (an NTFS drive) and 50MB of free disk space on a FAT system drive

❑ c. Alpha 21164 Windows NT member server with 1GB of free disk space on a FAT system drive

❑ d. Pentium Pro 150 BDC with 2GB of free disk space on drive D: (a FAT drive) and 500MB of free disk space on an NTFS system drive

❑ e. Pentium 133 BDC with 500MB of free disk space on drive G: (an NTFS drive) and 100MB of free disk space on a FAT system drive

Question 2

Which of the following Windows NT servers can be configured as a primary site server with a local SMS site database? [Choose all correct answers]

❑ a. Windows NT Server 4 (SP4) with SQL Server 6.5 (SP3)

❑ b. Windows NT Server 3.51 (SP5) with SQL Server 6.5 (SP4)

❑ c. Windows NT Server 4 (SP4) with SQL Server 7 and IE 4.01 (SP1)

❑ d. Windows NT Server 4 (SP4) with SQL Server 6.5 (SP4) and IE 4

❑ e. Windows NT Server 4 (SP4) with SQL Server 6.5 (SP4) and IE 4.01 (SP1)

Question 3

You want your users to install SMS client software manually on their Windows NT 4 Workstation computers. You will distribute SMSMAN.EXE to all users via email. Most of the users do not have Local Administrator rights to their workstations. Select the SMS feature(s) you should enable.

○ a. Windows Networking Logon Discovery

○ b. Network Discovery and Windows NT Remote Client Installation

○ c. Windows NT Remote Client Installation

○ d. Windows Networking Logon Client Installation

○ e. Windows Networking Logon Client Installation and Windows NT Remote Client Installation

Question 4

You want to use Performance Monitor to analyze the utilization of all your network segments. Which of the following should you install?

○ a. SNMP Service

○ b. Simple TCP/IP Services

○ c. Remote Tools

○ d. Network Monitor

Question 5

In which of the following cases should you install one SMS hierarchy with multiple sites? [Choose all correct answers]

❑ a. Two locations are connected via a fast WAN link. Each site is managed by its own administrator.

❑ b. Two locations with different language settings are connected via a fast WAN link.

❑ c. Two groups of users that require different client configurations are located on different segments of a fast routed LAN.

❑ d. Two groups of users that require different client configurations are on one IPX network. All of the users are serviced by a single NetWare 3.12 server.

Question 6

Which of the following optional SMS features are installed during Express primary site installation? [Choose all correct answers]

❑ a. SMS Installer

❑ b. NetWare NDS support

❑ c. SNMP Service

❑ d. Software Metering console

❑ e. IE 4.01 (SP1)

Question 7

Which of the following SMS features are enabled after Express primary site installation? [Choose all correct answers]

❑ a. Network Discovery

❑ b. Windows NT User Group Discovery

❑ c. Windows Networking Logon Client Installation

❑ d. Modify Logon Scripts (of Windows Networking Logon Client Installation)

❑ e. Remote Tools Client Agent

Question 8

Which of the following is installed by default on a secondary site server after manual installation using the SMS 2 CD-ROM?

○ a. SMS Administrator console

○ b. Software Metering

○ c. Secondary site server

○ d. Remote Tools

Question 9

Which of the following SMS features cannot be installed and configured to run on a secondary site server hosted on an Alpha machine?

○ a. Remote Tools

○ b. Software Metering

○ c. NetWare Bindery Support

○ d. NetWare NDS Support

Question 10

If you plan to use the Secondary Site Creation Wizard, what must you do prior to secondary site installation?

○ a. Install IE 4.01 (SP1) on a Windows NT server designated for the SMS secondary site.

○ b. Create an address from the primary site to the secondary site.

○ c. Create an SMS Service account on a Windows NT machine designated for the SMS secondary site, make it a member of a Domain Admins Global Group, and give it Logon as a service rights.

○ d. Create an address from the secondary site to the primary site.

Question 11

You want to establish a parent-child relationship between two sites connected via a T1 line. You also want to minimize the amount of SMS data sent on the T1 link. What should you do?

○ a. Configure both senders to use only 50 percent of the available bandwidth.

○ b. Configure both senders to operate during the off-peak hours.

○ c. Use Courier Sender to transfer packages from one site to the other.

○ d. Delete the Standard Sender and use Courier Sender only.

Question 12

You want to upgrade your existing three-level SMS 1.2 hierarchy to SMS 2. Which server(s) should you upgrade first?

○ a. Any secondary site servers

○ b. Any primary site servers

○ c. The central site server

○ d. Any site server

Question 13

You want to move your existing SMS 2 secondary site server from hierarchy A to hierarchy B. You want to perform this operation from a central location. What should you do?

○ a. Delete the secondary site from hierarchy A using the SMS Administrator console. Then, create an advertisement that installs a new secondary site and attaches it to hierarchy B.

○ b. Deinstall the secondary site using the SMS Administrator console. Then, install a new secondary site by advertising the unattended secondary site installation program.

○ c. Deinstall the secondary site using the SMS Administrator console attached to the central site of hierarchy A. Then, install a new secondary site using the Create Secondary Site Wizard from the SMS Administrator console at the new parent site in hierarchy B.

○ d. You can only perform this operation manually from the secondary site server.

Question 14

You want to use a remote SQL Server 6.5 for your primary SMS site configuration. Which of the following must you do prior to installation? [Choose all correct answers]

❑ a. Enable directory replication on all domain controllers.

❑ b. Create SMS data and log devices on the remote SQL Server machine.

❑ c. Create an SMS Service account, add it to the Domain Admins global group and the local Administrators group, and give it Logon as a service advanced user rights.

❑ d. Set the number of open database objects to 10,000.

❑ e. Create an SMS database.

❑ f. None of the above.

Question 15

You have obtained an updated version of a dynamic link library (DLL) file. You want to upgrade all computers that have the older version of this file, and you want to minimize resource utilization. What should you do? [Choose all correct answers]

❑ a. Enable software inventory and collect the old version of the DLL file.

❑ b. Enable software inventory.

❑ c. Distribute the new DLL to a collection that contains all machines with the old DLL.

❑ d. Enable software inventory and configure it to collect inventory of DLL files only.

❑ e. Enable hardware inventory.

Question 16

You want to collect information about the user accounts created on each of your 500 Windows NT computers. What is the easiest way to accomplish your goal?

○ a. Enable hardware inventory and modify the SMS_DEF.MOF file to collect the user account information.

○ b. Advertise a program that dumps the results from a **net user** command to a disk file and stores it in a central location for collection.

○ c. View the user accounts using User Manager for Domains.

○ d. Write a custom application that enumerates user accounts on each NT machine, creates a NOIDMIF, and dumps it to the NOIDMIF directory.

Question 17

You need to collect backup logs from your file servers. These files are generated weekly and are approximately 1.2MB in size. What should you do to collect these files and archive them for at least 30 days?

○ a. Enable the Software Inventory Client Agent and configure it to collect data files that are at least 1.2MB in size.

○ b. Enable the Software Inventory Client Agent.

○ c. Enable the Software Inventory Client Agent and rename the collected file every week.

○ d. Configure Scheduler to run under the system context and create a schedule job (AT) to collect the backup logs remotely.

Question 18

You created a custom application that enumerates computer memory slots and reports how many are available and how many are occupied. You want to report this information to the SMS site database and have it available to view through the SMS Administrator console. What should you do?

○ a. Create an IDMIF file and copy it to the client's IDMIF directory.

○ b. Create an IDMIF file and copy it to the CAP.

○ c. Create a NOIDMIF file and copy it to the client's NOIDMIF directory.

○ d. Create a NOIDMIF file and copy it to the CAP.

○ e. Create a NOIDMIF file and copy it to the logon point.

Question 19

You are the administrator of an entire enterprise composed of three SMS sites. John, the administrator of the lower level site (AB3), is supposed to be able view and remotely control only computers that are members of the AB3 site when he uses the central site server's SMS Administrator console. You decided to:

- Create a collection called AB3_Members that includes only members of the AB3 site

- Give John Read and Read Resource privileges to the AB3_Members collection

- Add John to the SMS Admins local group

- Remove John's rights to all collections except AB3_Members

Which of the following is the best answer?

- ○ a.   John will not be able to view members of the AB3 site.

- ○ b.   John will be able to view only members of the AB3 site, but he will not be able to remotely control them.

- ○ c.   John will be able to view and remotely control members of the AB3 site, but not any other clients.

- ○ d.   John will have access to all clients whose information is available at the central site server.

- ○ e.   John will not be able to access the central site's collections.

Question 20

You have not had a chance to replace all of the 700 older NICs that are causing problems on your network. Your network team can report only the MAC addresses of the faulty network cards. The problems become very frequent. You want to be able to quickly find the NetBIOS name of a computer with a specific MAC address. What should you do?

- ○ a.   Run the All Systems query and search for the specific MAC address. Then, find the corresponding NetBIOS name.

- ○ b.   Every time you are searching for a new NetBIOS name, create a new query that reports a NetBIOS name of a machine with a given MAC address.

- ○ c.   Create a single query that reports a NetBIOS name for a specific MAC address. Then, modify the query statement each time you look for a new MAC address.

- ○ d.   Create a MAC address-prompted query that reports a NetBIOS name.

Question 21

You have created a collection based on the **All machines with Outlook 98** query. After you upgraded the Outlook 98 application to the newer Outlook 2000, you modified the query to search for all machines with Outlook 2000. Your collection is not displaying any resources. What is the cause of the problem?

○ a. Your collection has not updated yet.

○ b. The Collection Evaluator thread has stopped working.

○ c. Your collection is still querying for all machines with Outlook 98.

○ d. Your collection has not yet synchronized with the modified query.

Question 22

You want to distribute an updated virus signature file to every client computer with anti-virus software currently installed. What must you do to accomplish this? [Choose all correct answers]

❑ a. Create a package with the updated virus signature file.

❑ b. Create a program that replaces the older file with the new one.

❑ c. Enable the Software Metering Client Agent.

❑ d. Enable software inventory.

❑ e. Distribute the package with the updated virus signature file to all distribution points.

Question 23

Your hierarchy is composed of a central site with sitecode 001 and a primary site with site code 002. You also have two secondary sites with site codes 003 and 004 that are attached to the primary site. You want to distribute a large package to the distribution points defined on each site. The uncompressed source files occupy approximately 550MB of disk space. The SMS compressed source files are approximately 300MB in size. You have created the package and specified to always obtain files from the source directory. You want to distribute the package to all distribution points at once and utilize fan-out technology. Approximately how much data will be passed between the central site and the primary site?

- ○ a. 550MB
- ○ b. 300MB
- ○ c. 1,100MB
- ○ d. 600MB
- ○ e. 1,650MB
- ○ f. 900MB

Question 24

You are concerned about the network utilization between the central site and the secondary site. The sites are connected with a highly utilized frame relay link and communicate using Standard Sender. You want to distribute a large package to the secondary site's distribution point and have decided to use Courier Sender. What should you do?

- ○ a. Add Courier Sender to the central site using the SMS Administrator console.
- ○ b. Add Courier Sender to the secondary site using the SMS Administrator console.
- ○ c. Create a Courier Sender address from the central site to the secondary site.
- ○ d. Delete the Standard Sender address from the central site to the primary site.
- ○ e. Delete the Standard Sender address from the secondary site to the primary site.

Question 25

You have created a set of Y2K advertisements. One of them is a Y2K BIOS verification program. You have since learned that this program will receive a major hot fix in a few days. You want to quickly prevent your clients from running this advertisement until you redistribute the new file source. Which of the following options will allow you to accomplish your task with the least labor?

○ a. Disable the Advertised Programs Client Agent.

○ b. Delete the advertisement.

○ c. Disable the advertisement on computers where it was advertised.

○ d. Delete the package.

○ e. Delete the program.

Question 26

You want to be able to deny use of an application for which there are no available licenses on your network. How should you configure software metering?

○ a. Enable real-time license verification—a property of the Software Metering Client Agent.

○ b. Enable full product version policy—a property of the software-metering server.

○ c. Enable license balancing.

○ d. Decrease the client configuration polling interval to one minute.

Question 27

You want to quickly view a summary of software used at your site. Which tool should you use?

○ a. Crystal Viewer

○ b. Crystal Reports

○ c. SMS Trace

○ d. Software Metering Tool

○ e. WBEM Viewer

Question 28

Your organization does not allow you to use logon scripts. You want to install SMS client software on all of the Windows 95 and Windows NT 4 machines on your network. Which SMS feature(s) should you enable to accomplish your goal?

○ a. Windows NT Remote Client Installation

○ b. Network Discovery and Windows NT Remote Client Installation

○ c. Windows Networking Logon Discovery

○ d. Windows Networking Logon Client Installation

○ e. None of the above

Question 29

You have two DHCP servers that provide both clients and servers with IP addresses. You also use SNMP to monitor your routers and switches. Your two Windows NT domains are configured with a two-way trust relationship. Which Network Discovery configuration will provide you with the highest number of discovered clients?

○ a. Both Windows NT domain names are specified.

○ b. All SNMP read community names are specified.

○ c. IP addresses of all of your routers and switches are specified.

○ d. IP address of one of the two DHCP servers is specified.

○ e. IP addresses of both DHCP servers are specified.

Question 30

Your central and primary child sites' boundaries do not overlap. The sites are managing computers that belong to one Windows NT domain with the Windows Networking Logon Client Installation method enabled and logon scripts modified from both sites. The central site is configured to collect inventory once a month. The primary site is configured to collect inventory twice a week. A user that has a Windows NT 4 Workstation laptop with the default SMS client settings and without local administrative privileges moves from the central site location to the primary site location. Where and how often will the client machine report inventory?

○ a. Once a month to the central site

○ b. Once a month to the primary child site

○ c. Twice a week to the central site

○ d. Twice a week to the primary child site

○ e. The client will not collect inventory until it comes back to the central site location

Question 31

Your machine has been an SMS client that belongs to a central site. The central site's Remote Tools Client Agent was configured to allow you to run commands on client computers and to restart them. You have now moved your computer to another IP segment that is shared between the central site and a secondary site. The secondary site's Remote Tools Client Agent is configured to allow you to run commands on client computers, but it does not allow for a remote reboot. Which of the following is true?

○ a. Central site SMS administrators can run commands and restart the computer. Secondary site SMS operators have no access.

○ b. Secondary site SMS operators can run commands, but cannot restart the computer. Central site SMS administrators have no access.

○ c. Central site SMS administrators can run commands and restart the computer. Secondary site SMS operators can run commands, but cannot restart the computer.

○ d. SMS administrators from both sites can run commands and restart the computer.

○ e. SMS administrators from both sites can run commands, but cannot restart the computer.

Question 32

You want to monitor disk activities on all of your Windows NT file servers from a central monitoring station. Which of the following can you do to accomplish your goal? [Choose all correct answers]

❑ a. Install Network Monitor on the monitoring station.

❑ b. Install Network Monitor Agents on all Windows NT file servers.

❑ c. Run DISKPERF -Y (or -YE) on all Windows NT file servers.

❑ d. Run DISKPERF -Y (or -YE) on the monitoring station.

❑ e. Install Health Monitor Agents on all Windows NT file servers.

❑ f. Install the Health Monitor console on the monitoring station.

Question 33

You have installed a primary site server using the Custom setup option with the default components on a Pentium Pro 200 server. You now want to create a remote CAP on an Alpha machine running Windows NT 4 (SP4). The DNS name of this machine is Alpha06.dev.softwarecomp.com. What should you do? [Choose all correct answers]

❑ a. Create a new Windows NT site system and specify the NetBIOS name of the Alpha machine.

❑ b. Create a new Windows NT share site system and specify the DNS name of the Alpha machine.

❑ c. Run SMS Setup from the Start menu and add support for the Alpha platform.

❑ d. Run SMS Setup from the installation CD-ROM and add support for the Alpha platform.

Question 34

You have initiated the distribution of a large software package to several distribution points in your SMS hierarchy. Which tool will help you view the progress of the distribution?

○ a. Network Monitor

○ b. Health Monitor

○ c. Network Trace

○ d. Status Message Viewer

○ e. SMS Server Manager

Question 35

Your SMS server is configured with the Event To [SNMP] Trap Translator Client Agent. You want your SMS server Windows NT Event Log to collect messages when the SMS site database is running low on disk space. Which of the following will help you achieve your goal?

○ a. Change replication priority of the Site System Status Summarizer to high.

○ b. Change the SMS_SQL_MONITOR warning threshold of the Component Status Summarizer to 1.

○ c. Enable the Report To The Windows NT Event Log option in the status filter rule called "Send a message when the site database is low on free disk space."

○ d. Set a filter to translate event 4707 to the SNMP trap.

Question 36

You want to create a report that summarizes the successes and failures of an Outlook 2000 advertisement sent to your 2,000 Windows NT client machines. You want to report the summary of the advertisement and the NetBIOS names of the machines that failed to run the advertised program. What is the easiest method for creating the report?

○ a. Collect Windows NT Event Logs from your clients, combine them into a spreadsheet file, and filter for the relevant events.

○ b. Export Windows NT Event system logs from the SMS site server and filter them for the relevant information.

○ c. View Failures and Program Success status messages of the Outlook 2000 advertisement and save the results in a tab-delimited file. Summarize the results in a spreadsheet file.

○ d. Create a Crystal Report showing the NetBIOS names of the machines that failed and succeeded running the advertised program.

Question 37

You have noticed that very few discovery records are processed after Network Discovery completes its activity. You want to observe the activity of Network Discovery during its next scheduled operation by tracing its log file. What should you do? [Choose all correct answers]

❏ a. Enable tracing for Network Discovery using Network Trace.

❏ b. Enable Network Discovery tracing using SMS Service Manager.

❏ c. Trace the DDM.LOG file using SMS Trace.

❏ d. Trace the NET_DISC.LOG file using TRACER.EXE.

Question 38

You have verified that a Windows 95 client runs hardware inventory and uploads it to the CAP located on the SMS site server with a sitecode W01. The inventory does not appear in the SMS Administrator console even two hours after the collection is uploaded. Which directory should you check first?

○ a. \SMS_W01\INBOXES\DATALDR.BOX

○ b. \SMS_W01\INBOXES\DATALDR.BOX\PROCESS

○ c. \SMS_W01\INBOXES\INVENTRY.BOX

○ d. \CAP_W01\INVENTRY.BOX

○ e. \CAP_W01\OFFERINF.BOX

Question 39

You have created an advertisement that targets a collection containing Windows 95 machines with at least 100MB free disk space. This collection is updated on a daily schedule. You have learned that only ten machines ran the advertisement. The remainder of the Windows 95 machines did not have enough available disk space. You advised your users to delete unnecessary temporary files. You would like to make the advertisement immediately available to them. What are the two best things you should do?

❏ a. Delete and re-create the advertisement.

❏ b. Delete and re-create the collection.

❏ c. Advertise a program that starts the Hardware Inventory Agent on all Windows 95 machines.

❏ d. Update the collection.

❏ e. Advertise a program that reboots all Windows 95 machines.

Question 40

Your have received several user phone calls reporting lack of access to the network. You cannot Remote Control them or ping them. You suspect that your new network assistant was practicing for the TCP/IP exam and might have enabled a DHCP server with the incorrect IP scopes. Which tool should you use to find if an unwanted DHCP server is present on the network?

○ a. Health Monitor

○ b. Network Monitor Control Tool

○ c. SMS Trace

○ d. Network Trace

○ e. WINS Manager

Question 41

You want to quickly learn the status of all of your SMS site systems and decide to use Network Trace. What must you do prior to using Network Trace?

○ a. Run Windows Networking Logon Discovery.

○ b. Run Network Discovery.

○ c. Install Network Monitor.

○ d. Install SNMP Service.

○ e. Install Crystal Reports.

Question 42

The size of your SQL 6.5 SMS site database (default SMS custom setup settings) has reached 1GB. You decide to change your backup strategy from running full backup every day to running a full backup weekly and an incremental backup every day. What should you do? [Choose all correct answers]

❑ a. Enable Truncate Log On Checkpoint for the SMS site database.

❑ b. Disable Truncate Log On Checkpoint for the SMS site database.

❑ c. Expand the SMS data device and then the database itself.

❑ d. Expand the SMS transaction log device and then the transaction log itself.

Question 43

The drive that hosts the SQL SMS data device has crashed. You need to re-store the SMS site database from the previous day's backup. What do you need to do after you replace the drive and before you run the restore process?

○ a. Start all SMS services and then start the SMS Administrator console from which to initiate the restore.

○ b. Re-create the SMS data device with the same name and the same size as the previous device.

○ c. Reinstall SMS and point to the backup dump during the installation process.

○ d. Restart SMS, which will re-create the database automatically.

Question 44

You have decided to move your SMS site database from the current local server to a remote server. How can you accomplish this?

○ a. Stop the SMS services, back up the SMS site database, restore the database on the remote SQL Server, and restart the SMS services.

○ b. Stop the SMS services, back up the SMS site database, restore the database on the remote SQL Server, rerun setup, and configure SMS to use the remote SQL Server.

○ c. Stop the SMS services, back up the SMS site database, rerun setup and configure SMS to use the remote SQL Server, and then restore the database on the remote SQL Server.

○ d. Back up the SMS site database, restore the database on the remote SQL Server, and use the SMS Administrator console to create a new SMS SQL Site System on the remote SQL Server.

Question 45

Your central SMS site communicates with its 10 secondary sites using Standard Sender. Every time you distribute a package, you send it to all distribution points in your SMS hierarchy. How can you configure the Standard Sender's concurrent sending settings to maximize the use of file caching?

○ a. All sites: 5; per site: 3

○ b. All sites: 3; per site: 5

○ c. All sites: 15; per site: 2

○ d. All sites: 2; per site: 15

○ e. All sites: 5; per site: 5

Question 46

You have two telephone lines available between your primary and secondary sites. How can you configure Asynchronous RAS senders and addresses on both sites to minimize the transmission time?

○ a. Set up two senders and one address on each site server.

○ b. Set up two addresses and one sender on each site server.

○ c. Set up each site server with one sender and one address using a multilink RAS address.

○ d. Set up each site server with one sender and one address. Configure the addresses to use different telephone lines.

Question 47

All of your Windows NT Workstation machines are locked when they are not in use, including at night. You enabled the Remote Tools Client Agent two days ago. Your helpdesk operators report to you that they cannot fully control the remote Windows NT Workstation machines (for example the ALT+key keystroke does not work). What is the most likely cause of the problem?

○ a. The Remote Tools Client Agent has not been installed on the client machines.

○ b. Logged on users don't have local administrator rights.

○ c. The Windows NT Workstation machines have not been rebooted yet.

○ d. Helpdesk support machines are configured with a different protocol than the SMS client machines they are trying to control remotely.

Question 48

You have manually installed a secondary SMS site server on a BDC of Windows NT Domain2, and after a few minutes you were able to view its configuration from the primary site's SMS Administrator console. The primary site is managing all computers in Windows NT Domain1 and the secondary site is to manage the computers in Domain2. You have enabled the Windows NT Logon Discovery method on the secondary site server and enabled the Modify Logon Scripts option. A number of clients have logged on to Domain2 since then, but you still don't see any discovery records from Domain2's clients. What is the most likely cause of the problem?

○ a. The domain controllers of Domain2 are not configured with the directory replication service.

○ b. You have incorrectly created the address from the secondary to the primary site.

○ c. You have not created an address from the primary to the secondary site.

○ d. The account you used for the secondary site SMS Service did not have Logon as a service advanced user rights.

Question 49

Your SMS 1.2 hierarchy was composed of one central, one primary, and three secondary site servers attached to the primary site. All sites were configured to report hardware inventory every seven days. After you upgraded both the central site server and the primary site server to SMS 2, you decided to change the secondary sites' hardware inventory collection frequency to one day. How can you accomplish this?

○ a. Change the secondary sites' hardware inventory collection frequency from the central site's SMS Administrator console.

○ b. Create an advertisement that modifies the inventory collection frequency and send it to the secondary sites.

○ c. Create an advertisement that modifies the SMS.INI file and send it to all of the secondary sites' clients.

○ d. Use SQL Enterprise Administrator to modify the inventory collection frequency at the secondary sites.

○ e. You cannot modify the inventory frequency without an SMS 1.2 primary site.

Question 50

You are the administrator of a central SMS site server. You have just noticed that the system status indicates a large number of Collection Evaluator errors, inventory resynchronization requests, and SQL Monitor errors on a primary site with the sitecode CH2. You think that the SMS site database of site CH2 might be corrupt. Which SQL command can you use to verify your suspicion?

○ a. **SP_CONFIGURE**

○ b. **DBCC CHECKDB**

○ c. **DBCC MEMUSAGE**

○ d. **DBCC SQLPERF**

Question 51

You plan on using SMS 2 to manage Windows 95 clients on a NetWare 4.1 network; all clients are configured with the IPX/SPX protocol only. You decided to install two Windows NT servers and configure them as a primary SMS 2 site server and a remote SQL Server. What must you do to prepare SMS to manage all of the Windows 95 client machines?

○ a. Install the TCP/IP protocol on all of the Windows 95 clients and NetWare 4.1 servers.

○ b. Install the TCP/IP protocol on the NetWare 4.1 servers.

○ c. Install the TCP/IP protocol on the Windows NT servers and configure them as member servers.

○ d. Install the IPX/SPX protocol on the Windows NT servers and configure them as member servers.

○ e. Install the IPX/SPX protocol and the Windows NT Server Gateway Service for NetWare.

Question 52

> You want to silently install a custom Visual Basic application on all Windows
> 98 computers on your network. The application doesn't provide an unattended
> installation setup option. What can you do to guarantee the successful comple-
> tion of your task?
>
> ○ a. Write a PDF file.
>
> ○ b. Create a program for the application setup routine and configure it
>   to run with administrative rights.
>
> ○ c. Use SMS Installer's repackage function.
>
> ○ d. Use SMS Installer's repackage and watch functions.

Answer Key

1. a, e	19. b	37. b, d
2. c, e	20. d	38. d
3. d	21. c	39. c, d
4. d	22. a, b, d	40. b
5. b, c	23. b	41. b
6. a, b, d	24. c	42. b, d
7. b, c, e	25. c	43. b
8. c	26. a	44. b
9. b	27. d	45. c
10. c	28. d	46. c
11. c	29. e	47. c
12. c	30. d	48. c
13. c	31. e	49. e
14. b, c	32. c, e, f	50. b
15. c, d	33. a, d	51. e
16. a	34. d	52. d
17. a	35. c	
18. c	36. c	

Here are the answers to the questions presented in the sample test in Chapter 12.

Question 1

Answers a and e are correct because they are the only answers that meet the minimum system requirements for SMS:

➤ Intel Pentium 133 (or equivalent/compatible) or Alpha class computer

➤ 100MB of available disk space on the system drive (either File Allocation Table [FAT] or New Technology File System [NTFS])

➤ 500MB of available disk space on any NTFS-formatted drive

Answer b is incorrect because the computer listed does not have enough available space on the system drive. Answer c is incorrect because the computer listed does not have an NTFS drive. Answer d is rather tricky. It lists 2GB of free disk space on a FAT drive and 500MB free disk space on the system NTFS drive. The requirements are at least 100MB available on the system drive with another 500 available on an NTFS drive. In order for SMS to use a system NTFS drive, there has to be at least 600MB free. This drive has only 500MB free, so it does not satisfy the requirement of 100MB available on a system drive and an additional 500MB available on an NTFS drive.

Question 2

Answers c and e are correct because they are the only answers that meet the following software configuration requirements for a primary site server with a local SMS site database:

➤ Windows NT 4 Server with Service Pack 4 (SP4) or above

➤ Internet Explorer 4.01 with SP1 or above

➤ SQL Server 6.5 (SP4) or above

You should also remember that the SQL Server does not need to be installed prior to the SMS installation. Answer a is incorrect because SQL Server 6.5 SP4, not SQL Server 6.5 SP3, is required. Answer b is incorrect because Windows NT 4 Server with SP4, not Windows 3.51, is required. Answer d is incorrect because Internet Explorer 4.01 SP1, not Internet Explorer 4, is required.

Question 3

Answer d is correct. You can install SMS client software using two primary methods: Windows NT Remote Client Installation or Windows Networking Logon Client Installation. You can accomplish manual client installation in one of two ways:

➤ Enable Logon Discovery and Windows NT Remote Client Installation. Then, run SMSMAN.EXE on each client to produce a Data Discovery Record (DDR). When Discovery Data Manager processes DDRs, it checks for the operating system of the client and the state of Windows NT Remote Client Installation. If Remote Installation is enabled and the operating system is Windows NT (either server or client), SMS client software will be installed.

➤ Enable Windows Networking Logon Client Installation. Then run SMSMAN.EXE on each client; the SMS client software will be installed automatically. This is also true if you do not have administrative privileges to the Windows NT client machine. In this case, Client Installation, which can install SMS client software under your context, creates a CCR request file and sends it to the client access point (CAP). The CCR is then forwarded to the site server, where CCM processes it. CCM then installs SMS client software on your machine remotely. This installation method does not require the Windows NT Remote Client Installation method to be enabled.

Answer a is incorrect because Windows Networking Logon Discovery is a discovery method that will not install SMS client software. Network Discovery and Windows NT Remote Client Installation will work for client installation. However, because the scenario specifically mentions running SMSMAN.EXE and not automated installation, answer b is incorrect. Answer c won't work because Windows NT Remote Client Installation works only if you provide a mechanism to create a DDR for each client using one of the discovery methods. Finally, answer e is incorrect because you do not have to enable both client installation methods; the question specifically asked about the features you *must* enable.

Question 4

Answer d is correct. The network segment object (with a percentage Network Utilization performance counter) is available in Performance Monitor only after you install Network Monitor. This is a trick question because Simple Network Management Protocol (SNMP) is also a required service for some Performance Monitor functionality. It is required to monitor Transmission

Control Protocol/Internet Protocol (TCP/IP) statistics on the network interface card (NIC). However, SNMP is not required to monitor segment utilization, so answer a is incorrect. Simple TCP/IP Services and Remote Tools are not required to use Performance Monitor. Therefore, answers b and c are incorrect.

Question 5

Answers b and c are correct. A configuration that requires multiple language settings requires a multisite hierarchy. In addition, two groups of users, requiring different client settings, that are located on separate IP segments must be separated into two SMS sites. Answer a is incorrect because only a slow wide area network (WAN) link requires a multiple site hierarchy. Having one administrator for each location is not a requirement for multiple sites either; the security features of SMS allow for very granular management settings. Answer d appears to be no different from answer c, but in fact it is very different. You need to recognize that clients located on the same Internetwork Packet Exchange (IPX) network can be split into two SMS sites and use different client settings. Unfortunately, only one NetWare 3.12 server is mentioned in answer d and it cannot be shared between two sites. Answer d would be a good candidate for a multisite hierarchy if it mentioned an additional NetWare server.

Question 6

Answers a (SMS Installer), b (NetWare NDS support), and d (Software Metering console) are correct. Only answers a, b, and d list optional SMS features and all of them are installed during Express setup.

Answers c and e don't list SMS features. Therefore, they are incorrect.

Question 7

Answers b, c, and e are correct. SMS Express setup installs all optional SMS features, and it enables Windows NT User Group Discovery, Windows Networking Logon Client Installation, and the Remote Tools Client Agent.

Refer to Chapter 4 for details about Express setup, SMS components, and their configurations.

Network Discovery is not enabled by default, as it might create unneeded traffic on your network and apply unnecessary load on your SMS site server. Therefore, answer a is incorrect. The Express installation process leaves script modification disabled to allow you to control client discovery and installation.

Therefore, answer d is incorrect. Another item that SMS Express setup does not create is the software metering server role.

Question 8

Answer c is correct. Secondary site servers can be installed remotely (from the primary site) or manually from the installation source CD-ROM. In the first case, the secondary site installs all optional components that are currently installed on the primary site and that can function on the secondary site. In the second case, the secondary site installation installs by default only the core SMS files. Secondary sites do not have an SMS Administrator console. Therefore, answer a is incorrect. Answers b (Software Metering) and d (Remote Tools) are incorrect because they are optional when you are doing a manual secondary site install. Other optional features on the secondary site server that you can install manually are NetWare Bindery Support and NetWare NDS Support.

Question 9

Answer b is correct. A software metering server cannot successfully run on an Alpha machine. It will run only on an x86 or compatible machine. All of the other listed features can be installed on Alpha machines, but only Remote Tools NetWare Bindery Support and NetWare NDS Support can be configured to run on it.

Question 10

Answer c is correct. The secondary site requires an SMS Service account and it must be a member of the Domain Admins Global Group and have Logon as a service rights. A secondary site server does not require Internet Explorer 4.01 (SP1) because neither the SMS Administrator console nor the electronic version of the *SMS Administrator's Guide* is installed on it. Therefore, answer a is incorrect. Both addresses between the secondary and the primary sites can be created during the setup process. Therefore, answers b and d are incorrect.

Question 11

Answer c is correct. Courier Sender could offload most of the heavy SMS traffic from the T1 link. Only inventory files (mostly deltas), status messages, and management instruction files will be transferred over the T1. In addition, that traffic can be scheduled for the lightest T1 utilization time window, though this would be a secondary solution. At first glance, answers a and b might appear to be correct. However, sender throttling can decrease the link usage only at a specific time rather than minimize the amount of transferred data. Answer d is incorrect because in order for Courier Sender to successfully carry on inter-site communication, another sender must supplement it.

Question 12

Answer c is correct. Because of the limitations of the mixed SMS 1.2 and SMS 2 site hierarchies, the only way to upgrade SMS 1.2 sites without detaching them from the hierarchy is to upgrade from the top down to the lowest level of the hierarchy. The central site has to be upgraded first. You cannot successfully upgrade a secondary SMS 1.2 site to SMS 2 because the parent's SMS 1.2 database cannot store SMS 2 data and site configuration settings. Therefore, answer a is incorrect. If you upgrade your primary site servers without upgrading your central site server, the sites cannot successfully communicate. Therefore, answer b is incorrect. Answer d is incorrect because the order in which you upgrade the servers is relevant.

Question 13

Answer c is correct. You can detach a secondary site from the hierarchy and remove it using the SMS Administrator console at the parent site. This process is called deinstall. You can then install the secondary site from its new parent using the Create Secondary Site Wizard. Answers a and b are incorrect because you can install secondary sites only by using the Secondary Site Creation Wizard or manually from the SMS source files at the secondary site server. You can attach the SMS Administrator console to any primary site (provided you have appropriate security privileges), so you can also install any new secondary site. Answer d is incorrect because it states you can perform this operation only manually at the secondary site server.

Question 14

Answers b and c are correct. You must do three things on the remote SQL Server 6.5 prior to installing a primary site server:

➤ Create data and log devices

➤ Create an SMS service account

➤ Configure the SMS service account with the appropriate privileges (member of the Domain Admins Global Group and the Local Admins group, and Logon as a service advanced user rights)

SMS does not require the directory replication service to be running. There-fore, answer a is incorrect. In addition, it does not require SQL Server to be configured with the number of open objects set to 10,000. Therefore, answer d is incorrect. Only SQL Server 7 requires you to create an SMS database (it is the only method of creating data and log files). Therefore, answer e is incor-rect. Answer f, none, is incorrect because there is an answer that lists the correct solution.

Question 15

Answers c and d are correct. In order to target the computers with the older version of the DLL, you need to enable software inventory and collect infor-mation about DLL files (answer d). Once you have collected the data, you can use the information to create a collection that includes all machines with the older DLL file. Then, you can distribute the newer version of the DLL to the collection (answer c). You could also enable software inventory, collect the old DLL file, and then create a collection including all of the computers where the old file was found (which leads to the same end result); however, this proce-dure utilizes too many resources and should not be used. Therefore, answer a is incorrect. Answer b also looks correct, but it does not provide a complete solu-tion. Therefore, answer b is incorrect. Answer e is incorrect as well because you do not need hardware inventory data to distribute a new DLL file.

Question 16

Answer a is correct.

Here's why answer a is the easiest way to accomplish your goal. The SMS_DEF.MOF file, a hardware inventory template, allows you to collect data about hundreds of computer properties. One of the property sets contains the information about user accounts created on each inventoried machine. Here is the relevant section of the SMS_DEF.MOF file:

```
      [SMS_Report(TRUE),
      SMS_Group_Name("User Accounts"),
      ResID(5900),ResDLL("SMS_RXPL.dll"),
      SMS_Class_ID("MICROSOFT|USER|1.0")]
class Win32_UserAccount : SMS_Class_Template
{
      [SMS_Report(TRUE)]
      uint32          AccountType;
      [SMS_Report(TRUE)]
      string          Caption;
      [SMS_Report(TRUE)]
```

```
string          Description;
[SMS_Report(FALSE)]
boolean         Disabled;
[SMS_Report(FALSE),key]
string          Domain;
[SMS_Report(TRUE)]
```

In order to collect the information available through hardware inventory, you need to make sure that the corresponding section is enabled in the SMS_DEF.MOF file. This is the easiest method for collecting user account data from a large number of client machines because the method uses features that already exist in SMS.

The total list of properties you can collect using the SMS_DEF.MOF file and hardware inventory is available in the *SMS 2.0 Resource Guide* that is part of the *BackOffice 4.5 Resource Kit*.

Each of the listed answers accomplishes the desired goal, so you need to choose the easiest solution. Advertising a program that collects the results of a **net user** command to a central location is relatively easy and not very time consuming. Unfortunately, viewing this data and using it for reporting becomes a rather large task. Therefore, answer b is incorrect. Viewing the user accounts on each machine would be a good solution if you had to view the accounts on only a few machines. However, this method is not the most appropriate when the number of machines exceeds five or so. Therefore, answer c is incorrect. Writing a custom application might be a bit time consuming. Therefore, answer d is incorrect.

Question 17

Answer a is correct. There is only one easy way to collect files on SMS client computers—enable software inventory and configure it to collect the appropriate file. By default, the Software Inventory Client Agent is configured to collect a maximum of 1MB of data from a single client. You will need to change this setting in order to transfer more data to the SMS site server. The log files will be collected based on the Software Inventory Client Agent schedule. Answer b suggests enabling the Software Inventory Client Agent. This is only one step in the total solution, so answer b is incorrect. File history will automatically keep up to five file versions, so you do not need to manually archive each set of collected files. Therefore, answer c is incorrect. Answer d will not accomplish the goal because the Scheduler has no access to networked resources when running under the site system account. Therefore, answer d is incorrect.

By default, collected files are deleted from the SMS site database as soon as they are 90 days old. This period is larger than the 30-day requirement, so deleting aged files is not a concern.

Question 18

Answer c is correct. Memory slots are a computer property (an architecture that is already defined in the SMS site database) so you should use a NOIDMIF to report this information. You can do this only by placing a NOIDMIF in each local computer's NOIDMIF directory. The Hardware Inventory Client Agent scans this directory every time it runs and includes collected data in the inventory file it passes to the CAP.

Most of the time only delta information is transferred from the client to the CAP.

Answers a and b suggest using an IDMIF file. You use an IDMIF file to create new architectures in the SMS site database. A NOIDMIF is a better choice because the property you want to collect belongs to an already defined computer architecture. Therefore, answers a and b are incorrect. Answers b, d, and e all suggest copying the file to a site system. You should remember that SMS 2 does not support passing custom inventory files (NOIDMIFs and IDMIFs) directly to any site systems. You should place these files in the appropriate local machine directories. Therefore, answers b, d, and e are incorrect.

Question 19

Answer b is correct. In order to remotely control the client machines in the AB3_Members collection, John must have the following permissions:

➤ Be a member of the SMS Admins local machine group

➤ Have Read, Read Resource, and Use Remote Tools access rights to the AB3_Members collection

John has everything required except the Use Remote Tools privileges needed to perform his administrative duties, and he has no rights to any other collection. Therefore, he can view only resources included in the AB3_Members collection; he cannot remotely control them. John can view some collections. Therefore, answer a is incorrect. John does not have the rights he needs to remotely control members of site AB3. Therefore, answer c is incorrect. John has been given rights to view only AB3 site members, so answers d and e are incorrect because d suggests that John will have access to all client information and e suggests that John will not be able to access any collections at the central site.

Question 20

Answer d is correct. SMS supports prompted queries. These are queries that ask you for query parameters during runtime. If you use the same query (with just one or a few parameters changed) very often, you should create a prompted query. Therefore, the solution listed in answer d is the most effective. Figure 13.1 shows the properties of a sample query for the specific Media Access Control (MAC) address.

You can use the results from answer a to find the NetBIOS name, but with 700 computers still having older cards in your site, you could spend a long time reading through the data for each computer to find the right one. Therefore, answer a is incorrect. SMS allows you to save queries, so re-creating a similar query over and over again is not practical. Therefore, answer b is incorrect. Similarly, answer c could also produce the desired result, but is not practical at a large site where you could end up creating a single query for each of the 700 computers containing the older NICs before you find the right one. Therefore, answer c is incorrect.

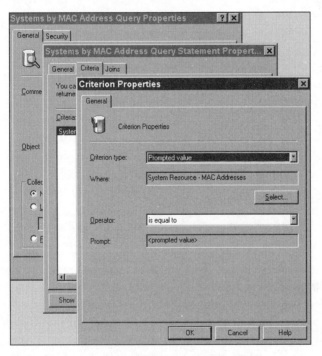

Figure 13.1   A prompted query—All Systems With A Specific MAC Address.

Question 21

Answer c is correct. When creating a collection based on a query, a WBEM Query Language (WQL) statement is copied to the collection query property; the collection and a query are not linked. By updating the query, you do not automatically update the collection, so Collection Evaluator is still querying for the old result set. In this example, the query has been updated so that it lists all machines with Outlook 2000, but the collection is still searching for machines with Outlook 98. To update the collection to the machines with Outlook 2000, you need to modify the collection's query statement manually or point the collection to the updated statement in the new Outlook 2000 query. Answer a looks like it could be correct because the collection might not have been updated yet. However, even after the collection updates, you will still not see the desired result set. Answer b is incorrect because you didn't properly modify the collection query statement. Answer d is incorrect because a collection does not automatically synchronize with a modified query.

Question 22

Answers a, b, and d are correct. In order to distribute software to SMS client machines, you must:

➤ Create a collection that targets the appropriate computers. This collection needs to be based on discovery data, software inventory data, or hardware inventory data (in this situation, you need to create a collection based on software inventory data).

➤ Create a software distribution package.

➤ Create a program.

➤ Distribute the package to at least one distribution point in each site to which the target clients belong.

➤ Create an advertisement.

Answer c is incorrect because software metering does not assist in the software distribution process nor does it provide the data required to target the desired computers. You could use software metering to see which virus applications are in use, but not to help update the virus files. Answer e is incorrect because you do not have to distribute the package to *all* distribution points. You need to distribute the package only to distribution points local to the clients that should receive the updated files.

Question 23

Answer b is correct. SMS transfers packages between sites in a compressed form regardless of how the package is stored at the origination location. SMS also uses fan-out technology to route packages between sites unless you create direct addresses to sites that are not direct subsites. In this example, only one compressed copy of a package will be sent to the primary site. The primary site will then route the package to each secondary site. The approximate (approximate due to network packet and protocol overhead) size of the sent packages will be:

➤ 300MB between the central site and the primary site

➤ 600MB from the primary to each secondary site

All of the other answers list numbers that are much higher than 300MB. The file will be sent over each link only once. Therefore, answers a, c, d, e, and f are incorrect.

Question 24

Answer c is correct. Only packages can be sent using Courier Sender and packages are sent only from the parent to the child site. Therefore, you have to configure a Courier Sender address from the parent site to the child site. Courier Sender is installed by default on each site. Therefore, answers a and b are incorrect. A Courier Sender address can be used to supplement communication between two sites only and only for software distribution. For Courier Sender to work, you have to maintain either the Standard Sender or create one of the Remote Access Server (RAS) Senders between the two sites. Therefore, answers d and e are incorrect.

Question 25

Answer c is correct. Each of the answers will solve the problem of not advertising the Y2K BIOS verification program. However, the question asks for the least labor-intensive solution. Answer c suggests disabling the advertisement, which will stop the software distribution process. Then, after you update the program files, you can enable the advertisement and make it available to all clients, making answer c the easiest and quickest solution. Answer a is quick, but disabling the Advertised Programs Client Agent prevents all clients from running all other advertisements. Therefore, it is not a good solution. If you delete the advertisement, you will have to create a new advertisement when the new program files arrive. Also, if you delete the advertisements, all of the clients that have already downloaded the advertisement can still run it. Therefore, answer b is incorrect. Answer d accomplishes the goal, but requires the administrator to do more work. By deleting the package, you also delete the program and the advertisements. You will then have to re-create all of these objects after you update the source files. By deleting the program, you also delete the advertisement. You will then have to re-create both of them after you update the source files. Answer e is a less labor-intensive solution than answer d, but it is still not the best answer.

Question 26

Answer a is correct. In order to deny usage of an application without available licenses, you have to enable real-time license verification (a property of the Software Metering Client Agent) and define the number of available licenses in the Software Metering tool. Full product version policy allows you to specify the granularity of software version matching, but it does not grant or deny software usage. Therefore, answer b is incorrect. License balancing allows you to balance the number of licenses available on each software metering server to more closely reflect software use at each site, but it does not allow you to deny usage. Therefore, answer c is incorrect. Finally, decreasing the client configuration polling interval has nothing to do with denying application use. Therefore, answer d is incorrect.

Question 27

Answer d is correct. The easiest way to view the summary of metered software use is by using the Software Metering tool. Although you can create a Crystal report that gives you a software metering summary, it is relatively difficult and definitely not very quick. Therefore, answers a and b are incorrect. SMS Trace allows you to watch the SMS log files write data in real time. Therefore, answer c is incorrect. There is no tool called the WBEM Viewer. Therefore, answer e is incorrect.

Question 28

Answer d is correct. If you use the Windows Networking Logon Client Installation method, you can modify logon scripts, or you can use manual installation by running SMSMAN.EXE on each client machine. Windows NT Remote Client Installation allows you to install Windows NT clients only after you have previously run one of the discovery methods (either Network Discovery or Windows Networking Logon Discovery). So, this method will not take care of your Windows 95 clients. Therefore, answer d is incorrect. Answer a, Windows NT Remote Client Installation, will not discover your Windows 95 clients, so it is incorrect. Answer b provides the discovery method to run with Windows NT Remote Client Installation; however, it will still not install your Windows 95 machines. Therefore, answer b is incorrect. Answer c is a discovery method rather than an installation method, so it is incorrect. Finally, answer e is incorrect because a correct answer is given.

Question 29

Answer e is correct. Using Network Discovery, you can set IP subnets, domains, SNMP community names, SNMP devices, and Dynamic Host Configuration Protocol (DHCP) servers to discover resources. A machine will be discovered only if its IP address and its subnet mask are recognized. The only three methods you can use to find this data are:

➤ Specifying the Windows NT domain(s) and having the SNMP agents running on the resources being discovered

➤ Using SNMP and retrieving discovery data from the ARP cache of routers and switches

➤ Specifying Windows NT DHCP servers and using their scope data to produce discovery records

By specifying the IP addresses of DHCP servers, SMS discovers all machines that have obtained dynamic IP addresses. You can specify as many DHCP servers in the Network Discovery Properties dialog box as you wish. For the best results, specify all of your DHCP servers. Therefore, answer e provides you with the highest number of discovery records.

All of your machines do not have an SNMP agent installed, so specifying domain names is not going to produce the desired results. Therefore, answer a is incorrect. Generally, the router or switch ARP cache is flashed quite often, so specifying SNMP read community names does not produce the desired results. Therefore, answers b and c are incorrect. Specifying the IP address on one of the two DHCP servers returns discovery information; however, the question asks which method will return the most discovered clients. This method uses only one DHCP server, and therefore, does not provide the most discovered clients. Therefore, answer d is incorrect.

Question 30

Answer d is correct. When a Windows NT 4 laptop user logs onto the network from a location that is included in the primary child site boundaries, the laptop becomes a client of that site and configures itself according to the client configuration in the primary site. Because the primary site collects hardware inventory every two weeks, hardware inventory is collected and uploaded to the primary site twice a week. If the SMS client software on the laptop were configured for traveling mode (not a default setting and not available for a non-administrator user to enable), the user could set the machine to lock its original site settings for a minimum period of 30 days. Answers a, b, and c are incorrect because they list lengths of time that are different from the setting at the primary site server. Answer e is incorrect because inventory is collected.

Question 31

Answer e is correct. When an SMS client belongs to more than one site, it assumes the most restrictive Remote Control Client Agent settings. For all other client agent settings, it retains the settings of its principal site. The central site allows running commands and rebooting the SMS client, and the secondary site allows only running commands on remote clients. Therefore, the most restrictive setting of the two is to allow an administrator only to run commands. This applies to the administrators of not only the secondary site but also the primary site. A client assumes the most restrictive Remote Control Client Agent settings, but both sites can still remotely control the client. Therefore, answers a and b are incorrect. The most restrictive settings apply to both sites. Therefore, answer c is incorrect. Answer d is incorrect because it assumes the least restrictive of the two settings, allowing administrators to run commands and restart the computer.

Question 32

Answers c, e, and f are correct. You can monitor disk activities on the remote computers using either Windows NT Performance Monitor or SMS 2 Health Monitor. In order to monitor any disk activity, the monitored machine must have disk performance counters enabled (answer c). You enable these by running DISKPERF -Y or DISKPERF -YE (for fault-tolerant disk configurations) on all Windows NT file servers. The question does not list Performance Monitor as an option, so you should focus on Health Monitor. HealthMon has two components: a client agent and a server HealthMon console. Answer e is correct because all monitored client computers must have HealthMon agents running. Answer f is correct because the HealthMon console should be running on the monitoring station. HealthMon does not require Network Monitor. Therefore, answers a and b are incorrect. Running DISKPERF -Y (or -YE) on the monitoring station allows you to collect disk performance data on your monitoring station only. You have to enable disk performance monitor counters on all servers to monitor their activity. Therefore, answer d is incorrect.

Question 33

Answers a and d are correct. The default installation does not install SMS server support for both the x86 and Alpha platforms, so you must rerun setup from the installation media to install support for Alpha (answer d). You cannot run SMS setup from the Start menu because no Alpha source files exist on the SMS server. Next, you need to create a new site system and specify the Alpha machine's NetBIOS name because SMS does not support Domain Name Service (DNS) names (answer a). Answer b is incorrect because you need to specify the NetBIOS name rather than the DNS name. Answer c is incorrect because the Alpha source files don't reside on the SMS server.

Question 34

Answer d is correct. Status Message Viewer is the most appropriate tool to monitor the progress of a software distribution. Network Monitor can show packets being sent over the network, but it does not report success or failure of the distribution. Therefore, answer a is incorrect. Health Monitor can show the status of the Windows NT system, but not the progress of the distribution. Therefore, answer b is incorrect. Network Trace, another SMS diagnostic tool, can report the status and the connectivity between SMS site systems, but it does not report on the progress of the distribution. Therefore, answer c is incorrect. Answer e is incorrect because SMS Service Manager can show the actual state of the SMS services and threads but not the status or progress of an actual package distribution.

Question 35

Answer c is correct. The SMS status system can report on many system conditions and processes, such as when the SMS site database is running low on disk space. You can use either the status system rules or status summarizers to control SMS's reporting capabilities. Status system rules control where status messages are reported. They can be reported to the parent site, the SMS site database, the Windows NT Event Log, the status summarizers, or an external user-specified program. So, the best choice is to use a status filter rule to report status messages to the Windows NT Event Log. Answers a, b, and d are incorrect because all are valid SMS settings, but they do not allow you to report status messages to the Windows NT Event Log.

Question 36

Answer c is correct. The status system has a predefined Advertisement Status reporting summarizer. The summarizer provides advertisement status information by advertisement and site. It also provides information about an advertisement's success, failure, how many programs have started, how many programs have been received, and so on. You can export the displayed messages to comma- or tab-delimited files and process them later in your favorite statistical program. Answer a is incorrect because no advertisement status is reported to the local workstations' NT Event log. Even if event messages were produced, it would be quite labor intensive to produce a distribution report using them. Answer b is incorrect due to the same reasons as answer a. Answer d would achieve your goal, but it is not the best answer because it is much more labor intensive to create a Crystal Report than to use the predefined advertisement progress status functionality.

Question 37

Answers b and d are correct. By default, SMS logging (tracing) is disabled. You can enable logging of any SMS component, including Network Discovery, from the SMS Service Manager (answer b). Network Discovery reports its activities to the NET_DISC.LOG file. You can, of course, view this file using any ASCII editor, but to monitor it in real time, you will need to use either SMS Trace or TRACER.EXE. Answer a is incorrect because Network Trace does not enable tracing or logging of component activities. Network Trace allows you to trace the connectivity between SMS site systems. Answer c is incorrect because DDM.LOG reports activities of the Discovery Data Manager (a thread that processes discovery records), not those of Network Discovery.

Question 38

Answer d is correct. Client inventory is uploaded to the CAP. The sitecode of the SMS site is W01, so the client uploaded the hardware inventory file to the CAP_W01\INVENTRY.BOX directory. This is the first place you should check for the unprocessed inventory file. If the file does not exist in this directory, you should follow it through its processing path on the site server. Answers a, b, and c are incorrect because SMS_W01\INBOXES\DATALDR.BOX, SMS_W01\INBOXES\DATALDR.BOX\PROCESS, and SMS_W01\INBOXESINVENTRY.BOX are site server directories, and you don't yet know if the hardware inventory made it to the site server. Finally, \CAP_W01\OFFERINF.BOX contains software distribution related files, and you are troubleshooting the hardware inventory process. Therefore, answer e is incorrect.

Question 39

Answers c and d are correct. Some of the Windows 95 clients could have freed up space on their drives to make them eligible for the advertisement. Therefore, the SMS system needs to learn of their new state and instruct the Offer Manager thread about new clients that should receive the advertised software. The following things have to happen:

1. Clients need to run hardware inventory (the SMS site database will automatically be updated with the information about the current disk space availability). Hardware inventory runs on a schedule (most likely not very frequently), so you need to initiate hardware inventory manually or automatically using software distribution (answer c).

2. Collection Evaluator needs to update the targeted collection and add new clients to it. The collection runs on a daily schedule, so you need to trigger the update manually (answer d). As soon as the collection is updated, Offer Manager recognizes new collection members and creates advertisements for them.

Answer a is incorrect because deleting and re-creating an advertisement will not change anything. Answer b is incorrect because you never have to delete and re-create a collection; you just need to update it or wait for the scheduled update. Answer e is incorrect because rebooting Windows 95 machines accomplishes nothing; all client agents work on a schedule rather than on reboot, restart, or logon script activation.

Question 40

Answer b is correct. The Network Monitor Control Tool has a Rogue DHCP and Windows Internet Name Service (WINS) Monitor that monitors DHCP traffic and compares the source destination to the prescribed list of valid DHCP servers. Answer a is incorrect because Health Monitor monitors the state of the remote system; it does not monitor the DHCP network packets. Answer c is incorrect because SMS Trace allows you to monitor appends to ASCII log files. Answer d is incorrect because Network Trace draws a map of your site systems and allows you to verify their state and the connectivity between them. Answer e is incorrect because WINS Manager is used to manage NetBIOS to IP name resolution.

Question 41

Answer b is correct. Network Trace uses information collected by Network Discovery to draw a network map with the SMS site systems on it. It also provides information about the health of the network connections between the site systems. Answers a, c, d, and e are incorrect because they are not required for Network Trace to operate.

Question 42

Answers b and d are correct. Incremental backup is accomplished by backing up transaction logs. By default, the SMS database transaction log is set to be truncated on checkpoint (flashed every minute), so you need to disable this option (answer b). Your transaction log will grow for a maximum period of one day between incremental backups. In order to accommodate this growth, you will need to expand it (answer d). Answer a is incorrect because it suggests enabling the Truncate Log On Checkpoint option, the opposite of what you need to do. Changes to the transaction log and your backup strategy do not affect the amount of data stored in the SMS data device of the SMS database. Answer c is incorrect because you do not need to adjust the data device space.

Question 43

Answer b is correct. Because the drive that hosts the SMS data device has been replaced, you need to re-create this device using SQL tools. The data device has to have the same name and size as the previous device. Answer a is incorrect because you cannot restore the database without re-creating the SQL device(s). Answer c is incorrect because you do not need to completely reinstall SMS to restore the SMS site database. Answer d is incorrect because SMS does not automatically recover from database device crash failures.

Question 44

Answer b is correct. The only method of moving the SMS site database to a different server is to do the following in the order listed:

1. Stop the SMS services

2. Back up the database

3. Restore the database on a different SQL Server

4. Run Custom setup

5. Modify the installation to point to a new SQL Server

Only answer b lists the above steps in the correct order. Answers a, c, and d are incorrect because they are either missing steps or list the steps in the incorrect order.

Question 45

Answer c is correct. Answer c gives us the highest probability of sending to all 10 secondary sites simultaneously; therefore, it is the best answer. If a file, or a part of the file, is to be copied to multiple locations within a short time frame, the chances are that this file will be read from the disk only once and then it will be accessed in the file cache. File cache access is much faster than disk access, so it is better to copy in a parallel fashion rather than serially. Because the sender is multithreaded, you can configure it to service multiple sites simultaneously. The default sender configuration allows for five simultaneous operations of which no more than three are to one site. To maximize file caching, you need to configure the sender for parallel communication with 10 sites and possibly with more than 1 session open to a single site. By looking at the available answers, you can easily recognize that answers b and d are incorrect because the number of connections to all sites must be greater than the number of connections per site. This leaves only three possible answers: a, c, and e. Answer a allows for communication to five sites simultaneously and allows for three open communication channels with a single site. The sender will have to read the files from the disk at least twice, but it might need to read them more than five times if multiple instructions are being transferred to a single site at one time. Answer c allows the sender to communicate with up to 15 sites at a time, but only with 2 open connections to a single site. In this case, it is possible for the sender to read the package files only once, but it might need to read them twice or more. The last answer, answer e, requires the sender to read the distribution files at least twice, but possibly 10 times (if 5 or more instructions are being sent to each site).

Remember that the more threads there are working on a single package, the longer it will take to transfer the package to each site.

Question 46

Answer c is correct. This configuration allows for the maximum bandwidth usage at any communication time. In this case, two phone lines to the site server act as one line with double the bandwidth. Remember that a single site can have the same type of sender configured multiple times if each sender is configured on a different site system. Therefore, answer a is incorrect. You can configure only one address to a site using a single sender type. Therefore, answer b is incorrect. Answer d is possible, but the two lines will be used simultaneously only if both servers dial their partners' numbers at the same time, a situation that almost never happens. Therefore, answer d is incorrect.

Question 47

Answer c is correct. Some Remote Tools Client Agent drivers are not completely installed before the client computer is restarted—the functionality of the ALT+key keystroke depends on one of these drivers. This has to be the cause of the problem because the help desk operators can use some but not all of the remote control functions. If the Remote Tools Client Agent weren't installed on the machines, your help desk operators couldn't access any Remote Tools functionality. Therefore, answer a is incorrect. The rights of the logged-on users do not impact Remote Tools functionality. Therefore, answer b is incorrect. Finally, if the help desk support machines had a different protocol than the client machines, SMS wouldn't function at all, so they certainly wouldn't be able to use Remote Tools on some of the computers. Therefore, answer d is incorrect.

Question 48

Answer c is correct. Answer c lists the most common problem encountered after secondary site installation—the secondary site has an address to the primary site, but the primary site does not know how to communicate with the secondary site. You have to manually create (using the standard installation method) an address from the primary site to the secondary site either before or after the secondary site is installed. The directory replication service is not required for SMS to integrate with Windows NT domains. Therefore, answer a is incorrect. If the address from the secondary site to the primary site were configured incorrectly, the primary site would not be aware of the secondary site. Therefore, answer b is incorrect. Answer d is not possible because the secondary site would not install if the SMS Service account didn't have Logon as a service advanced user rights.

Question 49

Answer e is correct. An SMS 2 site can view data collected at SMS 1.2 subsites and can send packages to their clients, but it cannot change their configurations. SMS 1.2 site settings can be changed only via the SMS Administrator

(SMS 1.2 Administrator console). The hierarchy in this question has no primary SMS 1.2 sites, so the secondary SMS 1.2 site settings cannot be changed until they are upgraded to SMS 2. Answer a is incorrect because it suggests using the central site to change the configuration of the SMS 1.2 site. You cannot use advertisements to change configuration settings at any sites. Therefore, answers b and c are incorrect. Likewise, you cannot use the SQL Enterprise Administrator to make secondary site configuration changes. Therefore, answer d is incorrect.

Question 50

Answer b is correct. You can check database or table integrity using **DBCC CHECKDB** (answer b), **DBCC CHECKTABLE**, or **DBCC CHECK-CATALOG**. **SP_CONFIGURE** is a stored procedure-calling function that is used for many SQL configuration operations, but not for consistency and integrity checking. Therefore, answer a is incorrect. Some database consistency checker (DBCC) functions are used for statistical purposes: **DBCC MEMUSAGE** and **DBCC SQLPERF** are two of them. Therefore, answers c and d are incorrect.

Question 51

Answer e is correct. SMS 2 can successfully manage NetWare clients provided that it is configured with one of the supported NetWare redirectors and the Internetwork Package Exchange/Sequence Packet Exchange (IPX/SPX) (or NWLink) protocol. If the SMS site is a primary site, it must communicate with the SQL Server using either the Named Pipes or Multiprotocol network library. Answer e is correct because it fulfills both requirements for an SMS server to operate in a NetWare environment. Answer a is incorrect because NetWare clients do not need to be configured with the TCP/IP protocol to be managed by SMS. Answer b is incorrect because Windows NT Servers cannot communicate with NetWare servers using the TCP/IP protocol. Answers c and d are incorrect because SMS must operate in a Windows NT domain. Remember that SMS does not have to be installed on the domain controller.

Question 52

Answer d is correct. Your application is written in Visual Basic, which requires some supporting libraries or controls that are not always included in the installation source files. Therefore, you need to use both the repackage and watch functions of SMS Installer. Answers a and b are incorrect because neither option will silently install a custom Visual Basic application. An SMS Installer executable created without the watch function could install successfully, but it wouldn't run due to some missing supporting files. Therefore, answer c is incorrect.

Glossary

. . . .

access account—A user or user group account that is given access to a package on a distribution point. Access accounts are optional and allow for configuration of each distributed package with specific access security rights.

address—An identifier that is used to connect to another SMS site in a hierarchy.

address priority—The order that SMS uses to select one of the many addresses defined for communication between SMS sites.

advertise—The action of making a (software distribution) program available to members of a collection.

advertised program—A (software distribution) program that is made available to members of a collection.

Advertised Program Monitor—An SMS client Control Panel applet that is used to check and modify (if allowed) Advertised Programs Client Agent settings as well as to view mandatory and executed advertised programs.

Advertised Programs—An SMS client Control Panel applet that is used to launch the Advertised Programs Wizard when advertised programs are available.

Advertised Programs Client Agent—An optional SMS client agent that allows clients to receive electronic software distribution.

Advertised Programs Manager—A client component that runs distributed software on SMS client machines. This component is used to install optional client agents and is used by the Advertised Programs Client Agent.

Advertised Programs Wizard—An application that guides users through the process of running advertised programs.

advertisement—*See advertised program.*

advertisement expiration time—The date after which an advertisement is no longer available. If the advertised program has an uninstall value specified, the program will be uninstalled from the SMS clients after this date.

advertisement start time—The date after which an advertisement is made available to members of the specified collection.

advertisement status—A set of status messages that is related to the activities associated with each advertisement. You can access advertisement status from the Advertisement Status node in the SMS Administrator console.

Advertisement Status—A node in the SMS Administrator console that displays advertisement status.

Advertisement Status Summarizer—An SMS component (thread of the SMS Executive service) that produces summaries related to distributed software. These summaries are displayed in the Advertisement Status node of the SMS Administrator console.

alert—An audio or visual indication of an event. An alert can be associated with advertised program availability, remote control session initialization, or software metering events.

aliasing—The ability of software metering to monitor multiple processes under one common name.

architecture—A term that is used in SMS to describe the top-level object in the database schema. Each architecture is composed of classes and their attributes. System resource is an example of an architecture.

assigned program—A program that is scheduled for mandatory execution; also called an assignment or a mandatory program.

assignment—*See assigned program.*

Asynchronous Remote Access Server (RAS) Sender—An SMS component (thread of the SMS Executive service) that manages site-to-site connectivity over an asynchronous RAS link.

attribute—A property of a class. An example of an attribute is NT file system (NTFS), which is a property of the logical drive class.

broadcast—A transmission that is sent to all recipients within a specific network area. For Internet Protocol (IP) or Internetwork Packet Exchange (IPX) networks, the area is limited to IP segment or IPX network numbers, respectively.

callback request—A request for notification when a software license becomes available.

CAP—*See client access point (CAP).*

capture—The process of collecting all network data that is passed by the network card of a computer that is running Network Monitor agent.

capture file—File that stores network data captured by Network Monitor agent.

capture filter—A filter that allows you to select the data to be captured by Network Monitor agent.

CCIM—*See Client Configuration Installation Manager (CCIM).*

central site—The SMS site that is at the top of an SMS hierarchy.

child site—An SMS site that reports to a different site, its parent site.

CIM Object Manager (CIMOM)—A primary component of Web-Based Enterprise Management (WBEM), also called Windows Management Instrumentation (WMI). CIMOM provides access to the Common Information Model (CIM) repository data store.

CIMOM—*See CIM Object Manager (CIMOM).*

CIM Repository—A WBEM (WMI) data store.

class—A container object that groups related attributes. Examples of objects within the SMS system architecture include a motherboard, logical drive, or NT service.

client—A computer with SMS client software installed.

client access point (CAP)—An SMS site system that serves as a communication point between SMS clients and the SMS site server.

client agent—One of several optional SMS client components that perform specific SMS functions; for example, the Hardware Inventory Client Agent.

client assignment—The process of assigning a system resource to an SMS site based on the network location and site boundaries.

client component—An SMS service, application, thread, or program performing a specific SMS function that is installed on an SMS client computer.

Client Configuration Installation Manager (CCIM)—An SMS client component (thread) that is responsible for synchronization of client component settings with the ones stored on the client access point (CAP).

Client Configuration Manager (CCM)—An SMS server component (a thread of the SMS Executive service) that initiates Windows NT Remote Client Installation.

client connection account—An account that client components use to access client access points (CAPs) and distribution points.

collected file—A file that is collected by the Software Inventory Client Agent and passed to the site server.

collection—A group of resources that is defined by membership rules.

Collection Evaluator—An SMS server component (a thread of the SMS Executive service) that is responsible for reevaluating collections and preparing them for replication to child sites.

collection membership rule—A rule (direct or query-based) that defines the result set of a collection.

Common Information Model Object Manager (CIMOM)—*See CIM Object Manager.*

complete inventory—A hardware or software inventory that enumerates and reports on all specified properties of a client machine.

component status—The status of an SMS component that is based on the number of informational, warning, and error status messages being reported.

Component Status Summarizer—An SMS component (a thread of the SMS Executive service) that produces a summary of component status messages.

compressed package source—A compressed version of distribution source file(s).

console tree—A hierarchical listing of objects that is displayed in the left pane of the Microsoft Management Console (MMC).

Copy Queue Manager—An SMS client component that copies client data—inventory, Discovery Data Records (DDRs), and status messages—to client access points (CAPs) and logon points.

Courier Sender—An SMS server component (a thread of the SMS Executive service) that writes a software distribution package to removable media.

Courier Sender Confirmation—An SMS server component (a thread of the SMS Executive service) that waits for confirmation from the subsite about the arrival of a Courier Sender package.

Custom setup—An SMS setup method that allows you to select and install any of the SMS optional components and use remote or pre-installed SQL Server.

database—*See SMS site database.*

database consistency checker (dbcc) commands—A set of SQL commands that perform many maintenance and monitoring functions.

database device—A storage area that is designated for a SQL 6.5 database.

database file—A storage area that is designated for a SQL 7 database.

data store—The storage location for SMS client or server data and configuration.

dbcc—*See database consistency checker (dbcc) commands.*

DDR—*See Discovery Data Record (DDR).*

delete aged objects—The action of deleting resources that are not updated within a specified period of time or that are outdated.

delta inventory file—A file that contains the difference between data in the current and previous (hardware/software) state of an SMS client.

dependent program—A program that is associated with another program. A dependent program has to be executed first.

Despooler—An SMS component (a thread of the SMS Executive service) that receives and decompresses files sent from other sites in the hierarchy.

direct membership collection—A static collection that contains directly selected SMS resources (as opposed to selected by query).

Discovery Data Manager (DDM)—An SMS component (a thread of the SMS Executive service) that processes Discovery Data Records (DDRs), evaluates site boundaries, and creates Client Configuration Requests (CCR files).

Discovery Data Record (DDR)—A file that contains information that identifies a resource.

Distribution Manager—An SMS component (a thread of the SMS Executive service) that manages software distribution packages.

distribution source—A source for files that make up the content of a software distribution package.

Euro compliance—Compatibility with the new European currency, the Euro.

Event To Trap Translator application—A graphical utility that allows you to select NT events to be generated in the form of Simple Network Management Protocol (SNMP) traps.

Event To Trap Translator Client Agent—An optional SMS client agent that generates Simple Network Management Protocol (SNMP) traps when selected NT events occur.

Express setup—An SMS setup method that installs and configures a fixed set of SMS features.

file collection—The process of collecting the contents of an entire file or files and passing them to the site server using the Software Inventory feature.

generic account—An account mapped to a specific set of Windows NT, NetWare Bindery, and NetWare Novell Directory Services (NDS) security accounts.

hardware history—Historical hardware inventory data stored in the SMS site database.

Hardware Inventory—An SMS feature or the action of collecting hardware inventory data from SMS client machines.

Hardware Inventory Client Agent—An optional SMS client agent that collects hardware inventory data.

HealthMon—*See Health Monitor.*

Health Monitor—A client-server application based on Windows Management Instrumentation (WMI) that provides real-time status of Windows NT computers.

Heartbeat Discovery—A discovery method that causes SMS client machines to produce Discovery Data Records (DDRs) on a configurable schedule.

hierarchy design—The process of combining SMS sites and creating parent-child relationships.

hop count—An integer that represents the number of routers separating two Internet Protocol (IP) segments or Internetwork Packet Exchange (IPX) networks.

IDMIF—A Management Information Format (MIF) file that contains a new SMS architecture or updates to a new architecture.

inbox—A working directory for an SMS server component.

Inbox Manager—An SMS server component (a thread of the SMS Executive service) that is responsible for moving files from the site server to client access points (CAPs). On NetWare site systems, Inbox Manager moves files to and from CAPs.

Inbox Manager Assistant—An SMS server component—a thread of the SMS Executive service that runs on Windows NT client access points (CAPs)—that is responsible for moving files from CAPs to the inboxes located on the site server; Inbox Manager Assistant works on a schedule as well as on directory change notification.

Info Agent—An NT service that is responsible for retrieving data from the SMS site database and making it available for report creation.

Info APS—An NT service that manages and schedules all of the Crystal Reports components.

Info Sentinel—An NT service that manages communication between the Microsoft Management Console (MMC) console where the Crystal snap-in is installed and Crystal (Info) services that run on the site server.

Installation Expert—An interface of SMS Installer that allows for automated creation of basic installation scripts on a reference computer. These scripts can later be edited and compiled to produce an installer executable file.

installer executable file—A compressed self-extracting installation executable file that is created by SMS Installer.

instruction file—An ASCII file that contains the identifiers of software distribution advertisements.

inventory—The information that SMS gathers about client properties and software that is running on clients.

Inventory Agent—An SMS client agent that is responsible for collecting hardware or software inventory data on client computers.

Inventory Data Loader—An SMS server component (a thread of the SMS Executive service) that processes binary hardware inventory files and enters their contents into the SMS site database.

Inventory Processor—An SMS server component (a thread of the SMS Executive service) that calculates the hardware inventory deltas of 16-bit SMS client inventory and updates all of the inventory (ASCII) files with a binary header.

IP address—A 32-bit binary number that represents a device's address on an Internet Protocol (IP) network.

IP network ID—An address for an Internet Protocol (IP) network segment.

IPX network number—An eight-character hexadecimal number that represents an address for an Internetwork Packet Exchange (IPX) network segment.

ISDN RAS Sender—An SMS server component (a thread of the SMS Executive service) that utilizes an Integrated Services Digital Network (ISDN) Remote Access Server (RAS) link to communicate with other SMS sites.

LAN Sender—An SMS server component (a thread of the SMS Executive service) that utilizes local area network (LAN) and wide area network (WAN) links to communicate with other SMS sites.

Lempel-Ziv (LZ) compression—A high-ratio math-intensive data compression method.

license balancing—The ability to move application licenses between two or more software metering servers or SMS sites.

logging—The process that SMS uses to report activities by writing them to ASCII files; also called tracing.

logical operator—A connector between two or more query expressions and/or subclauses. Three logical operators are used in SMS: AND, OR, and NOT.

logon discovery—A system resource discovery method that utilizes SMS logon points. It can be automatic through logon scripts or manual using the Systems Management Installation Wizard.

logon installation—An SMS client installation method that utilizes logon points. It could be automatic through logon scripts or manual using the Systems Management Installation Wizard.

logon point—An SMS site system used to initiate logon discovery and logon installation that is created on Windows NT domain controllers, NetWare Bindery, and NetWare Novell Directory Services (NDS) servers.

logon script—A file that is executed when a resource logs on to the network.

LZ—*See Lempel-Ziv (LZ) compression.*

Managed Object Format (MOF) file—An ASCII file that contains information about Common Information Model Object Manager (CIMOM) schema.

Management Information Format (MIF) file—An ASCII file that contains client inventory data.

mandatory assignment—A schedule of the program that is configured for mandatory execution.

mandatory program—*See assigned program.*

manual discovery—A type of logon discovery that is initiated using the Systems Management Installation Wizard.

manual installation—A type of logon installation for SMS clients that is initiated using the System Management Installation Wizard.

Microsoft Management Console (MMC)—A framework for various administrative programs (snap-ins).

MIF—See *Management Information Format (MIF).*

MMC—*See Microsoft Management Console (MMC).*

MOF file—*See Managed Object Format (MOF) file.*

Munger—Remote Tools Client Agent utility that reconciles differences between multiple configurations.

NAL—*See network abstraction layer (NAL).*

namespace—A grouping of Windows Management Instrumentation (WMI) classes and instances.

NDS Logon Manager—An SMS server component (a thread of the SMS Executive service) that manages NetWare Novell Directory Services (NDS) logon points.

NetMon—*See Network Monitor (NetMon).*

NetWare Bindery site system—A NetWare Bindery server that is configured to perform an SMS site system role.

NetWare NDS site system—A NetWare Novell Directory Services (NDS) volume that is configured to perform an SMS site system role.

NetWare NDS volume —A Novell Directory Services (NDS) object that represents a logical disk.

network abstraction layer (NAL)—An interface that manages the connectivity between two systems located on the network.

Network Discovery—A discovery method that scans the network for Internet Protocol (IP) devices using Dynamic Host Configuration Protocol (DHCP), Open Shortest Path First (OSPF), Routing Information Protocol (RIP), Domain Name Service (DNS), NetBIOS, and Simple Network Management Protocol (SNMP). It can also detect the operating system of certain machines using LAN Manager calls.

Network Monitor (NetMon)—A tool that is used for network data capture and analysis.

Network Monitor Agent—A program that runs on a machine that collects and monitors data passed on the local network segment; the statistical information about the captured data can be sent to the central monitoring station in realtime, whereas the captured data can be stored locally.

Network Monitor Experts—Post-capture network data analysis tools.

Network Monitor Monitors—Real-time network data analysis tools.

Network Trace—An SMS Administrator console tool that is used for displaying (based on server and Network Discovery data) diagrams of all SMS site systems and components as well as their connectivity status.

NOIDMIF—A Management Information Format (MIF) file that is used to extend the SMS system resource hardware inventory.

Novell Directory Service (NDS)—A hierarchical database that maintains information about and access to all network resources managed by the NetWare NDS operating system.

NT Logon Discovery Agent—An NT service, running on NT logon points, that forwards logon discovery Discovery Data Records (DDRs) to SMS site servers.

NT Logon Manager—An SMS server component (a thread of the SMS Executive service) that manages Windows NT logon points.

NW Logon Manager—An SMS server component (a thread of the SMS Executive service) that manages NetWare Bindery logon points.

Offer Data Provider—An SMS client component (a part of the Advertised Programs Client Agent) that checks for the availability of advertised programs.

Offer Manager—An SMS server component (a thread of the SMS Executive service) that is responsible for managing instruction files and other software distribution support files.

package—An SMS object that is used in the software distribution process. A package can contain programs and can be distributed to distribution points with the specific set of access account permissions; a package may or may not have source files.

package access accounts—*See access account.*

Package Definition File (PDF)—An ASCII file that contains the properties of (software distribution) packages and programs.

Package Status—A node in the SMS Administrator console that displays the status of package distributions.

parent site—An SMS site that has at least one site reporting to it, a child site.

PDF—*See Package Definition File (PDF).*

PerfMon—*See Performance Monitor (PerfMon).*

Performance Monitor (PerfMon)—An NT tool that collects and displays performance and activity data of NT computers.

ping test—A remote diagnostics test that is used to verify connectivity between an SMS Administrator console computer and an SMS client machine.

primary site—An SMS site that utilizes a SQL Server database.

principal site—An SMS site that dictates client agent configuration (with the exception of the Remote Tools Client Agent, which always uses the most restrictive settings of all sites of which the client is a member).

Product Compliance Database—A set of site database tables that contains information about the Year 2000 (Y2K) compliance of Microsoft products.

product version policy—A software metering setting that specifies the policy that identifies products by their version.

program—A set of instructions that describes the execution of an advertised program and its environment.

program name policy—A software metering setting that specifies whether the metering agent should report processes by the name of their files or by file header information.

prompted query—A query that is built without a specified expression value(s). The unspecified value or values has to be supplied during the query runtime.

provider—An interface that provides a communication link between Windows Management Instrumentation (WMI) and a managed object.

query—A set of criteria that specifies a desired result of a search operation.

query-based collection—A collection that is based on a query.

query builder—A set of dialog boxes that allows for the graphical generation of queries.

query expression—A statement that compares an attribute to a value using the query relational operator.

query relational operator—The part of an expression that defines how an attribute should be compared to a value.

rebuild indexes—An SMS task that rebuilds SMS database indexes.

relational operator—*See query relational operator.*

Remote Control—An SMS feature that interacts remotely with SMS client computers.

Remote Control Hardware Munger—A utility that reinitializes configuration of the Remote Tools Client Agent.

Remote Diagnostics—An SMS feature that is used to view a remote client's system properties.

Remote Tools Client Agent—An optional SMS client agent that provides remote control and remote diagnostics capabilities.

Repackage Installation Wizard—An SMS Installer feature that allows for the replacement of an application setup program with a new one that includes error checking, Registry changes, file modifications, and answers to questions the original setup would ask the users.

resource—An object that can be discovered and potentially managed by SMS.

resource discovery—The process of discovering resources.

Resource Explorer—A Microsoft Management Console (MMC) snap-in that is used to view SMS client hardware and software inventory.

RLE—*See Run Length Encoding (RLE) compression.*

roll back—An SMS Installer uninstall process that recovers system settings and files that were overwritten by the installation process.

Run Length Encoding (RLE) compression—A fast and efficient low-ratio data compression method; also called Run-Length Limited (RLL) encoding.

Script Editor—An SMS Installer interface that allows you to create and modify Installer scripts.

secondary site—An SMS site that does not utilize SQL Server directly; a secondary site uses SQL Server indirectly through its parent site.

Secondary Site Creation Wizard—An SMS Administrator console wizard that collects the information necessary to set up a secondary site on a remote server.

senders—SMS components (threads of the SMS Executive service) that provide communication between two SMS sites.

sender rate limit—The percentage of total link bandwidth that a sender can use.

senior site—An SMS site that is responsible for updating the logon points within an NT domain.

Server Component—*See SMS component.*

Server Discovery—A nonconfigurable discovery method for creating and periodically refreshing site systems discovery data.

Shared Applications—A feature of SMS 1.2 that allows for configuration of applications to be run from network servers.

site assignment—The process of assigning a resource to an SMS site based on network location and site boundaries.

site boundaries—A set of Internet Protocol (IP) network IDs and Internetwork Packet Exchange (IPX) network numbers that defines an area of SMS client site membership. Only supported clients located within the site boundaries can become members of the SMS site.

sitecode—A unique three-character code that identifies an SMS site in the hierarchy.

site control file—An ASCII file that contains site configuration settings; this file should never be edited manually.

site database—*See SMS site database.*

site hierarchy—The layout and relationships among multiple SMS sites. A site hierarchy is created by joining SMS sites, thereby creating parent-child relationships.

site reset—The process of resetting the site configuration defined during setup.

site server—A Windows NT Server on which SMS has been installed.

site server role—A role that is assigned to a site server computer; this is the primary role of the SMS site and cannot be moved to a different computer without deinstalling and then installing the new site.

site system—A Windows NT Server or share, NetWare Bindery volume, or NetWare Novell Directory Services (NDS) volume that provides functionality to an SMS site.

Site Systems Connection Account—An optional account or accounts that SMS components use to access site systems. If a Site Systems Connection Account is not specified, the SMS Service account is used instead.

site system role—An SMS role performed by an SMS site system.

Site System Status—A node in the SMS Administrator console for displaying the status of site storage objects.

site transaction log—A transaction log for the SMS site database.

SMS Administrator console—A set of Microsoft Management Console (MMC) snap-ins that allows administrators to manage an SMS site and hierarchy.

SMS component—An SMS service, program, or thread that performs a specific SMS task.

SMS_DEF.MOF—A Managed Object Format (MOF) file that is used to select the scope for hardware inventory.

SMS Executive—A multithreaded process that runs as an NT service and performs the majority of SMS tasks.

SMS Executive threads—The threads of the SMS Executive service that perform the majority of SMS tasks.

SMS Installer—An application bundled with SMS that creates customized, self-extracting compressed executables used for simplified software distribution.

SMS Provider—An interface between Windows Management Instrumentation (WMI) and SMS storage and configuration objects.

SMS Service account—An account that is used to run the main SMS services.

SMS Service Manager—An application that is used to monitor and manage SMS services and threads and their tracing settings.

SMS services—SMS processes running as NT services that provide functionality to the SMS site.

SMS Site Component Manager—An NT service that monitors and manages all of the other SMS services and SMS Executive threads that are running on the site server.

SMS site database—A SQL Server database that stores SMS data and configuration information.

SMS SQL Monitor—An NT service that monitors and manages the SMS site database.

SMS Unique Identifier—A unique identifier that is assigned to each discovered system resource.

SNA RAS Sender—An SMS server component (a thread of the SMS Executive service) that uses the existing Systems Network Architecture (SNA) Remote Access Server (RAS) connectivity to communicate with other SMS sites.

snap-in—*See Microsoft Management Console (MMC).*

SNMP agent—An agent that generates Simple Network Management Protocol (SNMP) traps based on predefined criteria and sends them to the specified monitoring station.

software distribution—The automated process of delivering and executing programs, batch files, and so on to SMS client machines.

Software Inventory—An SMS feature or the action of collecting software inventory data and files from SMS client machines.

Software Inventory Client Agent—An optional SMS client agent that collects software inventory data.

Software Inventory Processor—An SMS server component (a thread of the SMS Executive service) that processes software inventory files and updates the SMS site database with their contents.

software metering—The process of managing the usage of application licenses.

Software Metering Client Agent—An optional SMS client agent that monitors processes running on SMS client machines and communicates with the metering server(s) about the actions associated with these processes.

software metering database—A SQL Server database that stores licensing data.

Software Metering tool—A graphical interface that provides management and reporting capabilities associated with the Software Metering feature.

Software Patching—An SMS Installer feature that is used to create the installation difference (delta) executable rather than a new complete executable.

SQL database device—*See database device.*

SQL database file—*See database file.*

SQL tempdb database—A SQL database that is used for temporary purposes.

SQL transaction log—The history of data modifications to a database.

SQL transaction log device—*See transaction log device.*

SQL transaction log file—*See transaction log file.*

SQL user connection—A connection that is established between a SQL Server and an entity operating on a SQL Server.

status filter rule—A user-defined rule that determines the actions performed when a status message is processed.

Status Manager—An SMS server component (a thread of the SMS Executive service) that processes status messages and updates the SMS site database with their contents.

status message—A binary file that contains information about the state of an SMS component, about actions performed by an SMS component, or about actions performed on an SMS client.

status message ID—A unique ID that is associated with a specific SMS event or the state of an SMS component or SMS client.

status message severity—A measure of the urgency of information that is reported in a status message: error, warning, or informational.

status message type—The type of information that is reported in the status message: audit, detail, or milestone.

Status Message Viewer—An SMS application that is used to view status messages.

status MIF—A Management Information Format (MIF) file that is generated by a program being installed.

Status Summarizer—An SMS server component (a thread of the SMS Executive service) that monitors the severity and quantity of status messages and produces summary messages that are then displayed in the SMS Administrator console and/or forwarded up the SMS hierarchy.

status summarizer thresholds—The status message thresholds (numerical values) that generate status summaries.

status system—An entire system that collects, processes, summarizes, replicates, and displays SMS status messages.

storage object—Any device that can store data.

subcollection—A collection that is associated with another collection.

system resource—Any network device that SMS can discover.

Systems Management Server Setup Wizard—A wizard that guides you through SMS site server setup.

tracing—*See logging.*

transaction log device—A storage device that is designated for a SQL 6.5 transaction log.

transaction log file—A storage device that is designated for a SQL 7 transaction log.

trend analysis—The analysis of software license usage within an SMS site.

update statistics—The SMS task of updating statistics in the SMS site database.

User Account Discovery—A method and process for discovering user accounts that are stored in the Windows NT security account database.

user account resource—A Windows NT domain user account.

User Group Discovery—A method and process for discovering user groups stored in the Windows NT security account database.

user group resource—A Windows NT domain global user group.

Watch Application Wizard—An SMS Installer feature that allows you to capture all files necessary for program runtime; some files are not supplied in the setup packages, but are required for application execution.

WBEM—*See Web Based Enterprise Management (WBEM).*

WBEM Query Language (WQL)—A query language that is used to query data in the Common Information Model Object Manager (CIMOM) repository.

Web Based Enterprise Management (WBEM)—A set of standard technologies that is related to systems management.

Web Based Enterprise Management Permission Tool (WBEMPERM)—A graphical application that is used to set WBEM/WMI permissions.

Windows Management Instrumentation (WMI)—Microsoft's implementation of Web Based Enterprise Management (WBEM).

Windows NT Client Software Installation Account—An optional account used during software distribution when no users are logged on to the NT client machines.

Windows NT diagnostic tools—A set of tools that allows for viewing and monitoring system information of remote Windows NT machines.

Windows NT Remote Client Installation—A method for remotely installing SMS client software on Windows NT machines.

Windows NT Server site system—A Windows NT Server that provides functionality to an SMS site.

Windows NT Share site system—A Windows NT share that provides functionality to an SMS site.

WMI—*See Windows Management Instrumentation (WMI).*

WQL—*See WBEM Query Language (WQL).*

WQL wildcard characters—Wildcard characters that are used in the WBEM Query Language (WQL).

X25 RAS Sender—An SMS server component (a thread of the SMS Executive service) that uses an existing X.25 line and Remote Access Server (RAS) services to communicate with other sites in the hierarchy.

Year 2000 (Y2K) compliance—The compatibility with the date format past December 31, 1999.

Index